# Christian Concepts for Care

# Christian Concepts for Care

## Understanding and Helping People with Mental Health Issues

CONCORDIA PUBLISHING HOUSE · SAINT LOUIS

David J. Ludwig
Mary R. Jacob

Published by Concordia Publishing House
3558 S. Jefferson Avenue
St. Louis, MO 63118-3968
1-800-325-3040 • www.cph.org

Manufactured in the United States of America

---

Library of Congress Cataloging-in-Publication Data

Ludwig, David J.

 Christian concepts for care : understanding and helping people with mental health issues / David J. Ludwig and Mary R. Jacob.

  pages cm

 ISBN 978-0-7586-4416-9

 1. Church work with the mentally ill. 2. Mental illness--Religious aspects--Christianity. 3. Psychiatry and religion. 4. Pastoral psychology. I. Title.

 BV4461.L83 2014

 259'.42--dc23

                        2013050929

---

1  2  3  4  5  6  7  8  9  10          23  22  21  20  19  18  17  16  15  14

# Contents

The critical link between the spiritual and psychological is established in Part I, showing that the deep understanding of reality developed by the child's spirit underlies mental and emotional disorder. This important connection is explored with the introduction of the unique concept of *spiritual DNA*, giving a refreshing way to bring a person's faith into the healing process.

Disorder is the norm. Individuals shift up and down a continuum from relatively well to highly disordered during life. In this chapter, disorder is defined by constriction (as opposed to *neuroplasticity* and resilience) caused by both inherited problems and environmental stressors. A helpful way of understanding the need for various theories and approaches to therapy is given. A person's faith and faith community are seen as added benefits in developing wellness.

Each individual is born with a fatal flaw in creating reality. They are born without a relationship with God—missing *agape* in the formation of *spiritual DNA*. As a result, the person's spirit had to organize life without the guidance and surrounding love of God's Spirit. This chapter looks at the disorder *incurvatus in se* that creates a self-protective ME *orientation* in life. A healthy life demonstrates a WE *orientation* that cares for others. Damage to *spiritual DNA* occurs when high anxiety or feelings of entitlement result in *automated mood sequences* that show up in later life as dysfunctional strategies for handling situations.

This chapter looks closely at St. Paul's description of his own internal struggle in Romans 7:21–25, examining the war between the two internal forces: the *mind* and the *body*. The human spirit is the organizing force of the soul, and it can become dysfunctional if it allows the mind to dominate reality, causing *overcontrol* disorders. If the body is allowed to dominate, the result is *impulse-control* disorders. A spirit that is poorly formed because of genetic problems, excess privacy, or deceit will lead to *reality* disorders.

The standard categories of mental and emotional disorders are ordered into a developmental framework in this chapter to form an easy-to-understand classification.

# Dedication

This book is dedicated to all who care for and minister
to those in need and the faith communities they represent.

# Preface

This book is the culmination of the life's work of author Dr. David Ludwig in relating faith to life. The concepts grow out of his extensive study of both theology and psychology, and they put into practice over forty-five years' experience as a therapist, pastor, university professor, author, and retreat leader. Dr. Mary Jacob was recruited to add the perspective of an advanced-practice psychiatric nurse who worked extensively within a church counseling center and also gained expertise in health ministry and in the spiritual discipline area.

Both authors have worked extensively with Grace Place Lutheran Wellness Ministries (www.graceplacewellness.org). Many creative concepts grew out of a close and exciting association with its founder, John Eckrich, and with its chief program officer, Darrell Zimmerman. These concepts have been tried out during the many retreats that Grace Place has offered for professional church workers and congregations.

Of the many associates who have made contributions to this book with their suggestions, several deserve special recognition: Laura Eckerd, for her valuable insights and editing suggestions; Bob Reinhart, for his encouragement and editing comments; Mel Jacob, for his input in the PTSD area with returning military; Jim Otte, for his exciting visualizations of the concepts; Karl Brettig, for his insight into anxieties wired into children's brains; Bev Yahnke, for her perceptive reading of the manuscript and suggestions for other resources; John Oberdeck, for his helpful suggestions for additions to the manuscript; Rebecca Monfalcone, for her insight into faith community nursing; and Frances Hall, for her editing work and insights into caregiving for aging parents.

The concepts of the book are presented in such a way as to show that all persons have dysfunctional tendencies. Everyone is disordered, so everyone can find personal symptoms throughout the book. This is normal. In fact, it is healthier to realize personal dysfunction and the need for the healing presence of Christ and for a healthy faith community.

# Part I

## Understanding Disorder and the Role of a Faith Community in the Healing Process

# Understanding Disorder and the Role of a Faith Community in the Healing Process

The critical link between the spiritual and psychological is established in Part I, showing that the deep understanding of reality developed by the child's spirit underlies mental and emotional disorder. This important connection is explored with the introduction of the unique concept of *spiritual DNA*, giving a refreshing way to bring a person's faith into the healing process.

Current understanding of psychological problems relies heavily on scientific research, leading to increasing usage of evidenced-based practice to treat disorder. This has been a blessing in many ways to the field of therapy, but by definition, it focuses on observable data. The deep inner spiritual world of individuals (which includes faith) is somewhat ignored in this process, leading to the following mismatch: *most people seeking therapy value their faith, yet most therapists do not work with or value their clients' faith and have not been trained to do so.*

In Part I we develop the critical link between the spiritual and psychological, showing that the deep understanding of reality developed by the child's spirit underlies mental and emotional disorder. The unique concept of *spiritual DNA* is used to establish this important connection, giving a refreshing way to bring a person's faith into the healing process.

Careful attention is paid to the developmental nature of disorders, showing that the natural damage to spiritual DNA occurs when the child is faced with emotionally important situations that are handled privately. These become defining moments for the child's spirit in the formation of reality—of his or her belief system about life.

Within the context of the Christian faith, God created the world so that his loving presence—*agape*—would be with His people. Because of sin, the natural state for all lacks this agape, forcing children to handle situations in a self-protective manner (*incurvatus in se*). This leads to dysfunctional strategies for managing the resultant anxiety or feelings of entitlement. Careful connection is made in the first part of this book to such spiritual DNA damage and the various psychological disorders described in current literature.

The concept of *re-parenting* is introduced to show how a person's belief in the loving presence of Christ can be a healing force when applied to a concrete situation. This has the power to take the immature anxiety and self-protection out of the person's automatic reaction and allow for a new way of handling things so that the person's energy goes outward in healthy concern for others.

Sustainable spiritual growth is best accomplished in the context of healthy relationships. Special attention is given in this part of the book to establishing healthy faith communities and showing how they can be healthy partners in working with people struggling with various disorders.

# Understanding Mental and
# Emotional Disorder

## CHAPTER 1

IN THIS CHAPTER

- Disorder is a continuum, from relatively well to highly disordered, and individuals shift up and down the continuum during life.

- Disorder is defined by *constriction* (as opposed to *neuroplasticity* and resilience) caused by both inherited problems and environmental stressors.

- A helpful way of understanding the need for various theories and approaches to therapy is given.

- A person's faith and faith community are seen as benefits in developing wellness.

## HEALTH IS AN AMAZING GIFT

God's creation is wonderful. Amidst the intricacy of the physical world, He created man and woman to enjoy His handiwork and be in relationships with their Creator. Humans are *God-breathed* with a creative spirit that is endlessly curious and vibrant. God created people to love, with their energy going out in service to others. This is psychological health.

Even in a disordered world, people can have excitement about life, joyful experiences, and vibrant relationships. There is a good, loving side that people are usually able to express. Most relationships have a loving character about them. It is amazing how well the human spirit can function. Many are able to go about daily life, handling situations fairly well.

The stress of life and the ability to cope, however, have limits.

It had been three days since Graham was able to do anything constructive. Most of the time, he just sat there, staring vacantly at television. He had no energy to do anything else. He just sat there, sleeping fitfully from time to time, getting up only to get some food and water.

Graham was in a depressed state. He had crossed some line and was no longer able to function normally. He could not motivate himself. He felt an internal lethargy. He needed help.

## DISORDER AS A CONTINUUM

Emotional disorders are confusing. Daily mood shifts are puzzling. At times life seems good. Then there are days of depression.

The human spirit is mysterious and is the most complicated aspect of God's creation. To man, God gave the spark of creativity—of free will. A person's spirit creates reality, organizing all the information that impacts human consciousness. This is an intricate task that impacts emotions and mood states.

**NEED TO KNOW**

**Human spirit:** The *spirit* is the unifying force of the psyche, providing a creative organizing principle for the direction and purpose of life. It is the timeless observer, the center of consciousness that forms the basic attitudes of the person toward life and toward others. The *spirit* organizes the person's reality—what the person deeply believes to be true.*

God created humans to love and to have good relationships with their Creator and with one another. Much of the time there is a satisfaction about life and a good spirit for many situations. But life has its hardships, and relationships have their bad times. These affect mental and emotional well-being.

A person's well-being can be best understood by placing it on a continuum. Everyone experiences anxiety when faced with stressful situations. In a healthy personality, distress is usually situation-based and does not last long.

As distress increases, the person becomes caught in a negative cycle and emotions are more deeply affected, leading to elevated stress hormone levels. This can evolve into free-floating anxiety.

When anxiety becomes strong enough to affect normal life, disrupting sleep patterns and affecting the person's ability to function, the line is crossed.

---

\* Determinism is a construct of scientific methodology, making it popular to relegate human behavior to genetic, environmental, or internal forces beyond a person's control. This tends to take away responsibility for a person's choices, making confession somewhat obsolete. The "God-breathed" nature of humans does give *free will*: the capacity to ponder reality and make choices. Without the revelation of God and the work of His Holy Spirit, however, a person cannot choose to believe in or love (*agape*) God and desire to follow His will. This is God's work of faith.

Daily life is interrupted. Often there is obsessive thinking and inhibited social interaction.

Finally, when anxiety or depression becomes severe enough, the person can no longer function normally. There is debilitating internal distress. Some form of treatment is necessary.

Instead of labeling certain people as mentally ill, the best way of looking at mental and emotional disorder is to view it as a continuum, from relatively healthy to seriously disordered.

| Relatively Healthy | Mildly Disordered | Moderately Disordered | Severely Disordered |
| --- | --- | --- | --- |
| I | I | I | I |

During a person's lifetime, there can be considerable shift along this continuum. A relatively healthy individual can become disordered under periods of distress. An emotionally damaged person can become relatively healthy in a stable, loving environment. Relative emotional health varies with the degree of distress, especially relational stress.

There are varying levels of psychological disability, subjective distress, and inappropriate behavior. At any given time, about 20 percent of people could be considered well, 40 percent considered mildly disordered, 20 percent considered moderately disordered, and 20 percent considered severely disordered (about 6 percent of this category would be diagnosed with serious mental illness).[1] In terms of being able to function in life, there is a line between moderate and severe disorder that, when crossed, leaves a person somewhat incapacitated.

A good estimate is that about 20–25 percent of Americans ages 18 and older—about one in four adults—suffer from a diagnosable mental disorder in a given year (many have more than one diagnosis). Almost 50 percent of the population will experience a disorder during their lifetime that will interfere with normal functioning.

It is sobering to realize that one out of every four persons in any family or community will be facing significant mental and emotional problems and will be struggling to cope with their lives in any given year. And this does not even take into account the vast numbers suffering from seriously disordered family relationships!

## NEUROPLASTICITY VS. CONSTRICTION

There is a common denominator to all illness. The physical body, mental functions, and emotional expressions can become *constricted* when stressed or diseased.

Virtually all physical problems are associated with constriction and loss of plasticity. Asthma is a good example. Bronchial passageways begin to constrict, making it difficult to breathe. Blocked or constricted arteries inhibit blood flow. Blood vessels lose flexibility as disease sets in.

Emotional problems also constrict a person's life. The ability to consider alternatives decreases. Tunnel vision, obsessive thoughts, and rigid perception replace flexibility to adapt to new situations.

Depression is associated with changes in brain function. There is an actual decrease in the plasticity of the neural circuits in the depressed person. The brain cannot form new circuits as easily. A person's thoughts seem to get "stuck."

To be alive is to have excitement and vibrancy. To be healthy is to have energy and direction. Illness takes away this energy. It constricts mobility. When a person becomes depressed or has panic attacks, life choices are severely inhibited. There seems to be no choice except to withdraw into a more private world. This constricts life even further. Such a depressive cycle is hard to break. The amplification of this constriction process in a panic attack creates terrible inhibition of normal functioning.

> Jana could no longer go out in public. Her panic attacks had gotten more severe. The thought of being with other people was enough to send her stomach into flip-flops. She was a prisoner in her own home.
>
> She remembered the last time she had ventured out. She made it to the store, but as she walked in, a wave of anxiety hit her so hard that she had to lean against the wall to keep from collapsing. She thought she was going to pass out as her vision started distorting everything.
>
> She barely remembered getting back to her car. She sat for a long time, unable to drive. Finally her vision returned to normal, and the thought of being safely home again reduced some of the panic. When she walked back into her house, she knew that she would never venture out again. This was too stressful. She would rather just stay home.

The key to mental and emotional health is *neuroplasticity*. A healthy personality is open to new experiences. Situations can be handled as if they were merely interesting as opposed to stressful and overwhelming. When criticized, a person can genuinely search for ways to grow rather than get constricted and act defensively.

> ## NEED TO KNOW
>
> **Neuroplasticity:** A healthy body, a healthy soul, and healthy relationships are flexible, with energy flowing freely outward. Neuroplasticity is a similar concept for a healthy brain that is creative and flexible when processing new information. Constriction is just the opposite. In a disordered body, soul, or relationship, the flow of blood, air, or energy is blocked and turned back into self. Other terms for this constriction are "hardened arteries" and "a spiritually hardened heart."

It is interesting that antidepressive medication seems to work by facilitating the development of new neural connections.[2] The person has more options in thinking. Life seems less constricted and serious. The person can become curious again—a little more like a child.

## CAUSES OF DISORDER

It is very difficult to pinpoint causes of disorder. So many factors play a part. There are genetic problems, family background issues, and life stressors. Through all this, the human spirit has to navigate and struggle to keep a unity of consciousness.

Disorder is actually the norm. Disease is inevitable for the human body. The aging process brings on various kinds of constriction. Muscles gradually lose their elasticity. Veins and arteries become blocked and blood flow is inhibited.

Mental and emotional disorder is also the norm. Many life experiences are stressful and inhibit lifestyles. Relationships become constricted.

There should be no stigma attached to psychological disorders. Life is hard for everyone. All have varying degrees of disorder. All are in this together. It is part of the human condition.

## GENETIC BASIS FOR DISORDER

The problem actually begins before birth. Everyone has flawed DNA. Genetic inheritance is important. Susceptibility to alcoholism, for example, runs in families. Some disorders are actually caused by flawed DNA, like bipolar shifts in mood and childhood autism.

Medication is a gift of God. Antipsychotic drugs allow many to live improved lives, whereas without them they would not ordinarily be able to take care of themselves. Antidepressive medication has given energy and plasticity to the lives of many. Antianxiety medication certainly helps sleep patterns and normal functioning.

Subtle abnormalities in brain chemistry can be devastating. Abnormal levels of serotonin lead to unusual moods. A person can feel vulnerable and spend much unproductive time trying to be safe or protecting self.

The difference between *painters* and *pointers* is instructive. A painter will communicate by "painting a picture," processing thoughts out loud, giving detail and emotional content until the picture is complete. A pointer will think through things inside. The first words will be "the point."

## NEED TO KNOW

**Painters and pointers:** This is a typology that explores the difference in communication style that often leads to critical misunderstanding between two people. One "paints a picture" as they talk and the other "sticks to the point." Pointers misunderstand by focusing on the first word of the painter as the point, missing the rest of the picture. Painters dismiss the summarizing first word of a pointer, not realizing that this word needs to be unpackaged to get to the detail.[3]

In this communication typology, a painter has a sensitizing defense system. Surprises cause high anxiety. A painter will flash forward to situations in the future to anticipate what might happen. There is a definite feeling of vulnerability unless everything can be anticipated.

Her son was driving their car alone for the first time. He was going to pick up some friends and go to the mall. Coreen did not like the situation. She could picture him being distracted as he drove. He would take his eyes off the road as he bantered with his buddies. He would not notice a car pulling out in front of him. He would have a wreck and would be taken to the hospital. She would get a call . . .

Her mind kept flashing potential scenes as she anticipated her son's first driving experience. She had him driving too fast as a dare from one of his friends who liked to push the limits. She had him cruising around the mall and hitting a pedestrian when he was distracted.

As she voiced her objections and fears, her husband simply said that she was overreacting. That was no comfort to her as her mind continued to flash other potential dangers. She was ready for the phone call that told her that her son was in the hospital.

> A pointer's anxiety is totally different. With a repressive defense
> system, things can be handled without anxiety in a slightly
> detached fashion. A pointer feels anxious when things cannot
> be solved or when he or she has to react without a chance to
> think about things.

It took him totally by surprise. Jamell was looking forward to a relaxing day with his parents. Only a few minutes after they arrived, his mother brought up the subject of the next family vacation. The conversation was going fine until Mom showed her disappointment in the last vacation: "I don't know why the two of you had to bring your own car. We had plenty of room for you to ride with us. You could have helped us pay for our gas."

With that, Jamell's wife looked at him and said under her breath, "Aren't you going to say something? Are you going to let her get away with this?"

Jamell felt his stomach panic. He was not sure what was going on. He felt like a deer in the headlights. "What do you mean?" he whispered back, trying to buy some time.

His wife blew up at him. "Well, if you are not going to do anything, I am leaving. You always take your mother's side anyway." Jamell went into a full panic now, confused and totally uncertain as to what to do as his wife stomped out of the room.

Everyone feels anxiety when the situation is not safe. Humans are equipped with an automatic alarm system. Usually the person's stomach tightens up, leading to automatic internal reactions. Painters and pointers both feel anxiety, but they have different defense mechanisms. In both cases, the defense leads to constriction and loss of freedom.

## FAMILY-OF-ORIGIN ISSUES

Everyone goes through childhood within some type of family structure. This is perhaps the most important basis for disorder. There are so many situations that happen in each person's life while growing up that can lead to problems later in life.

> Jared was five years old. He was watching television when his
> mother told him to get in the car. They drove in silence. His
> mother was obviously agitated. Jared was confused and scared.
> They drove by a house and Mother exclaimed with emotion,
> "Your father is in there with that woman! He does not care about
> us." This was a defining moment in Jared's life. From that time
> on, he struggled to have a relationship with his father and was

"stuck" relying on his mother for emotional support growing up. He now lives with anxiety and uncertainty, and even at thirty-five years old, still feels the familiar childhood helplessness in many situations.

A child's spirit must take everything that happens growing up and make sense out of it. Often there are confusing family messages and behaviors that get passed down through generations. The result is strategies for life that are somewhat dysfunctional.

## LIFE STRESSORS

Think of a person's genetic makeup and family of origin as the basis for handling situations later on in life. To a person who is relatively healthy, a disruptive situation can be seen with curiosity and interest. To a person who is maladaptive, the same situation can be the source of considerable distress.

The stresses of life will take their toll on everybody. A relatively healthy person will show signs of disorder under prolonged stress.

Connie lost most of her energy. She was normally a vivacious and happy person. She was going through her son's long-term battle with cancer. The days ran together. They seemed to bring nothing but bad news. She had watched him turn from a healthy child into one who could barely move his head to look at her and smile. It had been a long time since she had gotten a good night's sleep. She knew she was obsessing over his blood count, desperately hoping that things would get better. She had a deep, helpless feeling that she could not shake.

## WHY SO MANY APPROACHES TO DISORDERS?

Unlike the study of the physical world, psychology does not have a unified theory to explain human behavior. Everyone agrees to the periodic table of elements for chemistry. Even a person's body has been scientifically studied, and its functions are fairly well understood with little disagreement.

A person's soul is a different matter. It is much more complex than the physical world. The problem is how to deal with consciousness.

Many gifted people have observed the functioning of the human soul and have come up with ingenious theories. All these theories are incredibly valuable and not only provide insight into dysfunction, but they also offer helpful ways of treating individuals with disorder.

To understand why there are so many theories, let's take a look at two basic philosophical questions concerning consciousness. These are unanswerable questions, but they provide insight into the different approaches to the study of psychology. These questions have been around for centuries.

The first is a basic question of reality: If a tree fell in the middle of the forest and no person was there to hear it, would there be sound? The answer to this question places reality either in the external world of sound waves or in the internal world of perception.

There is no right answer, but a theorist must make a judgment as to how important the inner world of perception is in forming the personality in contrast to the social environment.

It is a matter of emphasis. Some theorists start with an assumption that personality is formed by the contingencies of the environment. Behavior that is rewarded tends to become part of the person's reactions. Other theorists focus more on how the person views the situation. Such theories look to changing perception as the way to help the person in therapy.

The second is a question of free will: At any given moment, does a person have the choice to react a certain way, or is the reaction a product of predictable forces that determine the behavior? Again, there is no right answer, but a theorist must make a judgment as to how much of a person's behavior is a result of choices they make.

Again, this is a matter of emphasis. Some theorists start with an assumption that free will is not important. Predictable forces shape personality, and the goal of therapy is to change these forces. There is no need to work with the person's consciousness. Other theorists consider consciousness as most important in the therapy process.

The following chart is a way of picturing these different emphases in understanding mental and emotional disorder. The question of free will is placed on the vertical axis, going from a deterministic outlook to one that values human choice. The question of reality is placed on the horizontal axis, going from theorists that assume that the environment (external world) is more important in the development of personality to theorists that focus on the way a person perceives the situation (internal world).

Current theoretical orientations are placed in the four quadrants that are formed, suggesting that the answers to the two critical philosophical questions provide the basis of the assumptions of human nature that lie behind these theories.

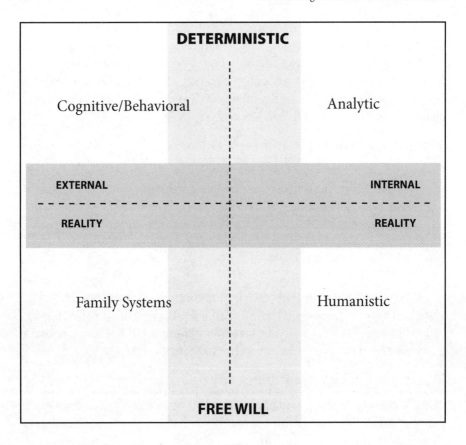

Cognitive/behavioral theories tend to be deterministic and emphasize the importance of the environment (external world) in the formation of personality. This is certainly a valuable insight. Habits obviously develop based on what is reinforced. Modeling explains a lot of the person's behavior. Automatic thoughts that can sometimes be depressive often come from high-guilt environments. Analytic theories also tend to be deterministic but emphasize the importance of internal conflict. Insight into defense mechanisms and unconscious motivations has been extremely helpful. The experiences of childhood certainly impact the adult life. The discovery of the "talking cure" to relieve internal distress is widely used.

Humanistic theories emphasize the value of free will and conscious choice. The human spirit can organize life in a healthy way if given the freedom to do so. People just need a chance to explore their own world without the usual conditions of worth that are placed on them. It is quite valuable to get into the other person's world and validate their experiences, seeing therapy as a partnering process. The therapy practice of "mindfulness" is another example of utilizing awareness to help the person enjoy the moment.

**Family systems theories** focus on the importance of the external family system and the individual's power to change the system by becoming a nonanxious presence. Self-differentiation is a way of using consciousness to change the family system by becoming less reactive.

## WHICH APPROACH IS BEST?

Each approach has its value. Given the complexity of the soul, an eclectic strategy is probably best. Some people respond well with one approach, while using a different approach may help others more.

Our current culture is biased toward a scientific approach. There is a movement toward *evidence-based practice*. There is good research into which approaches seem to help specific disorders the most. Since science relies on what can be observed, this movement favors a cognitive/behavioral approach.

Psychology cannot be purely scientific because of the nature of the human spirit and of consciousness. The soul cannot be studied with detached observation but also requires the artistic endeavor of intuition. The tension between psychology as a science and as an art has been long standing.

## WHAT IS THE GOAL OF THERAPY?

There is considerable agreement as to the goal of therapy: to help the person better adapt to his or her environment. This definition reflects a desire to help the person improve dysfunctional and maladaptive behavior. Since internal distress interferes with the person's life, there is also focus on helping the person's internal state.

This is a good goal. Most professional help will focus on this goal, even though the approaches may differ. Such help is a true gift to people in distress.

But there is a question that divides therapists: Should a person's faith be a proper focus in the therapy process? Therapists generally do not utilize a person's faith as a part of the therapy process and have not been trained to do so, yet most people seeking therapy value their faith highly.[4]

Many therapists are wary of bringing faith into the process. They have seen the damage that excessive religious dogma can bring to a person's life. There is a constriction process to a life of guilt and condemnation. It is true that some ways of presenting religious teachings tend to produce anxiety and guilt.

This does not mean that there is no value in a person's faith. There is a way of making faith a healthy part of the therapy process. The Christian faith and a healthy Christian community have gifts to offer those in mental and emotional distress. Faith communities can learn how to minister to those in distress, using faith as part of the healing process. A 2013 publication of the U.S. Department of Health and Human Services acknowledges: "Many turn to faith communities for support in dealing with mental health problems. Faith can provide important elements of solace and support for such individuals. Faith communities can also play a key role in educating their members about mental health problems. Supportive relationships, such as family, long-term friendships, and meaningful connections through faith can be important to building resilience and well-being."[5]

The *new self* is a blessing from God through faith. The fruit of the Spirit is love, joy, and peace. Individuals can be taught how their faith can impact daily life, taking away some of the anxiety of handling situations privately. This can help the therapy process.

The insight of Christian faith is powerful and provides a deeper goal for therapy than to better adjust to the environment. The wisdom of Christianity is that a deeply fulfilled life is a life of service. Leading people to reach out to others helps break the constriction cycles of their lives. Thanking God and loving others lead to neuroplasticity.

Therapy is also best when a supportive community is present. The healing power of a caring *faith community* can provide the atmosphere needed to help reorganize a dysfunctional life into a productive personality.

## NEED TO KNOW

**Faith community:** "For where two or three are gathered in My name, there am I among them" (Matthew 18:20). For most people, their primary faith community is a local congregation. This term is used in this sense, but is also used in a broader way to indicate the value of any gathering in Christ's name, sharing agape. Bible study groups, support groups, pastoral counselors, spiritual mentors, and deep conversations among Christian friends all qualify as elements of a person's faith community. Spiritual growth occurs within such faith communities that allow for intimate sharing and caring.

# The Spiritual Nature
# of Disorder

## CHAPTER 2

## In This Chapter

- The authors share a creative look at the *natural self*, born without a relationship with God—that is, missing *agape* in the formation of *spiritual DNA*.

- The authors identify the fatal flaw in creating reality: the person's spirit had to organize life without the guidance and surrounding love of God's Spirit.

- The self-protective *ME orientation* in life is discussed.

- The authors describe the healthy *WE orientation*, which cares for others.

- Damage to spiritual DNA occurs when high anxiety or feelings of entitlement result in *automated mood sequences* that show up in later life as dysfunctional strategies for handling situations.

## THE AMAZING HUMAN SPIRIT

God's creation is awesome. God "breathed into his nostrils the breath of life, and the man became a living creature" (Genesis 2:7). Created in the image of God, humans also have the incredible capacity to create. The organizing power of the human spirit shows up in the unity of consciousness. Each person has a deep personal world that ponders reality. All are very good with understanding what is really going on.

> Shayla was preoccupied. Something her friend said continued to puzzle her later on. She had indicated that Shayla's boyfriend was making fun of her at a party. Suddenly, it all fit together.

> Shayla had been feeling more distant from him and wondered
> why. Now it became clear that he was going to break up with her.

Like Shayla, all do a good job in understanding reality. That is the creative spirit at work. Children learn at an early age that people don't always tell the truth. They notice inconsistencies, ponder them in their heart, and then draw conclusions about what is real. This is how attitudes are formed.

"Bless the LORD, O my soul, and all that is within me" (Psalm 103:1). The soul is a rich inner world, filled with memories, attitudes, emotions, and deep understanding. The soul is an awesome creation of God. Human consciousness and its complexity are truly amazing.

The most remarkable function of consciousness is the unity of awareness. This is the astounding work of the human spirit. All of the richness of the soul must be organized to provide this unity. The spirit is the organizing force. Just as God's Spirit moved on the face of the earth, organizing chaos into our incredible creation, so the human spirit organizes the baffling data of life into a stable identity and orderly consciousness. People do a good job at organizing reality. This becomes what they believe to be true.

> Larson has been married for twelve years. Things haven't gone
> very well the last few years, and he has spent a lot of time puz-
> zling over the marriage. He finally concluded that his wife just
> has to be in control, just like her mother. It is obvious to him that
> everything is fine as long as it goes her way.

Larson is not making casual conversation when he talks about his wife. He is saying what he really believes to be true. As he goes through detail after detail, what he is saying starts to sound like a *litany*. His attitude is tightly constructed, based on many observations and repeated often in his mind. He has drawn a firm conclusion about his wife. Scripture calls this a *hardened heart* (Mark 8:17).

## THE FATAL FLAW IN PONDERING REALITY

Even though the human spirit is quite good at organizing and is also very accurate, the conclusions that are drawn have a fatal flaw. The words of 1 Corinthians 2:14 offer a good way of understanding this flaw. St. Paul uses the Greek word *psychikos* to describe the *natural self*. In this word picture, the rich raw material of the soul (*psyche*) had to be organized by itself. The organizing principle is thus "self-protection." Inevitably this turns the energy of life inward.

This is in contrast to the Greek word for "spiritual" (*pneuma*, 1 Corinthians 2:15), which describes the new self. In this word picture, God's Spirit helps to reorganize the soul. The organizing principle is now the love—agape—of Christ. With identity as a child of God, self-protection is no longer necessary.

## NEED TO KNOW

*Pneuma* (**New self**): This Greek term describes the soul that has been reorganized by the Holy Spirit and is a new creation. The gift of Christ's presence within the heart of the believer through faith has the power to create a new reality. The new self is not the human spirit, but God's gift of love that can influence the person by renewing a right spirit within (Psalm 51:10). This is the basis of an extraordinary WE orientation to life and is the proper order for the soul.

The new self is a gift from God. It does not have to get stronger, but is like the sun, shining all the time. It is God's grace.

The fatal flaw of the natural self is that all people are ultimately on their own, from childhood on, to understand a very complex world. Even as a child, the ability to ponder reality in a private inner world and form one's identity is done in the private regions of the heart.

## NEED TO KNOW

*Psychikos* (**Natural self**): This Greek term describes the development of a person's reality without the love of God and the direction of the Holy Spirit. This is a word picture that describes the struggle for meaning and fulfillment in life as the person is tossed about by cultural winds that blow promise for happiness. It describes one's sinful nature that is self-protective or curved back into self. This is the basis of a prevalent ME orientation to life and the dysfunctional order of the soul.

## NEED TO KNOW

**Heart:** This is where direction in life is developed (Proverbs 16:9) and where reality decisions are made. In this inmost chamber of the soul, the human spirit organizes reality and develops the person's attitudes and beliefs. This is the place of free will. What is pondered in the heart becomes what the person believes to be true.

Courtney was only seven and had never seen her father so angry. She had been playing in his office and spilled some of her milk on his papers. His anger scared her and she ran to her room, crying. From that point on, she never went into her father's office again. She concluded that his papers were more important than she was. She would stay away from him so she would not make him angry again.

This was a *defining moment* in Courtney's relationship with her father. She stopped being affectionate with him in order to protect herself from getting hurt again. But her conclusions came from her own private inner world, and they were not accurate. Yet she really, really believed that she was not safe with her father.

This fatal flaw of handling things privately creates anxiety and a personal sense of fairness. Everyone must protect and look out for self. Born without a relationship with God, without His loving presence, there is no other choice. This is why the natural self is ultimately ME oriented. The best way of describing this sinful condition is the Latin phrase *incurvatus in se*, which means "curved into self."

## NEED TO KNOW

*Incurvatus in se*: This Latin term was first used by St. Augustine and then by Martin Luther to describe the effects of sin. The term means "curved into self" and is a graphic description of the flow of energy inward that takes away from the joy of loving God and serving others (energy flowing outward).

Check out your own thought process for a moment. Remember some of the things that went through your mind during the past hour. Perhaps it was a situation that happened yesterday, which left you hurt and frustrated. Without wanting to, you replay that scene again and again, angry that it was not fair. Or perhaps you thought of a situation that's going to happen in a few days. Each time that situation comes to mind, you feel anxiety in your stomach, uncertain about the outcome.

So much of what goes on in one's internal consciousness reflects the need to defend self. Concern for self is automatic. Ultimately there is no backup. Fallen man has no choice except to be self-centered. This is the meaning of St. Paul's word *psychikos* (1 Corinthians 2:14).

This sinful condition is permanent. Nothing can be done to make the natural self more acceptable to God. The *psychikos* is the reality of life without God's loving presence.

## PROPER ORDER OF OUR SOULS

God created people as relational beings to be in relationship with their Creator and with one another. Relationships work when every person is thinking of the good of the whole (WE). Relationships don't work and they get into power struggles when each person is out for him- or herself (ME).

God did not create people to get depressed, to be anxious, to become resentful, or to stress about life. God did not create people to die, but to enjoy creation. God's will, as summarized by Christ, is that we love God with our whole heart and love others as we love ourselves (Mark 12:30–31). This reflects an outward flow of energy toward God and others in worship and service. Critical relationships in our lives function as they should when organized by selfless love. The word for this in Greek is *agape* and is used in such passages as John 3:16: "For God so *loved* the world" (emphasis added).

### NEED TO KNOW

**Agape:** This is an expression of a love that does not exist in its natural form on earth, but is a function of the new self as Christ dwells within the believer's heart through faith. This love seeks nothing in return but is completely selfless, its energy going outward in praise to God and service to one another. Such love is the basis for the fellowship within the Body of Christ and produces the unique healing possibilities of a faith community.

The problem is that agape does not exist on earth in its natural state. God is love, and without agape, all become ultimately self-centered. There is no other choice. Lives are stressful as people try to control things, endlessly worrying about what might happen. In other words, seldom is there a pause just to enjoy the moment.

In all relationships, especially within families, there is constant hurt, disappointment, and frustration. The most powerful forces on earth occur right here. Bad moods, hardened attitudes, and negative beliefs about others' motives dominate the family atmosphere.

Instead of being able to love self, there is usually a battle going on inside. Guilt, regret, and struggle for self-control are the things usually experienced in internal conversations. All of these forces lead to mental and emotional distress instead of allowing loving, joyful, and peaceful lives. Life is often hard and constricted. No one escapes this human dilemma.

## PHYSICAL DNA AND SPIRITUAL DNA

A good analogy to use in understanding the development of the *psychikos* and its inevitable struggle with disorder is *spiritual DNA*. Physical DNA is the blueprint for the organization of the body and its systems into a unified whole for a healthy physical life. Spiritual DNA is the blueprint for one's belief system: the organization of the spirit that produces a unified consciousness for a healthy life.

Physical DNA is the wonderfully intricate blueprint for the physical body. The precise organization of the genetic code at conception leads to the development of all of the body's systems and governs their function throughout a person's life. This precise code is replicated countless times and must always show the same exact order as cells divide and instructions are constantly given for cellular activity.

## NEED TO KNOW

DNA is the genetic "instruction manual" found in all our cells. If DNA becomes damaged and is not repaired properly, then the cell may get the wrong instructions and start to multiply out of control. This can lead to cancer. DNA is under constant bombardment, so it is vital that any damage be detected quickly and repaired. There are specialized damage and repair proteins, such as p53 and BRCA1. For more information, see www.cancerresearchuk.org.

The ability to organize the myriad experiences of life into a unified belief system is the function of the human spirit. The blueprint for such a belief system can be called spiritual DNA. The created capacity of the spirit to form attitudes and to make sense out of life is based on the amazing capacity to believe, to have faith in something, and to use this wisdom to organize. The ability to organize reality exists for every experience in the person's life, like physical DNA exists in every cell of the body. Spiritual DNA is the history of a person's construction of reality.

## NEED TO KNOW

**Spiritual DNA:** The history of the formation of reality by the human spirit over the developmental stages in life is called a person's spiritual DNA. Like physical DNA, spiritual DNA is a way of passing on characteristics of the parental behavior since the child's organization of reality begins within the context of the family unit. From early on, children form their own view of reality as they navigate through life experiences. This is the work of their creative spirit, and it forms the automatic habits and personality characteristics based on what they believe to be true about life.

Physical DNA is under constant attack that threatens to damage this code and its precise order. One example is that of carcinogens that damage elements of the code, leading to the disease of cancer. Such damage, if unchecked, brings illness to the body and eventual death.

To guard against attacks on its code, specialized agents are constantly checking the accuracy of the code, making sure that it is not damaged and changed from its original sequence. When such damage is found, other specialized agents will repair the damage, restoring the cell to health with its original code intact on the DNA strands.

Sometimes the DNA cannot be fixed and the damaged code remains, leading to various diseases to the body. In the case of cancer, the altered cell produces a substance that tricks the normal repairing mechanism into sensing that the DNA code is appropriate. This allows the cancer to spread since the immune system does not detect that these are dangerous cells.

The proper spiritual DNA code is reflected in God's Law. This purpose is revealed in this summary: to love God and to love others as one loves self (Luke 10:27). An outward flow of energy in worship and service is the proper order of one's spiritual life and leads to a fulfilled life of love, joy, and peace (the fruit of the Spirit, Galatians 5:22). A healthy spirit organizes life experiences around the belief that the person is loved by God and is always secure in His presence.

The proper order of the spiritual DNA code is reflected in the child's capacity to be curious, to love, and to respect (energy outward). This order is under constant attack as the child goes through the varied experiences of life. It is damaged when the child feels threatened or gains too much power, developing damaged automated sequences that are self-centered (*incurvatus in se*).

### NEED TO KNOW

**Spiritual DNA** is also an "instruction manual" for how to handle the experiences of life. It is damaged through threatening situations that produce anxiety or by poor boundaries that allow self-centered behavior to be rewarded. The love of parents and others functions like the damage-repair proteins of physical DNA for some of these situations. Without the constant presence of God's love (agape), however, many of these damaging moments have to be handled privately, leading to more-permanent damaged spiritual DNA that shows up later in life.

## DEFINING MOMENTS

Everyone goes through childhood. The human spirit has the awesome potential to organize experiences into a unified reality. Gradually, children become familiar with their environment, using each experience to better understand how things work and how they fit into the world.

The child's spirit must take all of these experiences and develop reality. In a deep, private place within the heart, a child will make sense out of life. The child will focus on voice tone and facial expression in order to determine what was really meant. Once formed, this becomes the child's reality. If a parent, in anger and at a critical developmental age, tells the child that he or she is stupid, the child will actually believe that. That becomes reality.

## DEFINING MOMENTS THAT LEAD TO HEALTHY SPIRITUAL DNA

A child develops relatively healthy spiritual DNA (1) within a loving environment that (2) has consistent boundaries and (3) where there are no secrets so that the child can be open and honest about things. In such a healthy family environment, everyone is more concerned about the good of the whole than personal welfare. A child learns to trust and have concern for others in such a WE-oriented environment. Such a child will be resilient, will have a healthy curiosity, and will form good relationships. The child's life will show plasticity rather than constriction.

There are many defining moments in such a family environment that lead to the formation of healthy spiritual DNA. A special birthday celebration, for example, becomes a defining moment for a seven-year-old child.

> Corie went to bed smiling. It had been her birthday, and her parents had made it so special. As her mind reviewed the events of the day, she could still see the look in her father's eyes when he swept her up in his arms and wished a happy birthday to his "little princess." She could still feel her mother's excitement as she presented Corie with a special doll that she would prize all of her childhood. She went to sleep knowing she was loved.

When a child has a potentially damaging experience but is able to be open about it in a loving family situation, the damage is healed or minimized. This experience will not lead to anxiety or excessive self-protection in the future life of the child. This process is similar to the processes that monitor the code of physical DNA to keep it healthy.

## DEFINING MOMENTS THAT DAMAGE SPIRITUAL DNA

Damage to spiritual DNA occurs when a child handles an emotionally important situation privately and is thus forced to develop personal strategies to handle the anxiety or lack of boundaries in this defining moment of the child's life. Moments of distress and anxiety are not forgotten, but become important in handling future situations. In this way the natural self develops.

Brandon had been a difficult child. He couldn't seem to concentrate and was usually defiant. When he was six years old, his parents were going through a difficult struggle. His mother was under extreme stress. Brandon came into the house, and his mother told him to pick up his jacket. He got angry and said he wouldn't do it. He stomped up the stairs to his room and slammed the door. He wanted to go and cool off like he normally did. But this time his mother stomped up the stairs after him. When she opened the door, Brandon yelled at her, "I wish I wouldn't have to come home to you!"

His mother replied, "Then just stay away! I would be happier without you!"

Of course his mother didn't mean this angry outburst, but at this critical point in his young life, it was a defining moment for Brandon. He saw the look in her eyes and heard the angry tone of her voice. He actually believed that his mother would be happier if he were not at home. This moment remained a vivid memory for Brandon, and it damaged his spiritual DNA. This became his reality. He really believed his mother did not want him around. He did not trust her, and later on in life, he had difficulty trusting anyone, especially women.

Every significant experience of the child helps form this spiritual DNA.* Without the constant security of God's love (agape), many of these experiences must be handled privately by the child. The child must develop reality privately, on his or her own. In other words, without the constant presence of

---

\* There is some recent scientific evidence that points toward this concept of spiritual DNA from the rapidly developing field of epigenetics, which quantifies the role of nurture in healthy development in addition to the genetic code acquired from nature. Neuroscience is demonstrating how relationships impact the way our brains are wired, particularly in the early years when parent-child attachment is critical in forming neural connections related to social and emotional development. However, very little is yet known from a scientific viewpoint regarding how relationships impact spiritual development, and that is where faith and science can complement each other in working with families. There is evidence from history and documented case studies as to how faith can improve outcomes for communities and individuals. This is difficult to quantify in terms of scientific measurement although some significant attempts are being made, as in the books *The Spiritual Brain—A Neuroscientist's Case for the Existence of the Soul* by M. Beauregard and D. O'Leary (New York: HarperCollins, 2007) and *The Spirit of the Child* by D. Hay and R. Nye (London: Jessica Kingsley Publishers, 2006).

agape, the spiritual DNA of every person is significantly damaged through-out life.† This is the effect of sin.

## AUTOMATED MOOD SEQUENCES

There are two basic ways in which spiritual DNA gets damaged, resulting in a faulty DNA coding that is self-centered and constricted, rather than resilient. Instead of a curious child that is in a good mood, such damage leads to predictable anxious, upset, angry, or entitled behavior in specific interactions.

The first type of damage is when there is high anxiety, signaling some threat or danger to self. Children must develop ways of handling such situations. When picked on or ridiculed at school, for example, the natural feelings of danger and vulnerability will cause considerable distress. The child's spirit must find a creative way to develop a degree of safety and protection. Depending on the age, the child will look away, walk away, or become defiant. Such nonverbal behavior then becomes an *automated mood sequence*. Later on in life, when faced with a similar situation, this automated sequencing will begin. In this way, spiritual DNA resembles physical DNA in the automatic nature of its sequencing.

### NEED TO KNOW

**Automated mood sequences:** Like the automatic sequencing of physical DNA, damage to spiritual DNA causes automatic thinking, feeling, and behaving when situations similar to the original one occur. This automatic response defines a person's belief system about the situation, justifying the reaction to the situation.

Damage to spiritual DNA also occurs when there are not healthy boundaries for the child. If the child can manipulate the situation to get what he or she wants, the child will grow up feeling entitled.

### NEED TO KNOW

**Damage to spiritual DNA:** Concrete, personal experiences that cause high anxiety or that give the child too much power (entitlement) cause dysfunctional strategies for later life. These are constrictive, self-protective strategies (the ME orientation) that turn energy inward. The natural self is on its own, without God's loving presence, and is forced to handle these situations privately. Such childhood strategies become the person's reality, forming personality traits that determine how situations are handled in the future.

---

† The only person without spiritual DNA damage was Jesus Christ. He was never alone, except during his last moments of life when His Father had to abandon Him to put the sins of the world onto Him. He always experienced His Father's love (agape) and presence in every other situation. Even the devil could not separate Him from His Father's mission and get Him to think about Himself.

Trevor was so angry that he was on the floor, kicking and scream-ing. He was at the mall and saw something that he wanted. He pestered his mother again and again until she got angry at him. So he flung himself on the floor and created a scene, knowing that his mother would give in. He didn't care that she was angry at him. He walked out of the store with what he wanted.

Repeated instances of anxiety or entitlement that occur at a vulnerable age become defining moments in the development of spiritual DNA. The strategy that the child's spirit develops to handle these situations is age-specific and becomes part of the personality. These are automated reactions that show up later in life when the person faces a similar circumstance.

## NEED TO KNOW

**Defining moments:** Concrete situations that remain vivid in a person's memory represent the moment when the child faced an emotionally important situation and had to develop a strategy to handle it. Some-times the child's only coping strategy is to disassociate or detach from the memory of the event. The child's coping strategy then becomes part of the spiritual DNA.

Let's go back to Trevor, who found out that a temper tantrum would get him what he wanted at age 5. He will become emotionally "stuck" at that age whenever his feelings are blocked. When he is thirty-five and married, he will give himself permission to express his emotions without consideration of the other person. His voice tone and mannerisms will resemble a five-year-old throwing a temper tantrum. This behavior is automated and plays out somewhat predictably whenever he is frustrated. This is his automated mood sequence. He is in a downward mood spiral and has *become oinkey*. He will believe that his behavior is normal!

## NEED TO KNOW

**Becoming oinkey:** When a person's mood shifts in a downward spiral in a relationship and one is blaming the other, a good term to use is that the person has become oinkey. The person is now in a bad mood that is justified because of the perceived hurt or "not fair" feelings that are felt in the stomach area as sinking, angry, and depressed energy.

Trevor got up early on Saturday morning since he and his wife had planned to clean out the garage and then go on an outing. His wife decided to sleep in. Trevor became increasingly upset as he cleaned the garage by himself. When his wife showed up to help, he blew up at her, calling her lazy and inconsiderate. His language became abusive, and he felt fully justified in his verbal abuse. At that moment, he had emotions, and they were going to be expressed.

Trevor had no insight that he was being abusive. His automated mood sequence felt natural to him. It was obviously his wife's fault for agitating him. After all, she was the one who had caused his feelings. If she had gotten up when they planned, he would not have gotten angry. That was his reality, so why would he stop himself from expressing his anger in this way?

Often there is no way for the person to be aware that his or her spiritual DNA code has been damaged. The person actually believes that his or her reaction is normal and blames others for the resulting bad feelings. Since this is now part of the belief system, the person is trapped with this automated reaction that seems normal. It is part of the spiritual DNA!

Every person has damaged spiritual DNA. There are multiple times in everyone's childhood when critical feelings of anxiety or entitlement result in automated mood sequencing.‡ This damage becomes embedded in the personality and feels completely natural to the person. That is why in every relationship, each person can see the other's dysfunction clearly, but his or her own is completely invisible. It is always natural to blame the other person for one's own emotional discomfort. People generally do not recognize their own dysfunctional behavior. This is what they grew up with, and so it seems normal to them.

## Repairing Spiritual DNA with Christ's Presence

What is missing from the spiritual DNA formation is the constant love of God (agape). Without God's loving presence, the child is often forced to handle stressful situations privately. This creates the damage that leads to immature automated sequences in the child's reactions in later life.

Recent advances in molecular biology have allowed repair of damaged physical DNA by external means, introducing the proper coding sequence into the DNA. In similar fashion, spiritual DNA can be repaired by external means,

---

‡    This concept is presented not to blame parents for spiritual DNA damage, but to give insight into the development of the natural self and its disordered state. Many times parents do or say things that normally would not do damage, but when the child is at a critical developmental stage, the impact may be more serious. Also, much damage occurs through interaction with peers and through unavoidable situations, such as accidents or sickness.

bringing the presence of Christ into the damaged area. This use of a person's faith can be accomplished either by going back to the defining memory and letting Christ be a part of that memory or by stopping an automatic sequence from the damaged DNA and letting Christ's presence change the progression of the sequence. This process is best accomplished within the relationships of a healthy faith community!

## NEED TO KNOW

**Repairing spiritual DNA damage:** Physical DNA is constantly being damaged and needs to be repaired. Specialized proteins recognize the damage and repair the DNA, restoring its original code. By analogy, damaged spiritual DNA (ME-focused energy) needs to be recognized by comparing it with God's will (the function of the Law), leading to confession. The damage can be repaired as God's presence is received (God's selfless love as expressed in the Greek word *agape*), restoring the original code (WE-focused energy).

A good analogy to use for the influence of the Spirit is that of a magnet and iron filings. Picture all of the thoughts, feelings, and memories of the soul as iron filings that are grouped together as the person's identity was gradually formed through life experiences. When a powerful magnet is placed under the iron filings, they are reorganized along the lines of the magnet's influence. In similar fashion, the witness of the Holy Spirit that gives a new identity as a child of God (Romans 8:15–16) reorganizes the soul to form the new self. This begins to reconstruct a person's reality based on this gift of faith.

There is now a proper ordering of the soul in the way God intended so that the energy goes outward. The "fruit of the Spirit" (Galatians 5:22) includes descriptive terms that represent this outward flow of energy. Love, for example, is selfless concern for others. Joy is reflected in praising God and serving others. Peace is shown in relationships where there is concern for the good of the whole and not for selfish gain.

# The Cause of Internal Dysfunction

## CHAPTER 3

### IN THIS CHAPTER

- St. Paul describes his own internal struggle in Romans 7:21–25.

- The authors examine the war between the two internal forces: the *mind* and the *body*.

The human spirit as the organizing force of the soul can become dysfunctional if it allows the mind to dominate reality, causing *overcontrol* disorders. If the body is allowed to dominate, the result is *impulse-control* disorders. A spirit that is poorly formed because of genetic problems, excess privacy, or deceit will lead to *reality* disorders.

> Pam could not remember affection growing up. She fantasized about closeness and tenderness, but her life was virtually devoid of those feelings. So, when Doug started talking to her at work one day, she felt hope for the first time.
>
> He was separated and found her easy to talk to. He told her of his struggles, and she listened. A few weeks later, they went out and he shared more deeply with her. For the first time, she experienced real affection. That unlocked something in her, and she wanted to be with Doug more and more.
>
> At first, he was amused at how she worshiped him, but he gradually tired of her constant attention. He demanded more from her.

He took money and favors and then became more open with his disgust. She grew more desperate, clinging more tightly, doing everything Doug wanted—even though his requests were degrading. Finally, when he flaunted other women in front of her, she broke off from him.

Deeply hurt, she could not trust herself any longer. She punished herself by remembering all the degrading things she had tolerated. Obsessed with thoughts like "You were so stupid!" and without hope of satisfying her need for closeness, Pam settled into a depressive state.

Her mind and body did not trust each other. In fact, these two forces seemed to hate each other as they struggled for control.

## SCRIPTURAL EXPRESSION OF INNER STRUGGLES

St. Paul was well aware of the reality of internal struggles. He wrote, "So I find it to be a law that when I want to do right, evil lies close at hand. For I delight in the law of God, in my inner being, but I see in my members another law waging war against the law of my mind and making me captive to the law of sin that dwells in my members" (Romans 7:21–23).

## THE MIND

The *mind* is an ever-present evaluating force. It monitors everything a person does. It also thinks back over what has happened and makes value judgments about actions. This is the voice inside that says, "That was really dumb." St. Paul calls this force the "mind."

The mind is essential within one's consciousness, giving practical application to a person's value system. It is a good force created by God that gives direction to life, separating right from wrong. It observes every situation and evaluates what is happening. It constantly monitors all behavior.

### NEED TO KNOW

**Mind:** The mind is the cognitive force within the psyche that knows what is right, operating out of the person's value system. This force relentlessly pushes toward what should be done and utilizes guilt in its effort to exert control over the impulses of the body.

The power of this force is pervasive. The mind provides motivation to do the right thing. But this is also where the perfectionistic "shoulds" and guilt feelings come from. The mind is powerful and relentless, constantly making the person aware of what should not have happened or of what should have been done.

## THE BODY

There is another force inside that pushes toward expression of energy. This force is more expressive of one's feelings or mood at the moment. An individual may have a distinct feeling, "I'm just not in the mood to clean things up." St. Paul calls this force the *body*.

The body is also an essential force within one's consciousness. It provides the impulse for action and gives emotional color to life. This impulse is felt in the body as direction for its energy. This passion—the zest for life—seeks expression on a moment-by-moment basis. It provides energy for the personality. It is also a good, God-created force.

### NEED TO KNOW

> **Body:** The body is the emotional force that searches for fulfillment of its energy. This force relentlessly pushes toward expression of its impulses (what it wants to do) and uses a "Who cares?" attitude as its rebellion over the controlling force of the mind. Impulses are sensed in the physical body, and fulfillment involves the physical body with its energy and actions.

At any given time, both of these forces inside are active. In any conversation, the mind is dealing with what is being said, and the body is dealing with the nonverbal aspects of the communication. If these two conflict, there is a double message.

The person's mind may give a good, socially acceptable response, "It's good to see you again," while at the same time, the body might give a nonverbal negative message by a flat voice tone. If there is not a good relationship with self, the person gives out double messages. This makes relationships with others difficult.

When these two forces inside are in conflict, the energy is blocked and an internal mood develops. Much time is spent fighting self. Such internal struggles are common. The mind and the body have different ways of looking at things. The mind is aware of one's goals as it looks at the past and considers the future. The body is aware of one's feelings and impulses at the moment.

### NEED TO KNOW

> **Internal disorder:** Faulty development of the personality can lead to internal struggle. St. Paul vividly describes his own internal disorder in Romans 7:21–23, identifying the natural war between the mind and

the body. If the mind can take charge of the personality, the result is an *overcontrol* disorder. If the body can take over, the result is an *impulse-control* disorder. If the spirit does not form properly, the result is a *reality* disorder.*

> Granger woke up angry at himself. He had eaten too much the night before and felt fat. He looked into the mirror and felt good as he felt a righteous anger and said to himself, "You are going on a diet."
>
> He had nothing but coffee for breakfast, then a small salad for lunch. His angry resolve was still firmly in place at dinner, so he had small portions and no dessert.
>
> But then, as he was watching TV that evening, another force took over. He had the wonderful thought, "Just a little wine and cheese won't hurt." As he started snacking, he felt so good as another thought took over: "Oh well, what does it matter? I'm fat anyway." He had that wonderful "I don't care" feeling.
>
> A half hour later, his mood shifted again. His mind was back in control, and he looked at all he had eaten. He was angry at himself again.

## THE HUMAN SPIRIT IS THE "THIRD FORCE" THAT UNIFIES

The *human spirit* is the unifying force of all relationships, linking together separate forces into a living, creative unity. It is also the organizing principle for relationships, forming basic attitudes, setting the atmosphere, and controlling communication. The oneness that couples experience, giving them greater energy for life, is the spirit of their relationship!

The forces of the mind and the body are powerful and relentless and need to be controlled by a third force. The spirit is the unifying force of the soul that produces an organized consciousness. It is a deep, creative power, forming the organizing principle of the person's life—the person's basic identity

---

* Such faulty development of one's internal conversation does not cause the sin that St. Paul describes as "making me captive to the law of sin that dwells in my members" (Romans 7:23). Rather, it is the natural condition of the sinful nature that takes the experiences of life and organizes them through a "ME-orientation" of both the *mind* and the *body* into a power struggle that St. Paul describes as "waging war" (Romans 7:23). The "law of the Spirit of life" (Romans 8:2) brings agape into this internal relationship, allowing for a "WE-orientation" of both of these forces. This is the work of the *new self.*

and purpose. It is related to a person's faith. It has the power to align the other two forces into a common direction, thus forming the basis of the will.

The spirit is not a static entity but is involved in the process of relating. Its effects are quite evident in the mood and energy level of the person. When the mind and body work in harmony, there is a good spirit within. Genuine warmth and a caring attitude toward others mark the existence of a healthy spirit. This allows the person to get into the spirit of things and be excited about different situations.

## NEED TO KNOW

**Human spirit:** The human spirit is the unifying force of the psyche, providing a creative organizing principle for the direction and purpose of life. It is the timeless observer, the center of consciousness that forms the basic attitudes of the person toward life and toward others. The spirit organizes the person's reality—what the person deeply believes to be true.

Without a healthy spiritual substructure to give direction and purpose, the personality loses its capacity for depth. The spirit can be weakened or damaged. Without a healthy mediating force, there is an inevitable power struggle inside with both mind and body trying to win and dominate the other. Such internal chaos and lack of self-control is debilitating.

In its battle for satisfaction, the body will settle for momentary pleasure—a pathetic substitute for the true fulfillment of its longing. In its battle for control, the mind will settle for following the letter of the law—also a pathetic substitute for the richness of life. Both of these give only surface satisfaction to the yearning of the soul but miss the depth of life.

## SPIRITUAL ALIGNMENT DISORDERS

The human spirit is the organizing force within the soul. Healthy spiritual development produces a good relationship between the mind and the body, both utilizing their power and gifts for the good of the whole personality. Proper spiritual alignment is reflected in this good relationship in which the spirit takes into consideration both the mind and the body in the final decision for action.

By analogy, marriage counseling is effective when the counselor keeps proper spiritual alignment. This means that the therapist is focused on strengthening the relationship (WE). Both spouses present their *litanies* in an attempt to get the counselor to align with them to change the other person. When the counselor does see the value of one of the litanies and allies with that spouse in the power struggle that has been going on in the marriage, the counselor's effectiveness is compromised.

## NEED TO KNOW

**Litany:** A person's attitude becomes hardened toward another person, a situation, or to self when sufficient evidence is gathered to support a belief system. The key defining moment(s) for the development of such an attitude is coupled with other observations that reflect this bias. Often, hundreds of hours are spent in this process. Once the person's heart has hardened, this attitude is presented in the form of a litany that is endlessly repeated, trying to get others to go along with the belief system. It is as if all words are being sung to the same tune.

As this plays out within the soul, the person's spirit will align with the mind against the body. During this phase, the person actually believes that thirty minutes spent in guilt and regret are necessary to stop the body from acting out again. But when the body builds up enough resentment, it will take over the personality in a similar way. Now the spirit aligns with the body, and the person actually believes that he or she is justified in fixing the mood. It is like there are two different people or moods inside.

> Hank could think of little else. He was at home with his wife, but the other woman was all he could focus on. He resented being trapped. He thought of the wonderful closeness and intimacy of this other relationship. He was sullen and angry, withdrawn and cold. He felt he deserved to be happy.
>
> He ended up getting very angry at his wife and, with his body in control, spent the night with the other woman. When he woke up and looked at the unattractive surroundings of her meager home, his mind took control, and all he could think of was how stupid he was. He was giving up a good life, his family, his nice home. He felt so guilty. He could not believe that he was doing this.

This alignment cycle is expressed in Romans 2:15: "They show that the work of the law is written on their hearts, while their conscience also bears witness, and their conflicting thoughts *accuse* or even *excuse* them" (emphasis added). When the spirit aligns with the mind, there is accusation. When it aligns with the body, there is excusing.

## OVERDEVELOPED MIND

Many circumstances lead to an overdeveloped mind. Defining moments coupled with anxiety during ages 7–10 will often create an overcontrolled personality.

> Her father moved out when she was eight years old. Maria remembers that day vividly. Her parents had a terrible fight. She hid in her bedroom with her five-year-old brother, comforting him as he sobbed uncontrollably. She remembers, as if it were yesterday, Dad blaming Mom for their financial difficulties and yelling as he went out the door, "I never want to see you again!"
>
> Mom went to her bedroom and curled up into a ball, sobbing with a deep moan. Maria went to her mother and began to comfort her. She knew that she would have to be the strong one now.

In an unsafe environment (abusive, alcoholic, or neglectful), the child's spirit can easily fall into the pattern of producing security by being responsible. Such a strategy allows the mind to overdevelop to reduce anxiety. The child can end up feeling responsible for everything and will gradually lose touch with the body. Such children are likely to become overcontrolled adults— much too serious, guilt-ridden, co-dependent, and wishing to please everyone.

An overdeveloped mind is also created when the parents live through their child, basing their worth on the child's success. The child is put on a pedestal. From being seen as the perfect child, his or her spirit can easily develop an organizing principle based on getting rewards for pleasing others.

> Her family referred to Connie as their "good little girl." To please her parents, she anticipated what they wanted her to do. She actually initiated this spiritual strategy in order to see the look of admiration in her busy father's eyes. She spent much of her childhood finding how to please him in order to get his attention. She would watch his face when he came in and would try to anticipate what he wanted. The strategy worked, and she was rewarded by being "Daddy's girl."
>
> She carried this strategy into marriage and set out to please her husband. Her husband, however, took her for granted and gradually paid less attention to her. She was trapped. The more she tried to be the perfect wife, the less interest her husband

showed. Even with her marriage in shambles, she pretended to her children and her friends that everything was fine. She was upset at her husband for not rewarding her efforts to please him, but deep down, she was angry at God. She had played by the rules, and the results were not fair.

This is not a healthy strategy for life. An adult will build resentment when a successful childhood strategy no longer gets rewarded.

An overdeveloped mind leads to *overcontrol* disorders. Perfectionism, obsessive/compulsive behavior, anxiety, and depression are examples of one's mind constantly dominating the personality.

## OVERDEVELOPED BODY

The delicate balance between the mind and the body also is upset when the child is pampered and is not given consequences. In this situation, the impulsive side, or body, will become overdeveloped. As an adult, this person will have problems controlling impulses and will stay immature, feeling that the world revolves around his or her needs. The organizing principle becomes "I deserve it." The person will even get angry if he or she has to face any consequences.

Sam could come up with a story at a moment's notice, and he was so convincing that he usually got his way. If anything went wrong, it was never his fault. He was always in a financial crisis, counting on his mother to bail him out. Sam's parents separated when he was three. His mother felt especially guilty, so she had a hard time saying no to him. When she tried to get him to follow through with anything, he would become angry and punish her.

Even after getting married and having several children, he was still a little boy—playing sports, hunting, and drinking whenever he had the opportunity, leaving family responsibilities go unattended. He would get angry with his wife if she expected anything from him. He just would not take responsibility for his family or his life.

Sam had difficulty with responsibility because he had little control over the overdeveloped, impulsive "kid" inside. He was out of balance—tuned in to his own needs but with little sensitivity to those of others. He continually made demands of his relationships and gave little back. He was a five-year-old believing that the world revolved around his emotions and needs.

An overdeveloped body leads to *impulse-control* disorders. Addictive and immature behaviors are examples of one's body constantly dominating the personality.

## INHERITED DAMAGE

To some degree, the formation of one's spirit—the relationship a person has with self—goes back to the relationship between the parents. The person's internal communication tends to pattern itself after this relationship. Each of the two forces inside often identifies with one of the parents. The mind will usually model after the permission-giving parent. The body will pick up the emotional reactions of the other parent.

Often, the organizing principle (spirit) of a dysfunctional marriage is based on a power struggle. Each spouse will have ways of getting even with the other. If one is highly critical, the other withdraws. This marital pattern is internalized and sets up an internal spiritual battle in the child. The child's body will take over and do what it wants, and then the mind will take over and make the child feel guilty—modeling the parents' power struggle.

If a child's parents had a warm, loving relationship, the conversation within the child will have a better chance of being healthy and productive, indicating the inheritance of the healthy marital spirit. Loving each other is one of the best gifts parents can give their child.

## DECEIT AND BETRAYAL DAMAGE A CHILD'S SPIRIT

Perhaps the greatest damage to a child's spirit comes from deceit and betrayal. The child's spirit knows what is true and seeks to express it. Deceit forces the child to create a *make-believe reality* that must stay detached from the deeper truth within the child's heart. This takes the child away from being free-spirited to being driven.

> Autumn remembered being a mouthy child, saying anything that came to her mind, and she was willing to challenge anything that did not fit her reality. Things changed when she was eight years old when, as she described it, "a lie came into my home."
>
> She came home from school one day, opened the apartment door, and found her father being very affectionate with a neighbor woman. Her father lied to her, saying the neighbor came over to borrow something. That evening, when she told what

she saw, her father became extremely angry with her for "making up a story." Her mother sided with the father, telling Autumn never to lie like that again.

"Darkness" was how Autumn described what happened inside her. No longer could she say what she knew to be true; instead, she learned how to fabricate "reality." She became deceitful as a teenager—totally different from her behavior as a younger child. She learned to live a lie very well.

Betrayal of trust does the same thing to a child's spirit. A child will trust adults and is normally open to parental guidance. If the adult misuses this trust for selfish desire, such as sexual contact, the child's spirit will be damaged severely. The child will try to believe the adult, but will feel that something is wrong, becoming confused inside.

Tara finally started remembering. She had always been afraid to sleep with her back toward the door, fearing that someone would come into her bedroom at night. She had idealized her father, but she always felt strange when he hugged her. The cues started making sense one day when her sister remembered that Tara had once talked of a "secret" that she and Daddy had.

Tara's spirit had detached from the repeated experience because her feelings were confused. Betrayal of her trust did serious damage to her spirit, forcing her to fabricate a different reality in her relationship with her father.

People who experience trauma as children often learn to detach, perhaps by tightening their neck and shoulder muscles, cutting off some of the emotional reality of the moment. This produces the effect of being a detached observer of the scene. It is as if their spirit is outside their body. Later in life, the person can still detach when there is anxiety, passively observing the war between their mind and body, feeling powerless to stop it.

## INTERNAL CONFLICT TAKES THE JOY OUT OF LIFE

Internal conflict forces a person's energy to turn inward (*incurvatus in se*). This struggle keeps the person focused on self. There is no joy in self-centeredness.

Josh realized he had just spent the last ten minutes in internal conversation. One of his friends at church wondered why he was not going to help with the church workday this coming Saturday. He mumbled that he was pretty busy, but that he would think about it. Now he felt guilty, but he really did not want to give up his Saturday. He had so much to do. He felt himself getting more worked up as he struggled with his guilt. He finally gave in and called his friend. "Count me in for this Saturday," he said with no energy in his voice. I guess I will put in my time, he thought, a little resentful about being somewhat forced to help out.

Joy is deep fulfillment of life as one's energy is going out in praise to God and in service to others. A true moment of joy comes when a person sees a tear of gratitude after performing an unselfish act of kindness. This is energy going outward that fulfills the soul.

Pete really did not have the time. He had so much to do, but he could not get Sarah's situation out of his mind. He heard at church that she had a water problem at her house but did not have the money to fix it. He knew he could help, but it would take all of his Saturday to dig around her house and put in a drainage system. He had so much to do around his own house and had decided not to offer to help.

He woke up early on Saturday with a warm feeling in his heart. In his early morning prayer time, he said, "Okay, God, I know what I am going to do." He called Sarah and asked if it was okay for him to come over and work on the problem. She protested, but he was insistent.

It was a hard day's work. It took him ten hours with his equipment to finish putting in the new drainage system. In the back of his mind, he knew that he still had so much to do at home, but there was warmth in his heart as he looked over what he had done. Then he saw Sarah looking at the finished work. She had tears in her eyes as she thanked him. That was when a true feeling of joy came over him.

Jesus showed the depth of such joy. His energy went out to save His people. In the midst of His terrible suffering and death, He felt joy in the fulfillment of His mission. "Who for the joy that was set before Him endured the cross" (Hebrews 12:2).

# Developmental Nature of Disorders

## CHAPTER 4

> **IN THIS CHAPTER**
>
> The standard categories of mental and emotional disorders are organized into a developmental framework.
>
> The categories developed in the previous chapter of *overcontrol*, *impulse-control*, and *reality* disorders are used to form an easy-to-understand classification.

## THE POWER OF A CHILD'S SPIRIT

Children are born to love and trust. Their initial reality is defined by parents. The child's spirit will adopt many of the parents' perceptions.

The child also has the capacity to form his or her own reality. Operating from the place within the heart that can ponder reality, the child gradually sorts through the confusing and sometimes contradictory family system.

> Conrad was a relatively easy child to raise. He usually went along with things and did not make many waves. By the time he was three years old, he had already learned that Mother would end up doing things for him. His favorite expression was "I will do it in a minute." As he procrastinated, his mother would finally get frustrated and do it herself. Conrad didn't mind that his mother was upset at him because that would not last long.

From early on, a child's spirit is constantly organizing. Each experience gives the child a better understanding of how to operate within the family dynamics. The child's spirit is very resilient and develops healthy strategies and attitudes if the family atmosphere is healthy. Healthy spiritual DNA grows out of a loving, consistent atmosphere where there are no secrets.

## WE-ORGANIZED ATMOSPHERE

A healthy family atmosphere grows out of a strong WE orientation. Each family member values the WE above ME. This is the wisdom of Ephesians 5:21: "[Submit] to one another out of reverence for Christ." The "one another" is the WE orientation. When concern for the good of the whole (the WE) is more important than concern for self-advantage, the family unit works and is healthy. This is the atmosphere that Christ's presence brings. His deepest prayer was that "they may be one" as He and His Father are one (John 17:22). Even on the cross, He did not think of Himself; He thought of those whom He would save with joy!

The child's mind thrives in a loving atmosphere. The basic curiosity of the child can meet new experiences with energy and excitement. With a sense of safety, there will be little anxiety to constrict the child's experiences. The child can develop healthy neural plasticity. The child can go through developmental stages without getting "stuck" because of anxiety.

The child's body thrives in a loving atmosphere that has appropriate, consistent boundaries. The child will learn to delay gratification for the greater good. The child will learn to be sensitive to others and not only concerned about self. The child can go through developmental stages without getting "stuck" because of feelings of unfairness or entitlement.

The child's spirit thrives in a loving, consistent, honest atmosphere where there are no secrets. The child is free to express self and explore things without having to keep things private. The child's experiences will match the reality that others present. The child can go through developmental stages without getting "stuck" because of having to detach from reality.

## AGE-RELATED TASKS FOR THE CHILD'S SPIRIT*

### AGES 0–3

**Task is to bond and trust**—to feel that the world is safe and to be able to risk being close and vulnerable. With a healthy spirit that grows out of a WE-oriented atmosphere, the child has the secure feeling of being wanted and can conclude that he or she is a gift to the family.

---

\*      Many theorists have proposed age-related tasks. The tasks and potential spiritual DNA damage for the various age categories presented in this book grow out of the author's own therapy practice, but obviously have some similarity to other theories.

## AGES 4–6

**Task is to assert self**—to discover impulses and find boundaries. With a healthy spirit that grows out of the WE orientation, the child is able to assert influence on the family.

## AGES 7–10

**Task is to develop responsibility**—to adopt family values and act them out. With a healthy spirit that grows out of the WE orientation, the child is proud to contribute to the family and is encouraged by parental approval.

## AGES 11–14

**Task is to develop internal independence**—to make up one's own mind about life and reality. With a healthy spirit that grows out of the WE orientation, the child is able to question things, spot inconsistencies, draw internal conclusions, and gradually voice them.

## AGES 15–18

**Task is to develop external independence**—to develop personal responsibility and independent living. With a healthy spirit that grows out of the WE orientation, young adults can now face their parents and express the value of their mature ideas. Children grow up when this can be done with respect and a good spirit and the young adult gets the parents' *blessing*!

### NEED TO KNOW

**Blessing:** All children yearn for parental blessing. As young people develop and form their own identity, parental interest and blessing are critical for the maturation process. Without parental blessing, the adolescent gets "stuck" trying to prove his or her worth, often in opposition to parental authority. An example of a blessing in the life of Jesus is recorded in Matthew 3:17: "A voice from heaven said, 'This is My beloved Son, with whom I am well pleased.'" A faith community can help with such a blessing from God in the re-parenting process.

## AGE-SPECIFIC DNA DAMAGE

Damage to a child's spiritual DNA occurs at specific moments in time. In general, when a family is going through a period of high stress, the child will get "stuck" at that developmental age. Examples of such stress would be serious bad moods, intense fighting, divorce, alcoholism, serious illness, or death. Each child is affected in different ways, partly because of the developmental age.

> Kendra was four years old when her mother died. She was protected from her death by going to stay with a relative when her mother got very sick. When it came time for the funeral, Kendra was told that her mother was just sleeping. She was fine until they closed the casket. Then she started screaming that her mother would suffocate if they did not open the casket. Kendra was taken away believing that her mother was going to suffocate. No one would listen to her. She had nightmares after that, and it was many years before she could go to sleep by herself. In her later life, she still felt like a four-year-old when people did not listen to her.

Even when the family unit is relatively healthy, spiritual DNA damage can occur. The child can misinterpret a situation and privately draw conclusions that affect his or her belief system.

> Brad was twelve years old and had never been so angry in his life. One of his father's golf clubs was bent, and he had been accused of doing it. He could still picture his father shaking the golf club in his face, upset with him for being so inconsiderate. Brad shook with his own anger at being falsely accused. Sure, he had played with his father's clubs, practicing hitting some balls. But he had not damaged them. He knew his little brother had done it, but his brother always got away with things. Later in life, Brad would have the same unjust anger, feeling like a twelve-year-old when he was accused of something.

Damage to spiritual DNA occurs during these defining moments. Such moments usually remain vivid to the person, as if time had stood still. Such moments help create the person's reality. The strategies developed at that age become part of the personality. Deep in the heart and wired into the brain,† this is what the person believes to be true.

---

† In a healthy, WE-oriented family environment, the child's brain develops healthy, flexible, and diverse capabilities. When there is disruption of normal developmental experiences, however, there may be devastating impact on neurodevelopment—and, thereby, function. For millions of abused and neglected children, automated pathways of the brain are developed that lead to future dysfunctional thought patterns, emotional reactions, and behavioral patterns. During the traumatic experience, these children's brains are in a state of fear-related activation. Persisting or chronic activation of this adaptive fear response can result in the maladaptive persistence of a fear state, resulting in hypervigilance, increased muscle tone, a focus on threat-related cues (typically nonverbal), and behavioral impulsivity. For more detail of these automatic brain sequences due to childhood trauma, go to the penetrating research of Bruce Perry: teacher.scholastic.com/professional/bruceperry/abuse_neglect.htm.

# Quick Guide to Where a Person Is "Stuck"

## Ages 0–3

Person reverts to being dependent and clingy and wants attention constantly. Voice tone is whiney. Body language shows helpless affect.

## Ages 4–6

Person reverts to an immature opposition, often with a temper tantrum. Voice tone is demanding, constantly asking, "Why?" Body language shows an immature defiance. Emotions must be expressed, whether appropriate or not.

## Ages 7–10

Person reverts to a "worrywart," constantly anxious about situations and wanting reassurance. Voice tone is worried and often high-pitched. Body language shows too much seriousness.

## Ages 11–14

Person reverts to lying, hiding feelings and actions. There are definite passive-aggressive tendencies—and undercover defiance. Voice tone is guarded and phony. Body language is closed in an attempt to reveal nothing.

## Ages 15–18

Person reverts to immature rebellion, getting upset at any attempts at enforcing the rules. There is a general negative reaction to authority. Voice tone is often dramatic with explosions of anger. Body language is defiant and challenging.

The strategy that is used later in life reflects the age of the child at the time when the spiritual DNA was damaged and when this strategy was first used to reduce anxiety or to gain power. Young children seek more attention to feel more secure. Children in grade school will try to make their own environments more secure. Middle school children will detach from the family to find security or power in friends. High school children will use their "attitudes" and gain power by controlling the mood of the house.

## Mental and Emotional Disorders

The *Diagnostic and Statistical Manual of Mental Disorders* (*DSM*) presents a well-organized categorization of mental, emotional, and personality disorders. When the child's thoughts, emotions, and personality were formed, something went wrong. The result is dysfunctional thinking and behavior later in life.

### NEED TO KNOW

**DSM-5:** The diagnostic categories that are used by most health professionals are delineated in the *Diagnostic and Statistical Manual of Mental Disorders*. This widely used classification is in its fifth revision and provides the most comprehensive description of the various mental and emotional disorders. These classifications are cited in this book.[1]

Remember, from the previous chapter, St. Paul's description of the natural self. In a vivid description of his own internal struggle, he sees his mind and body at war, both trying to control the personality (Romans 7:22–25). The human spirit can falsely align with either the mind or body ("their conflicting thoughts accuse or even excuse them," Romans 2:15) and cause greater internal problems.

St. Paul's description of the inner conflict can be interpreted along with the age-specific spiritual DNA damage. Using St. Paul's terms, mental, emotional, and personality problems can be classified into three areas: mind, body, and spirit disorders. Within each classification, there are age-specific disorders.

Anxiety, depression, and certain personality disorders (Cluster C‡) are the *overcontrol* disorders. This means that the anxious mind is trying to control the body's impulses by suppressing them. The effect on the body is the same as on a child whose angry parent is using guilt and intimidation to control the child. Since the mind is "unloving," it becomes selfish, reducing its own anxiety at the expense of the body's impulses.

Addictions, anger-management problems, and certain personality disorders (Cluster B) are the *impulse-control* disorders. This means that the entitled body is trying to control the personality by expressing its impulses directly without going through the reality check of the mind. The effect on behavior is immediate gratification at the expense of deeper fulfillment and social appropriateness.

Schizophrenia, paranoia, and certain personality disorders (Cluster A) are the *reality* disorders. This means that the spirit had trouble organizing reality to conform to social norms. The effect on the personality is perceptual distortions and eccentric behaviors.

As one closely observes disordered behavior in each of these three areas, there is often a definite age to the voice tone, body language, and thought process. The following is a way of putting these concepts together for a deeper understanding of the nature of personality disorders.

## Overcontrol Disorders

### Ages 0–3—Dependent Tendencies

Even though a person may not be able to remember the defining moments that

---

‡    Clusters A, B, and C are part of the organization of the *DSM* cited previously.

occurred at such an early age, his or her body will remember. If a child gets "stuck" at this early age, but has a healthy attachment to the parent(s), he or she will show tendencies to be anxious and whiney later in life, generally feeling helpless and looking to others to solve problems. When these tendencies become more severe, this can be called a *dependent personality disorder*.§

Some characteristics of this disorder include the following:

- Strong need to be taken care of by others
- Difficulty in making normal decisions without constant advice and reassurance
- Difficulty expressing disagreement, fearing loss of support or approval

## Ages 4–6—No Disorder, Since the Body Takes Control During This Age Range

Since the task of this age is to assert self, it is normal for the body to dominate the personality. Therefore there is no overcontrol disorder for this age group.

## Ages 7–10—Obsessive-Compulsive Tendencies

At about age 6 or 7, the child starts the identification process that produces internal control. Before this age, the child is controlled by external boundaries and the threat of punishment. During this age, an internal control system is developed that keeps the impulses in check with guilt. The child organizes a sense of right and wrong (usually in a very concrete sense) based on the family value system, trying to please the parents.

A child can get "stuck" at this age when there is high anxiety (such as a divorce, death, alcoholism, or neglect). As a result, the child will try to control the environment to reduce the anxiety.

There will be a preoccupation with orderliness and perfectionism. Rules, schedules, and details can become inflexible. There is expectation of perfect performance and rigid devotion to principles. Anxiety results from things going wrong, causing endless worry and regret. When these tendencies become more severe, this can be called an *obsessive-compulsive personality disorder*.

Some characteristics of this disorder include the following:
- Perfectionism
- Excessive work ethic, feeling guilty if not busy all the time

---

§    The disorders listed in italics in this chapter are the terminology of the DSM and can be found at www.dsm5.org.

- Overly conscientious, fearing criticism from others

## AGES 11–14—AVOIDANT TENDENCIES

At about age 10 or 11, the child will start questioning the parents' knowledge and authority. Inconsistencies in parental ideals and behavior will start being noticed. The child will disagree, but does not have the power to stand up to the parent, so will disagree internally. The child will find it easier to tell a lie than face the anxiety of confronting a parent. In a passive-aggressive way, the child will agree to something and then forget about it. The child will disobey in an "underground" way, hiding actions from parents.

The child will get "stuck" at this age if there are situations of high anxiety (such as divorce, death, or eruptions of anger). The mind is still more in control from the previous age and will handle things by withdrawing into fantasy. The automated ways of handling tension will become a personality trait. When these tendencies become more severe, this can be called an *avoidant personality disorder*.

Such a person stays in an inner world, spending much time in video games or private fantasy. Often there is social inhibition and hypersensitivity to criticism.

Some characteristics of this disorder include the following:

- Avoidance of social interaction, especially where there is conflict
- Evident reluctance when personally engaged, trying to escape the situation as quickly as possible
- High internal fantasy life that is much more emotionally rewarding than actual social interaction

## AGES 15–18—DEPRESSIVE TENDENCIES

At about age 14 or 15, the child begins to form his or her identity. If the adolescent is fixated at this stage, there are endless struggles to identify purpose and value in life. The pervasive feeling is that life has passed him or her by and there is no hope for the future.

Often this is accompanied by anger, since at this age, the natural rebelling process includes such energy for the person to break away from family and form his or her own identity. The result of this mixture of anger and defeated attitude is an angry depression, making the person at risk for suicide.

This is an overcontrol disorder since the mind has not let the body rebel to form its own identity. The mind is still trying to please the family unit, but its strategy has led to the depressive cycle. Often the teenager will not feel that he or she has received a blessing from parents and is struggling over feelings of self-worth. When these tendencies become more severe, this can be called a *major depression disorder.*

Some characteristics of this disorder include the following:

- Diminished interest or pleasure in daily activities
- Insomnia and listless affect with possible suicidal ideation
- Feelings of worthlessness and excessive self-reproach

# Impulse-Control Disorders

## Ages 0–3—Attachment-Seeking Tendencies

If there was not a healthy attachment during this young age, the person will spend the rest of life looking for a place to belong. Unstable relationships and emotions characterize this disorder. Like a young child, emotions can show dramatic shift from deeply hurt and angry to very happy and excited. Regard for others can go from excessive idealism to a very negative and devaluing attitude in a short period of time.

This person is looking for an attachment, but does not trust. From childhood there is a feeling of not being wanted. Emotions are used to get attention and to manipulate in order to keep the person responding. When these tendencies become more severe, this can be called a *borderline personality disorder.*

As is the case with individuals suffering from most of the other disorders, "borderlines" are not bad people, but they have developed a reality in which they are searching to belong. They will idealize a new relationship as their salvation, but their lack of trust and their manipulation will make it almost impossible for the relationship to work. Emotions have free reign and take over the person's reality.

Some characteristics of this disorder include the following:

- Fear of abandonment and poor self-definition
- Impulsive with such things as spending, sex, or substance abuse
- Manipulative, even using suicidal gestures to get attention

## Ages 4–6—Narcissistic Tendencies

A child in this age range will sometimes throw a temper tantrum. It is all about emotions getting expressed. Later in life, people "stuck" at this age will actually believe that they have the right to express their emotions in any way that satisfies them. An abusive husband is a good example of this. As he explodes in anger at his wife, he actually believes that it is all her fault. She caused his anger by not doing what he demanded.

Such a person has no insight into the self-centered and immature aspects of his or her behavior. It seems normal to have others respond to every emotional need. There is an exaggerated sense of one's own importance and a preoccupation with one's own success or brilliance. He or she commonly feels entitled to special treatment. When these tendencies become more severe, this can be called *narcissistic personality disorder.*

Some characteristics of this disorder include the following:

- Strong sense of self-importance and entitlement
- Emotions expressed freely without concern for others
- Idealized fantasies of success, beauty, or love

## Ages 7–10—No Disorder, Since the Mind Takes Control

This age group does not show an impulse-control disorder since during this age, the mind usually takes control for the identification process and organizes the internal value system around family values.

## Ages 11–14—Emotional Manipulation Tendencies

At this age, the child starts developing energy to break away from the family. The child uses the beginning emotional power of rebellion in order to form a new persona. The drama of these emotions is similar to an act that could be put on stage.

The main features of these tendencies are excessive emotionality and attention seeking. The rapidly shifting emotions are shallow, superficial, and exaggerated. Females in this stage are sometimes called "drama queens."

These people may assume either a "victim" or a "princess" role, seeking out novelty and excitement, but quickly becoming bored with routine. They love a crisis. When these tendencies become more severe, this can be called a *histrionic personality disorder.*

Some characteristics of this disorder include the following:

- Displays rapidly shifting and somewhat shallow expression of emotions
- Creates drama in situations, exaggerating emotional importance
- Is suggestible and easily influenced by situations

## Ages 15–18—Addictive Tendencies

When the teenager develops enough "I don't care" attitudes and does not have sufficient internal control, there is a good chance for addiction. Often this starts with partying (drinking, drugs, and sex) and develops into a habitual way of fixing the person's mood.

There is little insight into the pattern of addiction. Their behavior is rationalized as "just having fun." They are certain that the behavior can be stopped at any time.

There is often a growing dependence on the desired addictive object or substance in daily life. More and more time is spent in planning for such a controlled shift in mood. The person's life begins to center around the addiction. Addictions are usually related to mood-altering substances, but can also include sex, gambling, video-game playing, shopping, and so forth. When these tendencies become more severe, this can be called a *substance abuse disorder* or an *impulse control disorder*.

Some characteristics of this disorder include the following:

- Important social or occupational activities are affected by addiction
- Little desire to stop the addiction or insight into its disruptive effects
- Anger and denial at attempts to point out the addiction

# REALITY DISORDERS

## AGES 0–3—DISSOCIATIVE TENDENCIES

The first years of life provide a daily context of routines that the child's curious spirit utilizes to organize the myriad complexities of life experiences. Stable routines and predictable moods provide a safe background for the child's reactions to develop. When the routine is unpredictable and is accompanied by high anxiety, the child's spirit learns to detach to be safe and to organize experiences without the benefit of reality checks.

Physical DNA damage to the child's ability to organize leads to faulty reality organization. Also, lack of a stable environment leads to the need to detach. The child has to make up things internally to provide a more stable reality for self. This reality will often not match that of other people.

Detached children do not have a stable body image and will often have puzzling physical symptoms that do not match what is really happening to their bodies. They are able to detach from anxious situations and go into a private world. Memories from this part of a person's life will be seen as by an observer. When these tendencies become more severe, this can be called a *dissociative disorder*.

Some characteristics of this disorder include the following:

- Persistent recurrent feeling of being detached from self
- Inappropriate emotional reactions to situations
- Shallow reactions that seem to come from different personalities at times

## AGES 4–6—ODD BEHAVIOR TENDENCIES

As the child begins to develop his or her own view of reality and moves to the internalization of a value system, there is a definite need for parental and family input. If the child is withdrawn and does not get this feedback, he or she will be "stuck" in a private reality that increasingly does not reflect that of social norms and conventions.

Such persons do not fit well into social situations. Their thoughts and perceptions may seem unusual to other people. They usually lack close friends and show a restricted range of emotions. They may believe that they can cause events by thinking about them. Superstitions are common, and the persons may believe that they possess special powers. When these tendencies become more severe, this can be called a *schizotypal personality disorder*.

Some characteristics of this disorder include the following:

- Odd beliefs or magical thinking
- Unusual perceptual experiences, including bodily illusions
- Social anxiety and a lack of close friends

## AGES 7–10—INDIFFERENT TENDENCIES

As detached personalities move into peer relationships, the lack of good reality organization takes them to a greater detachment from social relationships and an even more restricted range of emotional expression. They may appear cold or aloof and seem to have little interest in family or friends. They remain indifferent to praise or criticism. When these tendencies become more severe, this can be called a *schizoid personality disorder*.

Some characteristics of this disorder include the following:

- Emotional detachment, coldness, and flattened affect
- Lacks close relationships and has little interaction with family
- Passive reaction to what is happening around them

## AGES 11–14—DISTRUSTING TENDENCIES

As these private personalities move into the development of their own inner worlds, there is a distinct distrust of others. They become increasingly isolated with their private thoughts and attitudes that are not shared by others. They lack a "reality check" to their inner world.

They are beginning to develop an oppositional attitude toward others, taking offense readily and holding grudges easily over some unintentional action. They seem angry much of the time and stubborn. They keep themselves isolated from others and typically have no close friends. When these tendencies become more severe, this can be called a *paranoid personality disorder*.

Some characteristics of this disorder include the following:

- Distrust and suspicion of others
- Reads hidden meanings into benign remarks or events
- Suspects others of exploiting, harming, or deceiving

## AGES 15–18—IRRESPONSIBLE, DESTRUCTIVE TENDENCIES

When a detached personality reaches puberty, there is the normal anger and "I don't care" attitude of someone ready to break away from the family and form a separate identity. These people come across as hostile, manipulative, irresponsible, and impulsive. They tend to violate the rights of others and often appear to show no empathy or concern for those around them.

Often they use dramatic ways of manipulating others that involve serious rule violations, deceitfulness, and destructiveness. There may be a history of violence and sexual exploitation with a lack of remorse for the suffering of others. When these tendencies become more severe, this can be called an *antisocial personality disorder*.

Some characteristics of this disorder include the following:

- Pervasive and reckless disregard for others
- Impulsivity and failure to plan ahead or to think of consequences
- Consistent irresponsibility over work or finances

# The Healing Power
# of Christ's Love

## CHAPTER 5

### IN THIS CHAPTER

- The authors share how the *new self* can heal *damaged spiritual DNA*.

- A *re-parenting* process as an adopted child of God daily practices "rising to a new life in Christ" is imbedded in St. Paul's use of the Greek word *pneuma*.

- The missing *agape* can rebuild damaged spiritual DNA through the presence of Christ, forming new strategies for handling experiences.

- The disorder can be healed gradually through the process of spiritual formation.

All need the loving support of a healthy community. No one has healthy spiritual DNA. Everyone was damaged growing up, and all face struggles with varying levels of anxiety, depression, addictions, and stressful relationships.[1] All are in this together. All need the healing power of Christ.

## MENTAL DISORDER IS NOT A MORAL WEAKNESS

Mental illness cannot destroy the soul. That is in God's hands. As bad as one's consciousness can become during the height of mental and emotional disorder, God's loving presence is still there for the Christian. Though it cannot be felt in the middle of this deep, agonizing struggle, there can be an awareness of God's love that cannot be taken away. This is hard to see and almost impossible to discern in private.

God does not love a person less during periods of deep depression or emotional distress. God does not promise to take the struggles of life away.

God's promise is to fill suffering with His loving presence. God's desire is that all things, especially the dark moments of life, be brought to Him: "casting all your anxieties on Him, because He cares for you" (1 Peter 5:7).

To a large extent, mental illness is a problem in defining reality—of what a person deeply believes to be true about self, others, and life. This reality is shaped by genetic inheritance and epigenetic modifications (interaction of genetics and environment) that set brain chemistry and neuronal circuits through DNA processes as the child's brain forms. This reality is also shaped through childhood experiences that set the private reality of the person through the spiritual DNA process. The child's spirit organizes the defining moments of life into a meaningful belief system. This becomes the person's reality.

## AGAPE MISSING IN SPIRITUAL DNA

St. Paul's use of the word picture *psychikos* for the *natural self* (1 Corinthians 2:14) is highly descriptive. There is a missing ingredient as the human spirit organizes the soul. God did not create people to be on their own, having to handle situations privately. Humans were created to be in relationship with their Creator and experience God's continuous love—agape.

Being born without a relationship with God is like being born without agape present in one's spiritual DNA. Without God's steadfast love, children learn at an early age that they are vulnerable and must look out for themselves. They learn how to stand up for their rights. No parent has ever had to teach a child to say, "That's not fair."

> **Agape:** Spiritual DNA requires agape (the loving presence of God) to organize a particular concrete experience to be interesting rather than anxiety producing. Agape heals potentially damaging experiences. Without agape, the experience must be organized to protect self (*incurvatus in se*), producing a dysfunctional inward flow of energy. The proper order of the soul is for the energy to flow outward, which is reflected in the fruit of the Spirit (Galatians 5:22–23).

The defining moments of childhood that help form spiritual DNA are usually accompanied by private distress. In the following two examples, a little girl develops her belief about dogs depending on how safe she feels in their presence.

**Example 1:** Brianna was walking alone when a big dog started barking at her. She stopped and was terrified as the dog came closer. She started running with the dog chasing her, her heart beating fast. She knew the dog would bite her if given the chance. She barely escaped into her house, and from that point on, she did not want to be close to any dog.

**Example 2:** Brianna was walking with her father when a big dog started barking at her. She was startled but held tightly to her father's hand, knowing that he would protect her. Her father picked her up in his arms. She felt safe and loved. Later in life, she was not afraid of dogs.

What the natural self organizes becomes that person's reality. This is what a person really believes to be true about another person, about self, or about life. *Automated mood sequences* develop as private ways of reacting to situations. Damage to spiritual DNA causes real impairment to what one believes to be real!

## HEALING POWER OF AGAPE

Healthy spiritual DNA develops as a person is loved, protected, and given good boundaries. St. Paul's use of the term "spiritual" (*pneuma*) in 1 Corinthians 2:15 is a description of the new self. Experiencing life situations with the loving presence of Christ makes all the difference in the world. The new self is never alone and does not have to handle situations with private distress. An experience that could arouse tremendous anxiety can now be seen as "interesting."

> A co-worker stormed into Bruce's office after a sales meeting. He was livid. "You are never going to do that to me again!" he shouted with his anger barely contained. "I'm going to make life miserable for you after what you've done!"

> Bruce's natural reaction to such an outburst would be to defend himself. He would have a variety of emotions, such as anxiety, anger, or disgust. He would react in ways that would amplify the situation and cause more damage to the relationship.

> His new self, however, gives Bruce another option. At that critical moment, Bruce can remember that he is the new self, protected by the love of Christ. He does not have to defend himself. The situation can become "interesting." He can be a nonanxious presence and change the way the situation will play out.

The power of the new self is absolutely awesome, but highly underused. For the Christian, Christ dwells in the heart through faith. His presence is constant, and the healing power of His love is always available for the believer.

The Holy Spirit does not manipulate. Christ's love may not have any effect on the next thought, emotion, or action of the believer. The Holy Spirit will not force this connection, but He is there to witness to the Christian's spirit, as a magnet will reorganize iron filings to conform to its magnetic field and its lines of influence. "By [the Holy Spirit] we cry, 'Abba! Father!' The Spirit Himself bears witness with our spirit that we are children of God" (Romans 8:15–16).

The new self can be active in any situation to reconstruct reality. The natural state of the believer is the old self. This is the "default drive." At any given moment, the old self will define reality and be reacting to the situation, convinced of the need to protect self. But the new self is always available to change this reality and take away the need to focus on self-protection.

St. Paul urges all to remember the new self in Ephesians 4:22–24. At any given moment, Christians can "put off [the] old self." In other words, they "don't have to do that anymore." They can get free from old ways of reacting, no longer forced to play out the automated mood sequence. This is made possible because Christ changes reality. The loving presence of Christ changes the heart.

## CONFESSION IS THE PROCESS OF PUTTING OFF THE OLD SELF

Sin is a condition that plagues everyone. Without agape, people have no choice but to think of self and defend self. Self-centered personality patterns developed over a lifetime are embedded in spiritual DNA. These become automated reactions that seem normal.

*Confession* is the extraordinary process of recognizing self-centered patterns of thought and behavior. Confession is hard since these patterns are invisible. Nothing appears to be wrong with one's behavior or internal conversation. It feels natural and normal.

> Karl had just spent the last fifteen minutes stressing over a presentation he was going to give the next day. He was plagued with fears that he would be a failure and that his job would be in jeopardy. His friend and co-worker Wally noticed his distress and commented, "Look, Karl, you always do a fantastic job. You are so much better than I am at making these presentations. Why are you worried about it?"
>
> Karl looked puzzled and replied, "I always stress over things." It was normal to him. "I guess it helps me sharpen up my presentation."

Wally chuckled. "I don't buy that. It looks like you are just sitting there, spinning in your own worry. You don't have to do that, you know."

Karl was getting more uncomfortable. For as long as he could remember, he had worried about things. He was not sure he liked where the conversation was going. "Look, it's no big deal. I will be fine tomorrow."

Wally pressed on, "I am sure it *will* go well tomorrow, but I am talking about today. I don't like to see my friend go through unnecessary stress. Remember the uplifting words of St. Paul, 'The Lord is at hand; do not be anxious about anything, but in everything by prayer and supplication with thanksgiving let your requests be made known to God' [Philippians 4:5–6]. God is telling you that He is with you and you do not have to worry anymore."

This touched Karl's heart. For the first time, it dawned on him that his life of worry was something he did not have to do anymore. He remembered when he had started worrying as a little boy. He told Wally, "I was only in second grade when my father got real sick. We thought he was going to die. I remember worrying about him every day and worrying about Mother and how we were going to make it without Dad."

Karl had now entered into confession. He realized the worrying was part of his old pattern. He tried to give it up, but things just did not feel right if he did not worry. "God, help me break this pattern," he prayed. "Help me feel more secure in You and not feel that I have to make everything happen myself."

Confession is counterintuitive. The old patterns were developed to be self-protective. They feel normal and necessary. Considerable anxiety develops when trying to break these patterns. It just does not feel safe or right.

Confession is good for the soul. Confession is best done in the presence of another person, like a pastor. Confession brings private thoughts, feelings, and behavior out in the open. Confession is the first step to spiritual growth and maturity. When absolution is pronounced, the healing presence of Christ is brought into the concrete reality of the confessed item. That is why the practice of Confession and Absolution is so deeply embedded in Christian tradition and practice.

**Spiritual growth and spiritual formation:** Spiritual growth is a gift of God that is passively received in the daily process of dying to sin and rising to a new life in Christ (Romans 6:4). This *renewal of a right spirit within* (Psalm 51:10) influences more of the thoughts, feelings, and behavior as the Christian grows in grace to be more Christlike. Spiritual formation is not a *doing* concept, but an outcome of *being* in God's Word: "Be still, and know that I am God" (Psalm 46:10). The "natural self" operates by the organizing principle that one's self must be protected. This "ME-oriented" stance toward life is a fatal flaw and cannot be corrected by trying to do better and live a life more pleasing to God. The "new self" is a perfect creation of God that sets a person free to consider the good of the whole.

## SPENDING TIME IN CHRIST'S PRESENCE HEALS SPIRITUAL DNA

There is a second step to break the old pattern of behavior. After stopping the old, natural reaction that is self-protective, St. Paul then urges, "Be renewed in the spirit of your minds" (Ephesians 4:23). Spending time in Christ's presence changes reality and can break old habits and allow for a new reaction to the situation reflective of the protection offered by Christ's love.

In this way, missing agape is put into spiritual DNA. This is *spiritual genetic therapy*. Call it *re-parenting* as a child of God. The presence of Christ reconstructs reality. A person's mood changes from defensive and constricted to open and interested. Neuroplasticity is restored for that given situation. Energy shifts from flowing inward to outward, expanding the experience of life.

The most dangerous aspect of mental illness is that it locks a person inside self. This creates a downward spiral of depression and hopelessness as a person's thoughts and sense of reality spin inward.

Renewal of one's spirit is a gift of God, shifting a person's flow of energy outward in thankfulness and love. This freedom from self is not instantaneous, but is a steady unblocking process that is initiated by God and helped by a loving faith community. It is a remembrance of God's love, even though a person cannot feel it. It is like a deep safety net, an anchor to the soul in turbulent, very difficult times. When a person's mind and emotions cannot find hope and a loving God seems far away, there is a comforting knowledge that deep inside, the soul is safe in His arms.

The power of this internal shift of energy from being curved inward (ME-oriented) to flowing outward (WE-oriented) comes from faith. Through Baptism, all have received the forgiveness of sin, their Savior Jesus Christ, and the Holy Spirit and His gifts. This new person is the constant, loving presence of Christ that can guide the spirit. The spiritual person of 1 Corinthians 2:14–15 is a new creation called into being through faith in Christ. It is a gift of God that can have a profound effect on one's daily life.

## The New Self Can Break Dysfunctional Patterns and Bring About Spiritual Growth

St. Paul's third step is to "put on the new self" (Ephesians 4:24) and react to the situation in a healthier manner. It is now possible, no matter how difficult the struggle, to think, How can I praise You, God, and love others, even in my current state? The brain may be ill, but the soul can show stirrings of spiritual health. A person can learn deep compassion from being in a helpless state.

The new self is a creation of God, created to be like Christ. With the new self, every moment can be enjoyed, no matter how difficult it may be. One way of measuring spiritual growth and health is to look at how many moments are enjoyed in any given time. Take a hundred moments in a span of time . . . how many of these are spent as the new self? The more situations that are faced with the awareness of the presence of Christ, the more moments will be enjoyed.

To a person suffering from mental and emotional distress, the concept of enjoying the moment seems foreign, even bizarre. How can a person in this state experience even a fleeting moment of joy? This almost seems cruel to suggest. To those suffering from intense mental illness, it seems like their brains are intent on destroying them. The suffering is intense and relentless. How can joy be possible?

Christ's suffering was the most intense anyone could endure. He had no defense. He did not detach from reality. He felt every physical pain and suffered from every disrespectful gesture. He was mocked and spit upon. Yet Christ could enjoy such persecution and even the horror of dying: "who for the joy that was set before Him endured the cross" (Hebrews 12:2). He experienced something deeper and more powerful than earthly pain and suffering. He exemplified the power of agape—of God's undying love. Suffering can deepen faith.

God's healing love is not given in an abstract way. Putting the presence of Christ into a concrete situation and reacting to it as the new self is the practical way of putting agape back into spiritual DNA. This is a process re-parenting that reconstructs the person's reality. Spiritual health means reacting to situations with more love, joy, and peace—the fruit of the Spirit.

## NEED TO KNOW

**Spiritual re-parenting:** Belief that God is the Christian's new Father leads to a re-parenting process. Such belief can heal some of the dysfunction of the natural self. Repairing damage to one's spiritual DNA is accomplished by bringing concrete situations to the loving presence of Christ, thus re-constructing reality. Spiritual healing is enhanced in the context of a Christian community. Another term for this is spiritual formation or the reorganizing of the human spirit by the witness of the Holy Spirit (Romans 8:16).

This new creation is no weakling. The new self under the Holy Spirit's guidance can yield one's spirit to follow the guidance of Christ's living presence. Within the heart, a spiritual battle takes place between the old and new persons. The old patterns of self-protection are quite tempting for the human spirit as it seeks to give direction to the natural forces within the soul. With the constant presence of the Holy Spirit, the human spirit can be led to give up the old ways (to die to sin) and override these selfish patterns with a life of loving service (to rise to a new life in Christ).

Through Baptism, the Holy Spirit is present to daily renew the spirit of the Christian: "[I pray] that according to the riches of His glory He may grant you to be strengthened with power through His Spirit in your inner being, so that Christ may dwell in your hearts through faith" (Ephesians 3:16–17). The "inner being" is the new self. A Christian's spirit is strengthened by God's loving Spirit.

The Spirit helps fight the daily battle between the old self and the new self (see Romans 6:1–14). As the new person comes forth daily, there is a change of heart so that the person wants to do what should be done according to the outward direction of God's will. The mind and the body work together in harmony with the energy going outward, making the person sensitive and caring toward others, which is what the Law requires.

The Christian's behavior does not make the new self more healthy. It is like the sun, shining all the time, whether experienced or not. But the new self can become more influential in the life of the believer. In other words, the new self can take over more of the heart and thus be a more influential source of strength for the human spirit in more of life's situations. The new self can lead to a "right spirit" (Psalm 51:10).

As the Spirit works in the person, efforts to obey God's will come as *a response to God's love* instead of being motivated by fear or an effort to earn

God's favor. The use of the Law as a rule for spiritual formation is important in guiding the new life so that a person's spirit can grow in Christ. The person is not under the Law (Romans 6:14), but because the Holy Spirit dwells in the heart through faith, God's Law becomes a friend. When our minds are right with God, we can "delight . . . in the law of the LORD" (Psalm 1:2).

This concept is not something that can be deeply understood by just hearing it. This concept must be experienced to be understood.

## RE-PARENTING

All personalities develop as the natural self, and so re-parenting is necessary for everyone. The damage to spiritual DNA can occur early in life as the child struggles to develop proper attachment to one or both parents.* Damage occurs if there is poor attachment or an abusive situation and the child does not feel safe. The deep anxiety coming from this age can be carried for the rest of the person's life. It is difficult to change such deeply wired anxiety by cognitive means.

The epigenetic modifications of highly anxious environments that set brain chemistry can be reversed so that these automated reactions do not determine dysfunctional behavior throughout the person's life.† The most promising approach to such healing is re-parenting.

Through faith, Christians are under the influence of the heavenly Father as their new Parent. His Spirit daily influences the lives of His people as He forms a new and right spirit within them. "Because you are sons, God has sent the Spirit of His Son into our hearts, crying, 'Abba! Father!'" (Galatians 4:6).

Baptism is a Means of Grace by which the Holy Spirit brings the person into the family of God. The person is born again with the assurance of salvation. Baptism gives a new organizing principle for the person's life: God's love

---

\* Attachment theory and the diagnosis of Reactive Attachment Disorder show how a dysfunctional relationship between an infant and caregiver can produce devastating results throughout the life of this infant. There are some similarities between this and the concept of damaged spiritual DNA. However, some of the treatment options that have been tried, such as re-birthing, are not at all similar to the concept of re-parenting developed in this book. A good short summary of attachment theory can be found in the 2011 article "Attachment Theory and Reactive Attachment Disorder" by Tiffanie Russell, MSW intern, for the New Britain (Conn.) Youth and Family Services; see nbcityjournal.com/archives/3470. See also www.attach.org.

† There is some evidence that epigenetic effects are reversible, so that inheriting a particular DNA sequence that is not myelinated does not sentence an individual to a lifetime of high stress reactivity and poor outcomes. To help unpack this, researchers have focused on attempting to identify the underpinning biology of secure and loving relationships. Ultimately the aim of this research is to use that knowledge to help shape appropriate supports for those children and families where there are significant risks for poor outcomes. This is the work being undertaken in Australia by initiatives such as Salisbury Communities for Children. See *Building Integrated Connections for Children, Their Families and Communities*, K. Brettig and M. Sims, eds. (Newcastle, U.K: Cambridge Scholars Publishing, 2011), 12.

will always be with that person. He or she will never be alone, forced to handle things by him- or herself.

Like any newborn child, Christians need a daily family life to help spiritual formation of the new self. This is how new habits and attitudes are formed. The modeling of a faith community shows how to handle situations in a healthy way. Old habits are hard to change!

In other words, a person does not go immediately from a weak, broken, or malformed spirit to a right, strong spirit. The right spirit is gradually renewed and strengthened through the daily process of the Holy Spirit's work in the heart to reorganize the Christian's spirit through the witness of faith.

"All who are led by the Spirit of God are sons of God. For you did not receive the spirit of slavery to fall back into fear, but you have received the Spirit of adoption as sons, by whom we cry, 'Abba! Father!' The Spirit Himself bears witness with our spirit that we are children of God" (Romans 8:14–16).

## HEALING SPIRITUAL DNA

The creative power of the human spirit to form reality is awesome. In the sometimes confusing atmosphere of family dynamics, the young child deeply understands how things work. Critical experiences let the child know whom to trust and what the real consequences are in certain situations.

The child is responsible for forming reality. The concept of *defining moments* is not presented to imply that parents are at fault for damage to a child's spiritual DNA. Such damage is inevitable for all. Depending on the child's developmental stage, his or her spirit will focus on a particular defining moment to understand reality. There is no way parents can keep a child from spiritual DNA damage. It comes from the child's perception of the situation.

These defining moments, which usually remain vivid in the person's memory, become the slice of life that the spirit uses to organize one's reality. Once formed, this becomes what the person really believes to be true. But these defining moments may have come at a specific point in the child's development. They were experienced without agape, resulting in deep anxiety or feelings of unfairness—the hallmarks of damage to spiritual DNA.

> Brandon was in the second grade and the smartest person in his class. He was somewhat shy and would attempt to avoid any conflict. One day, Darren decided to have some fun and got several of his buddies to put a scare into Brandon. As he was walking toward the playground, Brandon noticed several kids edging toward him. He looked around, heart pounding, and saw he was trapped by a fence.

This experience was a defining moment for Brandon. Even when he was in high school, he constantly scanned his environment for potential threats. And he made sure he had an escape, so he would sit next to the door in the classroom. He never told anyone about this vivid experience.

Every child has such DNA damage. For Brandon, this defining moment occurred when he was eight years old, causing his mind to become hypervigilant to protect him from another anxious moment. Scanning the environment for possible danger became his reality—it was an automated mood sequence that was part of his natural self.

Brandon's faith was a gift in his healing process. He lived with this free-floating anxiety of danger, and his hypervigilance got worse. He felt he had to scan to keep himself safe. This was his reality.

Brandon was now thirty-five years old. He had been on anti-anxiety medication for some time, but he never felt free of his need to constantly scan for danger. He could feel the comforting presence of Christ and knew that He brought healing to his anxiety, but the two just did not connect.

He shared his struggle with his men's Bible study group as they studied Philippians: "The Lord is at hand; do not be anxious about anything" (4:5–6). "You know," Brandon began, "Christ was there when those boys terrorized me. I never thought of that before." Something amazing happened when he pictured Christ in that scene he remembered so well. He felt Christ directing him to look straight at the boys without fear but with confidence instead. Putting Christ in the scene resulted in a change in his automated mood sequence.

He revisited this scene many times with Christ present. He felt something deep happening inside his soul. The scene no longer caused his stomach to tighten in fear and his mind to start scanning. He could look the fearful boys right in the eye. In fact, he enjoyed remembering this moment—enjoyed feeling the newfound confidence of being near to his Lord.

What happened to Brandon is profound. As the presence of Christ connected with this defining moment in his life, he did not feel the need to scan his environment as much. In fact, several months later, one of his friends in the men's group made the observation, "I noticed that you do not automatically sit next to the door anymore." His reality had changed. His anxiety had diminished. He felt a strange freedom to move about in his environment, free from the constriction brought about by the DNA damage experienced earlier in his life.

Such change in reality is not a cognitive process. It is a change in belief system. It is a change in the person's spirit—in what a person deeply believes to be true. This is hard—if not impossible—to do privately.

## RE-PARENTING IS A DAILY PROCESS

The natural self is one's normal personality: habits, attitudes, reactions, and emotions. These were all developed as the child struggled to function in the sometimes anxious or inconsistent environment. The amazing human spirit formed the personality, but was forced to do it in a somewhat private world— deep in the heart, where the child pondered reality.

If a child is left alone to frame hurtful defining moments, this experience becomes part of the child's spiritual DNA, forming belief about reality. Such belief will have damaged elements because it is framed in private without God's loving presence (agape) or community support. A violated or betrayed person will trust this private belief to be true.

An unhealthy defining moment is usually a time when a child is left alone to conclude a belief or attitude at an immature cognitive stage, leading the spirit to develop untrue beliefs. Changing such dysfunctional attitudes, emotions, and behaviors that become automated does not occur easily. It is a slow re-parenting process that takes intentional daily practice to alter such a tightly constructed belief system. God the heavenly Father is the new Parent, and the process of gradually reconstructing a person's reality takes place within his new faith family: the Body of Christ.

As we saw earlier in this chapter, re-parenting follows St. Paul's three steps to new life (Ephesians 4:22–24). First, there must be an awareness of the flawed nature of the person's natural reality. This first step involves confession—the painful process of stripping off the rationalizations and justifications that surround the attitudes of the old self.

> Jimmy felt things were so unfair. No matter how hard he tried, he just could not seem to please his wife, Jane. He had just finished cleaning the kitchen when Jane came home and remarked, "You never can get the sink clean." With that, he sighed, threw the washcloth down, looked away with a shake of his head, and walked out of the kitchen.

At that moment, Jimmy really believed that he had been treated unjustly and that looking away, sighing, and feeling powerless were all he could do. He was convinced that it was all Jane's fault for being so critical. This was natural behavior for him, and he did not know that he actually had other options. He was constricted!

When he was twelve years old, Jimmy's mother caught him in a lie. He was saving up for a new video game, and needed a few more dollars. On impulse, Jimmy used his lunch money to buy it. In the defining moment that he remembers as if it were yesterday, Jimmy felt his stomach panic as his mother asked where his lunch money was. He lied, "I lost it on the way to school . . ." but stopped short when his mother held the receipt for the video game in front of his face. Feeling powerless and trapped, he would never forget the disappointment on his mother's face. As he lowered his eyes, his mother walked away. Her reaction seemed so unfair. After all, it was only a few dollars, and he was going to pay it back. They never talked about it again.

As a result of this spiritual DNA damage, Jimmy returned to his twelve-year-old self whenever his wife criticized him. His automated mood sequence left him feeling powerless. He needed help breaking this constricted way of handling conflict. He needed to be aware of the dysfunction of his half of the relationship.

The second step is to receive help in order to heal the damage. Time spent in God's Word and in the presence of Christ is necessary for one to be made new in the spirit of the mind.

During one of their marriage counseling sessions, Jimmy shared the memory of being caught in a lie by his mother. As he talked, he felt his stomach tighten all over again as shame gripped his whole body. He knew his mother never trusted him after that. He felt the urge to lower his eyes. He felt twelve years old again.

The counselor directed him to put Christ into that scene. He felt the warmth of forgiveness and some relief from his shame. As he continued to imagine Christ's presence, he felt the confidence to face his mother. In a breakthrough moment, he pictured himself looking right at his mother, confessing what he had done, and asking her forgiveness. With that expression of confession and honesty, something started changing inside. The feeling had moved from his stomach to his chest, seemingly brought closer to his heart (where Christ lives through faith).

This moment of freedom was deep. He felt a confidence and power that he had never felt before with his mother. He was growing up! He went back to this defining moment in his life again and again, each time feeling more confident as Christ and His presence became more of a reality in the memory. This confidence began to change the way he interacted with his wife. Instead of looking down and feeling helpless when she was disappointed, he could look right at her and be interested in her feelings.

After there is a change in mood and in the perception of reality, the person is able to put on the new self that is "created after the likeness of God in true righteousness and holiness" (Ephesians 4:24).

Jane pointed out that he had forgotten to call the restaurant for reservations as he had promised. Normally, he would have gotten defensive or just looked away and sighed, feeling helpless.

Jimmy now had other options and could act more like a man in conflict with his wife than like a young boy who felt criticized. He found himself wanting to become passive, but then remembered that he did not have to do that anymore. He paused to remember that Christ was present. Then he smiled and looked directly at Jane. "Thanks for reminding me, honey," he said. Then he went to give her a hug as he added, "You are the best thing that ever happened to me."

Instead of the usual bad mood that would have dominated the evening, Jimmy found that he could change the mood by reacting as his new self. Some of the damage to his DNA had been healed. His reality was changing.

## Growth of the New Self: Spiritual Formation

The natural self is a well-developed personality organized around the basic principle of self-protection. Defending self, feelings of things not being fair, and anxiety are all part of the habits and strategies of the old self. This is true of everyone.

The new self is a gift of God. With the repairing power of agape now present, every experience now can have a new organizing principle: a Christian is never alone, but is in the constant love and care of God.

Spiritual growth is the daily process of the new self taking over more territory—taking over the old habits, emotions, and attitudes. This process does not happen in abstract. The love of Christ must be personally, concretely connected to each situation, relationship, thought, and attitude. The human spirit must be completely reformed and molded with the new organizing principle.

There is actually no moment that a Christian cannot enjoy. The fruit of the Spirit is love, joy, and peace. Christians can rejoice in the Lord always. They are to be like Christ, who "for the joy that was set before Him endured the cross" (Hebrews 12:2).

The power of the new self is a gift of God's grace. Long-standing reactions of resentment, anxiety, or anger can be broken. As each concrete situation is connected with God's love (agape), healing takes place. Anxiety is replaced by confidence. Resentment is replaced by concern and sadness. This is spiritual growth through the power of Christ.

## THE ROLE OF A HEALTHY FAITH COMMUNITY IN RE-PARENTING

Mental and emotional disorders are helped by sustained interaction within a healing community that functions much like a healthy family in the re-parenting process. Professional counseling sessions are quite valuable, but usually provide a limited number of contacts. A healthy faith community sustains a loving, safe atmosphere for the long term.

The re-parenting process is not a short-term "quick fix." Slow spiritual growth that affects the deep reality within a person's spirit occurs over months and even years. In that way, it is similar to the years of development of the child's spirit within a family unit. Reality that is formed in this slow, deliberate fashion is also changed in the same slow, deliberate fashion. All the habits and cognitive processes of the personality that are related to childhood reality are changed slowly by the new reality of faith experienced in the context of a healthy faith community.

Spiritual mentors, spiritual disciplines, and deliberate interest in a person's spiritual growth and maturity are the marks of a healthy faith community. These provide the sustained, loving, yet firm atmosphere that helps the healing process of mental and emotional disorders.

# Understanding the Value of Spiritual Formation

## CHAPTER 6

**IN THIS CHAPTER**

- The authors review the developmental stages.

- The authors share an understanding of how a healthy faith community can assist the re-parenting process of spiritual formation by its loving atmosphere and through teaching and modeling.

- The authors offer a deep look at the traditional *spiritual disciplines* that can be used in this process of re-parenting.

## FAITH FORMATION DURING THE DEVELOPMENTAL PROCESS

A child can know God. A young child can feel the comfort of His love. A developing child can sense Christ's presence and be able to handle anxious situations with more confidence. Faith is made personal by questioning and thinking things through. A preadolescent should be encouraged in this process of confirming his or her belief system. An adolescent can grow in faith while struggling with the more powerful issues of life.

In all ages of life, a healthy faith community can help influence the formation of the child's spirit. Such community effort can provide concrete experiences that lead to the development of healthy spiritual DNA. When periods of struggle and questioning enter the person's life, spiritual mentors and guides can help lead the person through them in an honest, forthright confrontation of the issues.

## Ages 0–4

As a young child[1] growing up attending church on Sunday with my family, I learned to sing the words of the liturgy with familiar melodies week after week, month after month, year after year. I have a vivid memory of sitting with my older brother beside my grandmother, who loved to sing hymns and liturgy with gusto (though not always exactly on pitch), while my mom sang in the choir and my dad conducted worship as pastor of the congregation. This was the early phase of my spiritual formation that I remember. I did not know exactly what was meant by the words "Create in me a clean heart, O God" or what "a right spirit" was, but as a child, I sensed that in singing those words, we were asking God to do something important for us.

As I listened to the words being sung around me, I was also gazing at a huge portrait behind the altar—a painting of Christ kneeling in prayer in the Garden of Gethsemane. Jesus was very real to me as a child, and I suppose I thought He lived in the church, in that picture where He prayed. I was not able to conceptualize God living in me; first I had to learn about who God was and why we were asking as we sang and prayed to be given a clean heart.

Young children are developing spiritually, just as they are developing emotionally and physically. In infancy, a child is aware of his or her environment and responds to it. He or she soon discriminates between a loving, relaxed voice tone and facial expression and one that is filled with stress.

Gentle, loving touch and talk for the infants, healthy play and clear limits for the toddlers, and interest in and encouragement to parents all contribute to the spiritual formation of children within the faith community. Young children can experience the church as a safe place where they can receive the care they need. There they can learn to trust.

## Ages 4–6

As children begin to distinguish what is "me" and what is "not me," they become capable of participating in relationships. Their thinking is concrete, so looking at a life-size picture of Jesus might mean to them that they are really looking at Jesus. Images of God begin to develop early on in life. Young children are in the most rapid learning phase of their lives, and so can readily learn spiritual disciplines, just as they learn physical and emotional discipline.

A faith community can become a village that helps raise the child, teaching that God is real. Children this age learn of God's love by the way they are treated by the community. They respond to kindness, knowing they are viewed as a gift to the church. They also experience healthy boundaries that help move them from self-centeredness to concern for others.

## AGES 7–10

Christian education flourishes during this age. Children love to learn about Bible stories. They are so real to them at this age. The rich, powerful stories of God working in the lives of His people become part of the reality of the concretely thinking child.

Through these stories, the children learn moral living. They begin to understand how to treat one another. They learn about forgiveness. Jesus and His sacrificial life becomes a real model to them.

For some children, the church becomes an oasis during this critical time in their anxious and chaotic childhood.

> Bill was a college student preparing for seminary study after graduation. As part of his application process, he wrote a reflection on his own faith development. He shared that he had been an orphan adopted by an aunt and uncle who mistreated him. They permitted a neighbor to take him to church with her family on Sundays, and Bill developed a sense of belonging at church, where he learned about a loving God through the teaching he received and by participating in the youth activities. He viewed the church as his safe place, and he wanted to spend his life serving in the church. He wanted to lead people to Christ as he had been led.

## AGES 11–14

As students begin middle school and faith instruction, new challenges arise. The developing child develops a capacity for abstract thinking along with a healthy need to define self. The church can challenge these preadolescents to search out the truth of their faith during this critical period of exposure to the culture. Youth at this age love to challenge things. This is a wonderful time to inoculate them to the barrage of messages they receive each day that are opposed to their faith.

Jenny has served her congregation for many years as a confirmation mentor. Her gifts are patience, love, kindness, and joy (including a sense of humor). She is a crucial part of the "village" at her church—listening to the students' life stories and being with them in many of the life changes they are experiencing.

Her favorite thing to do is what she calls "inoculation." She will show a TV commercial and then ask, "What is this commercial trying to get you to think?" The class gets excited as they search out the hidden messages that make the viewer think that the product is very important in his or her life. Inevitably, one of the class members will reach the usual conclusion: "It is obvious that they are not really interested in us, but only in selling us something."

Then Jenny will show a segment from a TV show or cartoon, showing how to handle conflict. "I get it," one of the students says with excitement. "The person came out the winner by that sarcastic remark, but ruined a relationship in the process."

Jenny also will show scenes that depict suggested sexuality to the thirteen- and fourteen-year-old youth. "What is the message here?" she asks. The class sees through this scene also. "They are showing this to make the show more popular," one boy almost shouts. "They do not care what they are teaching us." With that, Jenny points out that this casual way of handling sexuality misses the wonderful mystery that God created in males and females.

## AGES 15–18

High school and college students are discerning among many paths in their lives—what to study, how to be in relationships that support them, developing their bodies and relating to family members as life changes occur. This is a time to form their identity. Friendships and romantic relationships take a lot of energy to create, maintain, and understand. The pain of loss is always present, yet often misunderstood or unprocessed. This age group has one of the highest rates of suicide.

Questions arise within many young adults as they struggle with their childhood belief system. This time of life can be marked by a denial of spiritual needs and a suppressing of childhood religious teachings as the young person continues his or her journey of self-definition in a confusing and Me-focused world. Opportunities to serve (such as mission trips) are helpful for the spiritual growth of this age group.

Bible study time for this group can focus on the real issues these high school students are facing. There is no other opportunity in their life to voice their deep struggles and inner anxieties. At school they have a reputation to keep up, and at home there are the usual patterns of communication that usually do not allow for such frank conversation.

The unique atmosphere that the Holy Spirit can develop as the students gather around God's Word can provide the needed forum for frank disclosure and discussion of the real-life issues of this age group. With a healthy leader who models a disarmingly honest style, issues of sexuality, breaking from home, and forming identity can lead to exciting discussion.

## AGES 19–29

Faith communities can reach out to those in this age group through college campus ministries, young adult activities, and learning opportunities that meet the young adults' needs. There are defining moments in young adulthood when life plans are thwarted, a friend dies, a parent or sibling becomes gravely ill, and simply coping with life becomes a challenge. These moments may become windows of opportunity for spiritual growth. Young people can realize that life does not have to be lived privately.

For many in this age group, religion seems somewhat superficial. As these young adults struggle to find out what is real for their lives, the church often seems restrictive and dogmatic. Most stay away from organized religion, searching for something that speaks more to their struggles and their life.

Instead of seeing this reality as distressing, a healthy faith community can see the questioning of this age group as a gift and a needed force to produce growth within the Church. As a faith community welcomes the challenges of this age group, these young adults will feel more like a gift to the Church.

## SPIRITUAL DISCIPLINES AS EXERCISE FOR THE SPIRIT AND HEALING FOR DAMAGED SPIRITUAL DNA

Since ancient times, Christians have sought to learn and practice ways to grow spiritually—to become more like Christ, to experience a relationship of intimacy with God. We know that Jesus prayed, practiced solitude, engaged in fellowship, spent His life in service, and gave glory to His Father. All of these activities can lead to a closer relationship with God.

*Spiritual disciplines* can be practiced internally, in interaction with the environment, or with other believers. Individuals are drawn to particular disciplines naturally. For example, a person with a preference for drawing energy from other people (*painters*) will enjoy service, group study and prayer, and worship. Those who naturally draw energy from time spent alone (*pointers*) will be attracted to solitude, meditation, and private prayer and devotional practices.

One way of categorizing spiritual disciplines is to use St. Paul's own terms in Romans 7 and 8: law of the spirit, of the mind, and of the body.

Certain disciplines may help to strengthen the organization of the person's spirit by witness of the Holy Spirit. Such practices include prayer, study, worship, and guidance.

Other practices might be adopted to provide rest for the mind that suffers with overcontrol. Examples of these practices are meditation, solitude, simplicity, and celebration.

For the person with impulse-control problems, practices such as fasting, submission, service, and confession are good exercises to attain healthy self-control of the body.

## DISCIPLINES TO RE-FORM THE SPIRIT

### PRAYER

Prayer, in its various forms, brings us into awareness of God's presence. As a spiritual practice, prayer creates communion with God. Prayer is joining the conversation that is going on in God and being invited into an intimate relationship.

Prayer is responding to God's open invitation—not just to converse, but to sit together in intimate companionship. As with the closest friend one can imagine, there may be silence, resting together, freely sharing feelings, and different kinds of talk. There can also be asking for help, giving affirmation, and expressing our love.

Prayer is something learned. From the first act of folding tiny baby hands until the hearing of the last words of prayer before death, those seeking to experience God's presence are learning and practicing prayer ("Lord, teach us to pray," Luke 11:1).

God uses prayer to change His people. It is through prayer that spiritual formation takes place, and spiritual re-parenting can happen in that intimate, loving relationship with God.

## STUDY

"If you abide in My word, you are truly My disciples, and you will know the truth, and the truth will set you free." (John 8:32)

The discipline of study brings one to Scripture in order to be changed ("transformed by the renewal of your mind," Romans 12:2), not merely to gather information. Study involves centering attention on a subject repeatedly, then understanding the meaning of what is being studied and pondering that meaning. This process leads to depth and wisdom.

For the Christian, study focuses upon "whatever is true, whatever is honorable, whatever is just, whatever is pure, whatever is lovely, whatever is commendable, if there is any excellence, if there is anything worthy of praise" (Philippians 4:8). This renews the spirit. The inner transformation (new self) occurs as a gift of God.

## WORSHIP

"God is spirit, and those who worship Him must worship in spirit and truth." (John 4:24)

As God's Spirit bears witness to one's spirit (Romans 8:16) and produces the confidence of faith, the natural response is one of joy and gratitude. Worship is the expression of thanksgiving and celebration of the relationship with God that heals and makes whole the spirit that was broken.

Participating in corporate worship allows the Body of Christ to tell the story of God's redeeming love, inviting others into relationship with God and celebrating the healing and the daily renewing of a clean heart within. Worship offers time and space, rituals and forms that support spiritual growth. Such forms and rituals are designed to gently lead the worshipers into the realm where God touches and frees the human spirit.

Worship involves the body, mind, and spirit. The body is engaged with movement—sitting, standing, kneeling, walking, tasting, touching, smelling, hearing, and seeing. The mind is engaged in worship with hearing and understanding words and ideas—singing words, praying words, repeating liturgy, listening to the reading of Scripture. The spirit is engaged through the senses and with music that is imbedded into the deepest places of human awareness.

## GUIDANCE

"Again I say to you, if two of you agree on earth about anything they ask, it will be done for them by My Father in heaven. For where two or three are gathered in My name, there am I among them." (Matthew 18:19–20)

Receiving divine guidance through other believers is a gift from God. Guidance can be received from the Scriptures as they are heard in preaching, through Bible study, or in the context of small-group ministry. Guidance is one way in which a believer can experience the power of the new self as Christ changes the heart and changes a person's reality. Guidance can be found in a network of trusted friends or in a community of believers.

Guidance may be sought from a spiritual director or companion. Spiritual direction is the process of accompanying a person on a spiritual journey. This unique type of guidance invites a deeper relationship with God. It offers a place to explore prayer practices, meditation, and spiritual experiences and allows us to serve with authenticity and grateful hearts.

A person might seek out a spiritual director or companion and meet on a regular basis over time. The purpose of the meetings is to explore how one views God, how God is acting in one's life, and how one is experiencing a relationship with God through prayer. One may seek out spiritual direction at any point in life. Often life transitions are times when persons are open to pursuing intentional spiritual growth with spiritual direction.

Spiritual direction or companioning, as a specific practice of receiving guidance, enables persons to discern where God is in their life story and to identify how the Holy Spirit is at work. This opportunity for spiritual growth can work hand in hand with counseling or medical therapy to engage the person's body, mind, and spirit in healing.

## DISCIPLINES TO HELP AN OVERCONTROLLING MIND

### MEDITATION

"Be still, and know that I am God." (Psalm 46:10)

Meditation is the process of quieting the mind and the body in order to contemplate the presence of God. The practice of meditation is intended to fill the mind with thoughts of God. It can provide spiritual refreshment for the soul.

One can meditate on (quietly contemplate) a Scripture passage by selecting a verse and reflecting on it prayerfully, exploring it in depth. Another way to meditate is to spend time in a setting where there is beauty, such as a natural setting, an art gallery, a sanctuary, or a chapel, while noticing God's presence in that place. Any situation in which one ceases "doing" and focuses on "being" can be conducive to meditation.

Meditation can be learned through practice. It comes more naturally for some than for others. Natural and repetitive rhythms, such as breathing and some sounds or movements, can be woven into meditation. Quieting the mind can be a real challenge in this age of multitasking and attachment to technology. With the cell phone turned off and out of sight, meditation can allow for the opening of one's mind to hear God's voice and obey God's Word.

## Solitude

"For thus said the Lord God, . . . 'In returning and rest you shall be saved; in quietness and in trust shall be your strength.'" (Isaiah 30:15)

Solitude is the discipline of being alone and silent. Spiritual growth can occur through stillness: "Be still, and know that I am God" (Psalm 46:10). Solitude is more than being alone and quiet; it is a state of mind and heart.

In solitude, awareness of the nature of one's sinful condition has a chance to surface. Even though this becomes the dark night of the soul, God can use this experience to show how the person needs to be free. He invites the yearning sinner into a closer relationship with Him.

## Simplicity

"Therefore I tell you, do not be anxious about your life, what you will eat or what you will drink, nor about your body, what you will put on. . . . Seek first the kingdom of God and His righteousness, and all these things will be added to you." (Matthew 6:25, 33)

In today's culture, the advertising industry works to create desire for their products. Happiness is defined by owning stuff, pampering self, or having exciting experiences. Success is having thousands of followers on the Internet.

The life of Jesus exemplifies the discipline of simplicity. Simplicity as spiritual discipline flows from the attitude that all is a gift from God. Renewed by a right spirit within, the Christian will desire to make personal goods available to others, rather than amassing them for a sense of security.

The practice of simplicity extends beyond material possessions to the amount of activity we take on and how we use our time and personal gifts. It is a practice of prioritizing. It is taking the unnecessary busyness out of life to leave room for enjoyment of the moment.

## Celebration

"Rejoice in the Lord always; again I will say, rejoice." (Philippians 4:4)

With the joy that comes with knowing that Christ is present, one can celebrate the simple goodness of life. Celebration invites the Christian to be carefree and thankful. Celebration is the experience of real joy in the moment. As the Holy Spirit shifts the mood of a believer from closed and defensive to open and interested, the new self can enjoy the moment in the presence of Christ—each and every moment! There is always something to celebrate.

Sharing the joy of God with others with a spirit of carefree celebration can occur when getting together with friends without an agenda. With celebration comes laughter!

The discipline of celebration invites one to consider the things in life that are easy and those not so easy to celebrate. When a Christian dies, the memorial service may be called a celebration of the life of that person. While feelings are mixed at such a celebration, thanksgiving and deep joy can be found as well. Practicing the discipline of celebration may generate gratitude and real joy—aspects of well-being that go beyond emotional experience.

## DISCIPLINES TO HELP THE BODY WITH IMPULSE CONTROL

### FASTING

"Man shall not live by bread alone, but by every word that comes from the mouth of God." (Matthew 4:4)

Jesus fasted for forty days in the wilderness. The practice of fasting allows one to learn by experience that God's Word can be sustaining apart from food that is consumed. Fasting can be a way of showing devotion to God's Word. One may choose to combine fasting with an aspect of meditation or prayer.

For one who has not fasted before, a fast of one or two meals' duration, consuming only water and fruit juice, is recommended. The duration of a fast may be determined prayerfully as that length of time that is right for an individual's purpose.

As an alternative to fasting from food, something else may be chosen, such as fasting from behaviors or attitudes or actions that are not nourishing to the spirit. Being completely dependent on God for sustenance for a period of time can be a powerful way to exercise spiritual discipline.

### SUBMISSION

"[Submit] to one another out of reverence for Christ." (Ephesians 5:21)

Submission as modeled and taught by Jesus is being able to lay down the burden of controlling one's life. Scripture teaches a mutual attitude of subordination—Christians living as citizens of a new order. Jesus calls His people to self-denial as a way to understand that they are free to give to others. Happiness does not depend on getting one's needs met. Self-denial can lead to the discovery of the true self—the identity God has given.

Service to others flows out of submission. The cross is a sign of submission. Living as Jesus lived in voluntary submission is to live a life of servanthood.

The believer submits to the triune God, to the Word of God, to our family, friends, and neighbors, to the body of believers, to the broken and despised, and to the world.

## SERVICE

> "If I then, your Lord and Teacher, have washed your feet, you also ought to wash one another's feet. For I have given you an example, that you also should do just as I have done to you." (John 13:14–15)

The discipline of service creates the grace of humility. When a believer consciously chooses a course of action that places the good of others first, a change occurs in the spirit, bringing deepened love and joy in God.

Service is freely given and needs no recognition or reward. True service lies in hiddenness, in small things, such as common courtesy, hospitality, and listening. True service bears the burdens of others and shares the Word of God. Jesus said, "But whoever would be great among you must be your servant . . . even as the Son of Man came not to be served but to serve" (Matthew 20:26, 28).

In every congregation and neighborhood there are people who are grieving loss—death of a loved one, loss of a job or home, a divorce, loss of health. Often the weight of the burden of loss becomes so heavy that illness or depression develops. One practical aspect of the discipline of service is to find ways to help these people. Service could be simply bringing meals to the home, visiting in the hospital or nursing center, serving Communion at home for the sick and bereaved, or listening and offering words of encouragement.

## CONFESSION

> "If we say we have no sin, we deceive ourselves, and the truth is not in us. If we confess our sins, He is faithful and just to forgive us our sins and to cleanse us from all unrighteousness." (1 John 1:8–9)

The practice of confession is fundamental to living in fellowship in God in a right spirit. A person's spirit is damaged by sin, leading to internal dysfunction as the body and mind struggle for control of the person. Examining one's life for the sin that needs confession can be a fearful thing. Overcoming this fear is possible through God's grace. Prayer and meditation in solitude can lead to the discovery of one's deep longings for forgiveness. Listening to one's own inner conversation can lead to the truth about what needs forgiveness. With careful listening, the Holy Spirit provides guidance. It is in this way that the new self participates with the Holy Spirit to create a right spirit.

Confession can be practiced in private or in community. Confession practiced as a part of the discipline of worship allows for words to be spoken in unison, reminding worshipers of the need for forgiveness and cleansing. This leads to receiving the Sacrament of Holy Communion.

Sometimes confession is practiced appropriately as a private discipline. In choosing those to whom we confess, we look for certain qualities: spiritual maturity, wisdom, compassion, common sense, the ability to keep a confidence, and a wholesome sense of humor. The one receiving confession may be a close friend, a fellowship group, or a spiritual mentor, such as a pastor or a spiritual director/companion. "Therefore, confess your sins to one another and pray for one another, that you may be healed" (James 5:16).

## INTEGRATING THE SPIRITUAL DISCIPLINES

Many of the disciplines can be practiced together. When several disciplines are integrated into a spiritual practice, a creative process can happen. For example, to engage the body, mind, and spirit, a *prayer* walk may be taken. One mode of walking prayer is to walk a labyrinth—a circular path based on an ancient form of prayer. The path leads in concentric circles to the center, where the person praying may pause and *meditate* on God's presence. While walking the labyrinth, verses of Scripture are repeated that have been memorized through *study*. Upon leaving the prayer walk, the pray-er may *celebrate* the time with God with gratitude for the gift. This spiritual practice incorporates two of the disciplines that help strengthen the organization of the new self.

An example of a practice that focuses on strengthening the mind suffering with overcontrol disorder is to combine *meditating* alone in *solitude* for a designated period of time on a regular basis, gradually increasing the time spent. For the person with an impulse-control disorder, practicing disciplined *service submits* one's own desires to the will of God and strengthens the body, as well as the spirit, by *fasting* from addictive substances or behavioral patterns.

# Congregation as a Healing Community

## CHAPTER 7

### In This Chapter

- The authors describe how a congregation can become a healing community.
- The model of the Early Church is examined, showing that the congregation is in the relationship business.
- The authors describe the marks of a healing community.
- Specific help for overcontrol disorders, reality disorders, and impulse-control disorders is outlined.

## A Congregation Is in the Relationship Business

Sustainable health changes are more likely to occur in a group setting than in private. A faith community provides a setting for healing and wholeness, as long as its atmosphere is healthy. The spirit of a congregation is determined by the relative well-being of all of its relationships.

The congregation is in the relationship business, worshiping a relational God (Trinity) who created humans to be in a loving relationship to their Creator, to self, and to one another. The Hebrew word *shalom* describes the peace that comes from this proper order of life. Fulfillment (joy) comes from living for God and others—for worship and for service.

Instead of energy flowing upward and outward, self-protective tendencies always turn the flow inward (*incurvatus in se*). The temptations of Christ were intended to get Christ to think of Himself (ME) and break the loving relationship of obedience to His Father (Matthew 4:1–11).

Sin is a relational concept. The first commandments show how a relationship with God is damaged by disrespect; the next commandments show how family and community relationships are damaged by selfishness; and the last show how a relationship with self is damaged by coveting—not appreciating the good gifts that God has given to each of His people.

## MODEL OF THE EARLY CHURCH: A CULTURE OF WE

The Christian life is not a private one, but one lived within the Body of Christ, with each person concerned for one another and considering the good of all. This is made possible through the power of Christ, who is the Head of the Body.

The apostles gathered in one another's homes daily. "They devoted themselves to the apostles' teaching and the fellowship, to the breaking of bread and the prayers" (Acts 2:42). Throughout the New Testament Epistles, there are nearly sixty "one another" exhortations given to churches. All of them imply the ideal of close-knit community of the Holy Spirit that will be a witness as it reaches out to others. These exhortations called the members of the Early Church to

- live in harmony with one another (Romans 12:16; 1 Peter 3:8);
- care for one another (1 Corinthians 12:25);
- serve one another (Galatians 5:13);
- bear one another's burdens (Galatians 6:2);
- speak to one another with psalms, hymns, and spiritual songs (Ephesians 5:19);
- submit to one another (Ephesians 5:21); and
- forgive one another (Colossians 3:13).

In Colossians 3:15, Paul expresses his prayer for God's people: "And let the peace of Christ rule in your hearts, to which indeed you were called in one body." The Church is one and so enjoys community, a precious gift in our society in which isolation and loneliness, animosity and hatred, individualism and division seem to be the order of the day. In the face of an ever-increasingly ME-oriented culture, the exciting model given to us by Christ and the exhortations to the Early Church is to develop a WE-oriented culture within our congregations.

For example, today's parents are a product of a ME-oriented culture and think in ME-oriented terms for their child. They want their child to have the best possible benefit to succeed in the world. They are unaware that this logic comes from evolutionary theory—that the purpose of life is to survive and that their child has to have every advantage (such as dance lessons, soccer lessons, etc.) to come out on top. What parents can learn from a healthy faith community is that a functional WE-oriented atmosphere will produce a healthy spirit within their child, a spirit of love and service rather than a spirit of self-centeredness.

"Rather, speaking the truth in love, we are to grow up in every way into Him who is the head, into Christ, from whom the whole body, joined and held together . . . makes the body grow so that it builds itself up in love" (Ephesians 4:15–16). Spiritual growth occurs in the context of the Body of Christ as it functions as a WE orientation in all of its relationships. This represents an actual cultural shift from the power struggles and negative, disrespectful attributes of a ME-oriented culture. This WE-oriented shift is a different way of thinking, a different set of emotions, a different way of perceiving, and a different way of acting—all taking into account the best for all concerned. A WE-oriented shift is what the new self helps accomplish in the mind and heart of the believer.

The markers of a healthy faith culture are similar to the attributes of a healthy Christian family: (1) loving in the agape sense, (2) honesty, "Speaking the truth in love," and (3) having good WE-oriented boundaries. A child from a home that has these three markers has good internal control, a healthy self-image, and a genuine concern for others.

## MARKER 1

### A Healthy Community: Loving

The word is *agape*. It describes a love that does not exist on earth. It is the love of Christ that is totally selfless, thinking always of the best for all concerned. It is the gift that the Holy Spirit brings to the Christian community that makes it a healing community.

Building community is the practice of agape as articulated in Romans 12:9–21. Love is genuine; it is mutual (vv. 9–10). It contributes to the needs of the saints and expresses itself in hospitality (v. 13). It rejoices with those who rejoice and weeps with those who weep (v. 15). With humility, it seeks to live in harmony with all (v. 16). Recognizing that relationships are not just dependent upon us, it urges us to do our part in living peaceably with all (v. 18). Further, love's conduct is not determined by a "get even" mentality, or a desire for revenge, but it is motivated by the mercy of God. It seeks to bless rather than curse (v. 14), to respond to evil with what is noble (v. 17), to let God do the judging (v. 19), and to be kind to our enemies, thus overcoming evil with good (vv. 20–21).

Like money put in the bank, gracing one another with words of respect and kindness makes people want to get together and share their lives. These are the marks of a healthy faith community.

A loving atmosphere always occurs in the context of relationships. Relationships require constant communication to stay fresh and alive. Curiosity and excitement over God's Word keeps our relationship with God growing and deepening. A healthy congregation has vibrant Bible study opportunities that allow for personal reflection and conversation.

## PERSONAL CONVERSATION

People must get to know one another and stay in touch to keep their relationships growing. In practice, this means that half of all church meetings should be spent in relationship building. The best way to change this part of the congregation's culture is to start every meeting with a devotion or Bible study to work on the relationship with God. Then ask everyone to respond to these questions: "What can we pray for in your life? What is on your heart?" Leaders model this process by answering the questions first, disclosing their personal life.

Personal communication with appropriate self-disclosure is necessary to develop healthy relationships. As leaders model such personal expression, gradually the culture shifts from the pretense that things are fine in everyone's life to emotional conversation about personal hopes and struggles.

Time and energy spent in listening is also a vital part of being loving. Listening skills can be taught and modeled so that everyone feels understood. This is especially important in "painter/pointer" conversations to keep misunderstanding from occurring.

Pointers can learn not to focus on the first thing said and draw conclusions, but to recognize that this is the first brushstroke of a picture and not the main point. Rather than solving, disagreeing, correcting reality, or getting defensive, pointers can just sit back and enjoy the picture being painted.

Painters can learn to actually listen to the exact word or words of the pointer and then ask for more detail so that they can understand what is being said. Instead of asking a number of questions to dig for detail, painters can "double-click" on the logical word, as one does to an underlined word on the Internet.

## MOTIVATION BY LOVE, NOT GUILT

It is common for counselors to devalue faith and a faith community because of the unhealthy guilt that is sometimes fostered there. When a faith community focuses on appropriate behavior (rules orientation) as its goal, it is easy to use guilt to enforce such guidelines. Christian families can also fall into this orientation. Guilt is a powerful motivator and can be overused so that community or family members behave properly. It is natural to think that God will love a person more if he or she lives a good life. Such motivation is law oriented and leads to outward compliance. Jesus did not speak kindly of such shows of righteousness by the Pharisees of His day (Matthew 23:27).

Guilt is sometimes utilized as an emotional manipulation technique, shaping another person's behavior by being critical or by showing disappointment. Utilizing such guilt to control behavior creates an unhealthy environment.

> Yvonne was stopped short by the comment. She had just joined a Bible study group and questioned the leader's interpretation of a Scripture passage. She assumed that such openness was appropriate. The leader took offense and observed in a slightly sarcastic tone, "Are you sure you know what you are talking about? I spent many hours in preparation." She suddenly felt guilty about being so open and hurting the leader.

> Yvonne would not be back. She did feel guilty about her comment. She felt she had nothing to offer. She no longer felt welcome in the group.

When congregation members are going through a bad time, struggling with addictions, family struggles, or even depression, many stay away from church. They often feel that they should be doing better and that they will be judged for not being able to control themselves or their family.

A healthy faith community focuses on agape as its motivator. There is a clear message that all are in this together. All have fallen short and need God's love and forgiveness. This allows members to be open with the struggles they are having and to feel the healing power of Christ's presence.

Such a focus does not minimize sin or its effects on lives and relationships. Rather, an agape environment allows the freedom of deep confession with the assurance of God's love and forgiveness. When guilt is the motivator, motivation to change comes from the old self trying to do better. With agape, the motivation to change one's life flows out of the new self.

## MARKER 2

### A Healthy Community: Honest

Relationships thrive on honesty. Pretense and secrets prevent people from forming good, deep relationships based on trust. Sharing personal concerns with one another helps the community pray for one another.

Leaders model such disclosure by letting others know what to pray for in their lives. Appropriate sharing of such personal information bonds and solidifies relationships.

> I grew up in a pastor's family[1] with the unspoken message that we were to present a good model to the rest of the congregation. With this background, it has been easy to give out the message that our family is fine and does not need anything.
>
> This strategy worked well until my wife, Kathy, and I received the devastating news that our grandson was near death with a vicious form of leukemia. During the months that followed, we all were beaten up, tired, scared, and in need of support. Our congregation and Christian friends stepped up and surrounded us with their love.
>
> We learned that such caring connections are what a faith community is all about. Even now, years later, with our grandson doing well after a bone marrow transplant, we feel the deep connections forged during those difficult years.

Hurt feelings always get in the way, so the Christian community does not allow this anger to stay private, but will get people together to talk through things. In fact, relationships grow when things are confronted and forgiveness can happen. A good concept to use is *disarming honesty*. This allows things to be brought out of private thoughts and into the open, where they can be discussed in a helpful fashion. Key to such honesty is the lack of any hidden agenda; things are expressed for the purpose of helping the relationship grow.

## PROBLEMS WITH STAFF RELATIONSHIPS

Staff relationship problems are a daily occurrence. Feelings are hurt, turf is threatened, favoritism is suspected, and liaisons (some sexual) are developed that create tension and power struggles. These problems must be caught early and confronted in love so the air can stay "clear."

> Pastor Martin was hesitant at first, but felt strongly that the staff should have a regular time to clear the air. This had been a bad year for conflict. He could feel the tension in the air. They had regular staff meetings on Friday mornings, but it was normally a short meeting after a brief devotion, devoted to programmatic concerns. This Friday, it would be different.

Pastor Martin began with a devotion on Ephesians 4, emphasizing the need for dealing with issues "before the sun goes down." Then he suggested that they put this into a concrete form: "We are going to take at least fifteen minutes of our staff devotions each week to share anything that hurt our feelings or that did not 'set right' within our ministry. Let me begin with something that happened to me this week that still causes me distress."

With that, Pastor Martin modeled disarming honesty about a situation that he was personally involved in: "I must admit that I am still upset about the lack of interest in our special evening fellowship event last week." He was open with his frustration and invited others to give their feelings and reactions.

The talk was difficult at first, but it became very honest in a short period of time when everyone realized that Pastor Martin was not trying to establish blame or induce guilt, but was being vulnerable with his feelings. Other private frustrations were shared in this area, resulting in a better understanding among the staff. As one of the staff members put it after the meeting, "I looked down and felt tense when the fellowship dinner was brought up. I thought, Here we go again, expecting to feel guilty. But we all had a chance to say what we really felt. It did clear the air."

For the first several weeks, Pastor Martin was the only one to raise issues, but after several months, this became precious time to talk through things that usually got ignored or took the form of gossip. The time often extended well past the allotted fifteen minutes.

## PROBLEMS WITH RELATIONSHIPS BETWEEN MEMBERS

Often, there are long-standing factions that go back ten or twenty years that cause power struggles. A WE-oriented community does not allow such factions or hurt feelings to stay under cover, but confronts them in a spirit of love. The parties involved will be tapped on the shoulder and asked to sit down together to clear the air. The attitude is always "It is not good for *us* that this tension exists between you two, because the spirit of the whole Body suffers."

Hurt feelings and anger that have been long standing are deadly to the spirit of the congregation as such moods linger. In fact, it is descriptive to picture the emotional state of the congregation in terms of *mood particles** that begin to accumulate in areas where conflict has not been resolved. These are spiritual forces that build up and bring resentment to a relationship. Picture them as remnants of a bad mood between two people that did not get resolved. The hurt feelings do not go away, but instead compress into a mood particle that lingers indefinitely in the atmosphere. When hundreds of these particles build up after repeated bad interactions, they have the power to shift the mood of any situation. When activated by a new situation, the mood shifts at lightning speed, making good discussion of the issue impossible.

The accumulation of mood particles usually has a definite starting point (*defining moment*), when immature spiritual DNA of two people touched. Both had feelings hurt and felt wronged. This shifted the mood of the relationship. Since these hurt feelings are usually kept private and not talked through, the result is a mood particle left between the two people. Some trust is lost, and the two no longer feel like allies.

For the good of the faith community, addressing these issues can be pursued, bringing both parties to confession so that reconciliation can occur. But the conversation has to get past the individual *litanies* and get to the defining moment when the original hurt and upset occurred.

> Fred and Granger finally sat down together with the pastor. They represented the two factions of the congregation that had been at odds with each other for many years. There were constant issues that sometimes exploded into a battle of words. Several days earlier, Fred and Granger had gotten into a shouting match in a meeting. That issue was replacing carpet in the sanctuary.
>
> The pastor began with prayer, thanking the two for responding to his firm suggestion that they meet face-to-face. As both tried to share their litanies against the other, the pastor stopped them kindly with the question, "When was the first time either of you remember being very upset at the other?"

---

* "Mood particles" is a term developed by one of the authors, Dr. Ludwig, to show the effects of earlier unresolved conflicts on future situations. Particle physics uses terms like "quarks" to indicate subatomic forces that cannot be seen (except as traces in a cyclotron cloud chamber). The term is used here to indicate powerful spiritual forces that cannot be seen, but are very real in affecting the mood of future situations. See two of Dr. Ludwig's works for more information: *The Power of WE* (2009) and *Renewing the Family Spirit* (1989), both available from Concordia Publishing House, St. Louis, Mo.

After a pause, Fred said quietly, "There is something that happened fifteen years ago that I still remember vividly." The pastor thanked Fred for his honesty and asked that he share his memory.

Fred began: "We were considering a building program. I had just spoken at a congregational meeting and requested that the existing building be preserved and expanded. Then Granger got up and seemed to sneer at my presentation, saying that this was stupid. I still get a sick feeling in my stomach when I remember the look on his face and the sarcasm in his words."

"Was there something about the existing building that you wanted to keep?" the pastor asked softly. Fred broke into tears. "My father built the old church with his own hands. He loved that building. This was my father's legacy."

Granger had tears in his eyes as he spoke. "I didn't know . . . I didn't know," he began. "I was somewhat new to the congregation and was upset at the condition of its finances. I felt it was my calling to get the congregation on a better financial footing, so when you suggested a much more expensive project that would preserve the old building, I reacted to the cost."

Fred and Granger's eyes met, tears in both. The years of conflict melted at that moment. The defining moment was out in the open and reconciliation was evident. The situation was now in the hands of the Holy Spirit, not the devil!

The defining moment is incredibly powerful. Trust breaks down at that critical time, and gossip and litanies begin against each other. It is critical to bring the defining moment out of private thought and feeling, and into shared conversation. When such hurt is kept private, the devil builds a base of operations (Ephesians 4:25–27).

## CONFLICT CAN BUILD INTIMACY AS TRUTH IS SPOKEN IN LOVE

Whenever people get upset with each other, it can become a common practice that both are invited to talk things over face-to-face so that reconciliation can occur. In this way, conflicts are talked through before deeper problems develop.

"Be angry and do not sin; do not let the sun go down on your anger, and give no opportunity to the devil" (Ephesians 4:26–27). Pervasive bad moods cannot be allowed. These destroy the community.

Talking through conflicts helps relationships grow when forgiveness is given and received. Power struggles often stem from childhood sensations of powerlessness (damaged spiritual DNA).

> Pastor Tim and the church council president were locked in conflict. They had trouble agreeing on anything. Joan, the president, felt discounted and unimportant, despite her efforts to provide leadership. It seemed that Pastor Tim took matters into his own hands and disregarded council decisions too often. Joan had let her anger and frustration build. She was upset that Pastor Tim was not being a team player.

> Pastor Tim had difficulty trusting that council decisions were in the best interest of the congregation. He felt compelled to exert leadership in making sure things were done the right way. He believed he was acting in accord with his calling.

> Finally, Joan reached her limit and could no longer tolerate her frustration. She blew up in a council meeting and submitted her resignation. It was too painful to continue feeling powerless and unappreciated. The council members were upset. Pastor Tim told them that Joan could not work with him, and it was best that she go. Both Pastor Tim and Joan had abandoned the practice of the WE and were focused only on the ME. Their self-protective tendencies had turned inward.

> As the faith community prayed for its leaders and brought these two together to be open about their frustration, the Spirit began its work. Reflecting on her deeper hurt, Joan realized how she had longed for Pastor Tim to respect her leadership. When he ignored her and pushed through on issues, she felt personally disrespected. She was unable to reconcile her need for Pastor Tim's respect with his inability to work through differences. It was just easier to end the relationship.

> Pastor Tim prayerfully reflected on his part in the separation, and he saw that he felt insecure when his vision for the church did not predominate. He feared others would view him as less than effective as a pastor. He felt impatient with drawn-out processes for solving problems and preferred immediate action.

How can the faith community support those who are locked in conflict without taking sides? Such situations are very painful for all involved when it happens in the faith community—a place that people want to be a safe and healing space. Sometimes people turn against the church and distance themselves from it because it no longer feels safe or loving. Such an experience can create spiritual pain as well as emotional pain. There can be anger at God as well as at the church and individuals in it. Without an honest and open attempt at resolution, such situations are likely to be repeated in the future. Anger and sorrow remain, and the community becomes a grieving community. Conflicts dealt with in love and honesty can prevent the deep feelings of loss from occurring.

Although conflict-management skills are not innate in humans, such skills can be learned. Conflict resolution as taught in Scripture can be practiced, taught, and modeled. Conflict management may be thought of as a *spiritual discipline*—to be approached prayerfully, humbly, lovingly, and openly, with clear boundaries for behavior in the relationship. Effective conflict management will focus more on the facts in a situation and less on the personalities. When differences are openly faced and feelings are named clearly and worked through, the experience can build a sense of intimacy for all involved.

Anyone on the church council, Pastor Tim, or Joan could take the initiative and ask, "How are we going to handle this conflict we are experiencing?" since the conflict affects everyone. Addressing their differences in a spirit of love could have produced a different outcome than separation. Because both Pastor Tim and Joan were convinced that each was right, a third party was needed to help them look honestly at what was happening, be listened to with respect, and listen to each other.

> After prayers for God's healing, both Pastor Tim and Joan experienced a softening in their harshness toward each other. In a courageous step toward seeking healing, they agreed to invite a trained conflict manager to meet and assess their situation.
>
> Will, a psychologist with a passion for service to hurting churches, met with them and outlined an approach to seek a peaceful resolution. When he was a high school student, Will had

experienced a confusing, angry separation in his own church. While studying psychology, he had learned principles of conflict management that fit with his understanding of Scripture. This awareness of God's Spirit working in conflict situations energized him, and he began to offer his services to congregations. Will's hopeful spirit, loving attitude, and skill in working through a process with clear boundaries were gifts he offered over and over as a deep calling to care for the Body of Christ.

Dealing with natural differences between adults before strong emotions erupt is a mark of a healthy community. Being willing to ask for help and submit to a healing process is also a mark of strength. Pastoral leaders and others who are able to exert a nonanxious presence in the face of differences being expressed among church members are a gift of God. Knowing how to recognize and deal with one's own anxiety is an important self-care skill incorporating spiritual disciplines of silence, prayer, and meditation.

## MARKER 3

### A Healthy Community: WE-Oriented Boundaries

In order to model the Body of Christ, the staff of the church (and school) can deliberately form a WE and model this WE focus in all of their interactions and decisions. In other words, the staff *thinks WE, not ME!*

The cultural models for life are obvious: Think ME. Virtually every situation that is modeled in TV sitcoms, reality shows, movies, and so forth is carefully scripted to show how to look out after self. The character gives just the right put-down and walks away the winner. But the process has just destroyed the relationship.

Modeling within the WE-oriented culture of a faith community is critical for the re-parenting process that all Christians need in order to live more as the new self. Leaders can model the practical aspects of living a life of service. "Let each of you look not only to his own interests, but also to the interests of others. Have this mind among yourselves, which is yours in Christ Jesus" (Philippians 2:4–5).

The staff first works on its internal relationships so that it can function as a unit and can think, say, and act as a community with a WE focus. This means regular staff meetings where relationships are addressed. This means making decisions as a WE. This means dealing with an upset member as a WE. This means that strained relationships between staff are not allowed to stand without being addressed in a spirit of love!

The real test of a functional WE-oriented community is how the congregation handles the various problems that arise in its daily functioning. Are all of the problems handled with the basic question "How is our WE-oriented community going to handle this?"

Leaders model good boundaries. When someone tries to manipulate, leaders work together, focusing on the good of the community.

> It was the third phone call of the day. Belinda needed some advice from the pastor again. His secretary tried to dissuade her, but she insisted. When the pastor picked up the phone, Belinda launched into a nonstop description of her situation.
>
> The pastor knew this would be another thirty-minute phone call. He listened for two minutes and then broke in, "Belinda, I know this is important to you. Right now, I have other things to do. It will not be good for our church, for me, or for you if I take your call and not really be listening to you."
>
> Belinda started to get upset. "You are always too busy for me," she whined in her pathetic, childlike voice. "I thought you cared."
>
> The pastor was loving, but firm. "I do care. If I talk to you now, I will not really be listening, so it will do you no good. It certainly will not do me any good either, since I have other things that are pressing. Call me back tomorrow at 10 a.m., and we will talk for ten minutes."
>
> Belinda started protesting, "I have no one else to talk to ... "The pastor cut her off: "I am thinking about the good of all of us. I will expect your call tomorrow. God go with you." And he stopped the phone call.

## IN A HEALTHY FAITH COMMUNITY, EVERY PERSON IS SEEN AS A GIFT

Every Christian has a calling. Basic to this vocation is a passion for service and outreach. God places passion in everyone's heart for His purposes. Each person is to search the heart to find the passion God has already placed there (Acts 1:24). Working out of that passion produces energy and excitement for the congregation where people do not "keep score," but are generous with their time and efforts.

St. Paul uses two Greek words to describe the importance of each member of the Body of Christ to community wellness. "Now concerning spiritual gifts," he begins in 1 Corinthians 12:1, using a form of the Greek word *pneuma* (spiritual). As discussed earlier, this is the word for the new self and the gift it brings to the Body of Christ. The presence and good attitude of the member is a gift to the congregation. That's what makes a loving community.

In verse 4 he uses another word, *charisma*, as he writes: "There are varieties of gifts, but the same Spirit." The Greek word *charis* represents God's "grace" that gives life and passion to the new self. Putting these two words together, it is the presence and passion of the new self that is the gift that each member brings to the community. These are human treasures showing agape as they reach out to one another.

A healthy congregation perceives every member as a gift to the church and values this work of the Holy Spirit. Opportunities are given for members to search out their passion. In that way, all members can see their presence as a gift and enjoy their role in the ministry of the church. Worth is granted, not earned.

One of the best ways of modeling this is in the way that leaders handle gossip. This can be a gift that the Holy Spirit can utilize for the good of the congregation.

"Some people have been talking," Tom began as he caught the pastor between services, "and they do not think your new stewardship ideas will work."

The pastor stopped and looked at Tom. "Wow!" he began with genuine excitement. "People have been talking! That means there is passion about this subject. We need their ideas and passion for the program. Give me their names, and I will invite them to share their ideas."

Tom was taken aback. "Oh, I can't give their names. They told me this in confidence."

Genuinely saddened, the pastor replied, "But we need their ideas and passion so that we can be successful in this area." After a pause, he continued. "I know what. Go back to these people and get permission to share their names. Our congregation really needs the gift they have to bring to this program."

There was obvious passion that was driving the gossip, but it was misplaced and was in the devil's hands. The faith community preserves its passion as hurt feelings and gossip are handled as gifts that can be reclaimed for ministry.

## RECLAIMING TURF FOR MINISTRY

The culture has changed. Personal problems are not perceived as spiritual in nature. The concept that the Church is a healing place for damaged souls has dramatically eroded. The Word of God and the Sacraments are often seen as having no real power for the healing of personal struggles.

Yet the soul is also the domain of the Church, not just of psychology. The following is a personal story of Dave, one of the authors of this book:

> My father was a pastor. He saw himself as a *Seelsorger*. His ministry reflected that. Even though he had no formal psychological training, he knew that sin damaged the spirit. He knew that confession was good for the soul.

### NEED TO KNOW

*Seelsorger:* A German word that means "one who cares for the soul"; used to describe a pastor.

Confession and forgiveness were central to his ministry. For example, he required each family to register before coming to Holy Communion. He sat in his office on Saturday afternoon so that parishioners could drop by to sign up for the Sacrament the next day. He would ask each to sign the list and then sit down. "How have things been going?" he would begin. It was time for confession, and the person knew it.

Sometimes the person would walk out within five minutes. But often there would be things on the person's heart, and the door would stay closed for a while. It was an opportunity for soul-searching. At times they moved to the altar rail, where tears indicated the depth of contrition. My father always ended the session with the pronouncement of forgiveness through Jesus Christ.

While not always handling personal problems in the best way, he saw such struggles as spiritual in nature. Sin was seen as the root of things; confession and forgiveness were absolutely essential to cleanse the soul of resentment, bitterness, and hard feelings that damage the person's spirit.

# Developing Wellness Ministries

## CHAPTER 8

**IN THIS CHAPTER**

- The authors describe practical ways for existing members of a faith community to be a part of a *Wellness Circle*.
- The process of creating a healing community is examined.

How can a faith community build a strong caring ethic? Leaders who value a caring community will give priority to the planning, education, and culture change necessary to establish and maintain such an environment.

A way to begin is with the *Wellness Circle*. The image of a circle is one of continuous flow, without a beginning or ending. Wellness is a continuous process that may begin at any point. Wellness encompasses all aspects of the person: physical, spiritual, emotional, social, ecological, financial, vocational, and intellectual.

Everyone lives in the tension between the old self (disorder) and the new self (wellness). For example, a person living with accumulated belly fat related to lack of exercise and dietary imbalance can benefit from disciplined help from a faith community in living as the new self, gradually adopting healthy lifestyle changes. Also, a person with chronic depression who, with the help of his or her faith community, manages his or her moods using available resources can enjoy life more as the new self.

The healing power of the new self can be exercised on a daily basis. The Sacraments of Baptism and the Eucharist bring this new creation to all of life. God has a greater wholeness than perfect health to offer—wholeness established in healthy relationships with our God, with ourselves, and with one another.

A faith community that is focused on agape will embrace and exercise the health-giving power of the new self. For example, studying Bible stories of healing, such as those of Jesus healing the sick (John 5:1–14), provides individual and group opportunities to reflect on (1) what Jesus' healing stories say to each person about personal healing and wholeness and (2) what the healing stories say about the community. With an ever-growing understanding of the gifts of healing that the new self brings and a willingness to embrace them, a congregation can establish its own plan for wholeness, wellness, and healing.

## EVERY MEMBER IS A GIFT TO THE COMMUNITY

As the *new self* (*pneuma*) with passion that God has put into the heart for service (*charisma*), every member of the Body of Christ is a gift to the community.* A healthy faith community searches out these gifts and provides training and opportunity for such passion to be utilized. Through such orientation toward serving one another, the fruit of the Spirit is realized ("love, joy, peace . . ." Galatians 5:22–23).

Most members of a congregation do not realize that they are a gift to the faith community. They can be taught that as the new self, their loving presence and passion is the gift. They can be encouraged to search out the passion that God has placed in their hearts for service.

Congregational leaders start with prayer, asking God to reveal the passion He has given to the individual members of the Body of Christ. Each member is invited to join a prayer group to search out the gifts and passion that each person has been given. The leaders of the prayer groups first express a sense of their own passion and then ask, "What is God calling you to do? Where do you feel led to serve? What has been on your heart? What has come back to your mind again and again as a way to help others?"

As members begin to share an initial sense of their passions, the potential of their gift is immediately valued and pursued by the leadership. Those who have similar interests are invited together into one of the areas of the Wellness Circle. Some may have passion in an area in which they have received special training; others may have a strong passion but no training.

Once spiritual gifts and passions are identified, "wellness teams" can be formed to promote the various aspects of well-being within a congregation. Examples of those who may serve on these WE-oriented wellness teams include the following:

1. The Spiritual Wellness Team might consist of a pastor, a lay spiritual

---

\* See the end of the previous chapter for the background to the use of *pneuma* coupled with *charisma* to show that every member is a gift to the community.

director (companion), individuals who are known "prayer warriors" chosen from various age groups, and a teacher with deep interest in spiritual disciplines.

2. The Physical Wellness Team might consist of a nurse, a physician's assistant, a fitness trainer, a dietitian, and some who have experience in healthy cooking.

3. The Emotional Wellness Team might consist of a pastoral counselor, a mental health nurse, an empathetic mother, and a student who is interested in a counseling career.

4. The Social/Relationship Wellness Team might be made up of a social worker, a family life minister, and several who have a passion for coordinating social and recreational events.

5. The Vocational Wellness Team might include vocational counselors, human resource workers, job service personnel, a teacher, and a person who is currently out of work.

6. The Financial Wellness Team might include a financial planner, an accountant, a banking professional, and a layperson interested in fiscal responsibility.

These human treasures can gather and share their experiences and visions of wholeness in this particular area of life. Each wellness team can develop a group vision for wellness in that aspect of life, and out of that vision can develop learning opportunities: classes, temple talks, retreats, sermons, worship themes, and individual consultations. Bringing together the various groups and weaving their treasures into the life of the congregation can coordinate the Wellness Circle initiatives.

Most congregations will not have members with expertise in all of these aspects of wellness; many do have members with life experience and a heart for service who can be effective in serving on those teams. To illustrate the possibilities for creative health ministries using a Wellness Circle model, the following descriptions of congregational wellness committees are offered. The descriptions that follow serve as examples of health promoters who may be found within congregations.

## Spiritual Wellness

Spiritual wellness is focused on a person's relationship with God. Establishing opportunities to grow spiritually contributes to a healthy faith community.

> Faith Church was on a quest to nurture wellness among its members. The leaders believed that spiritual wellness was a dimension of personal wellness that would influence every other aspect of well-being. They formed a spiritual wellness initiative.

Faith's pastor was committed to the quest, and he identified some members who had shown passion in this area to form a team. A church staff member, Ellen, was a trained spiritual director/companion and loved to help others on their spiritual journeys through listening and prayer. June, a retired teacher, taught classes on spiritual disciplines over many years and had a passion for sharing spiritual practices with others. Jim, a middle-aged businessman, led men's prayer groups at Faith. Susan, a mother of three and a musician, assisted at women's spiritual growth retreats. Pastor Tom convened the group and served as the group's spiritual adviser.

Through prayer and study, members of the group shared spiritual practices that had meaning for each of them. They also discussed spiritual practices they wished to try. They answered questions designed to help them think about their spiritual life— examining both their strengths and areas for desired growth.

They looked at what spiritual growth opportunities existed in the congregation and what the strengths and needs were. Then they designed a survey for the congregation to help them identify unmet spiritual needs. They gathered information with a written survey and by listening to what spiritual longings were expressed.

Based on what they learned, a plan was developed to add one new spiritual growth opportunity each month for the upcoming year. In conjunction with the education ministry, June would teach a class on spiritual disciplines that focused on a different spiritual practice each month. During that month, the spiritual practice (whether it be worship, prayer, fasting, service, celebration, or something else) would be lifted up in every aspect of the church's ministry, including worship services, fellowship, learning groups, and servant events.

The challenge of the spiritual wellness team was to weave the spiritual practice of the current month into the life of the faith community. This required another level of commitment and action. During each monthly emphasis, Pastor Tom would lift up in sermons, and in all other communications to the congregation, the spiritual discipline being studied and practiced that month.

Jim agreed to enlist his prayer group to give a presentation about the power of prayer. Each would invite a new person to join a group and be available to form new groups. Susan offered to plan a retreat for women to explore different forms of prayer.

Ellen volunteered to give a presentation and write a blog linked to the church's online newsletter and website explaining "spiritual companioning" and inviting members to contact her to learn more and experience a session with her. She provided videos of spiritual directors and examples of sessions. Ellen offered to be a resource for referral to trained spiritual directors in the area who were known to have a grace perspective on how God's love empowers lives.

The Spiritual Wellness Team agreed that as members were helped to cultivate a closer relationship with God on an individual level, the faith community as a whole would be stronger and healthier for service. In turn, it was evident to anyone who came to Faith Church that this was a faith community that cared deeply about spiritual wellness.

## PHYSICAL WELLNESS

Physical wellness encompasses a healthy body, which in turn influences the health of the mind and spirit. Exercise, nutrition, use of health care, and managing health conditions are all parts of physical wellness. Exercise and movement are known to release brain endorphins that promote a sense of well-being.

The natural leader for a Physical Wellness Team is a trained faith community nurse[1] (FCN). Many congregations are adding an FCN to the staff; others are sharing the services of an FCN among congregations. Other staff and volunteers can be leaders in health ministry if they have a passion for promoting whole-person health and are willing to learn to integrate faith with health. Joining a support network with those who have training in health ministry best does this.[2]

The leaders at Grace Church were committed to creating a wellness initiative that focused on physical health. Grace Church had a trained FCN on its staff. Ellie, a registered nurse, had been trained in a fifty-hour faith community nursing program to minister to the whole person—body, mind, and spirit. She knew that when people of faith nurtured their physical health, they were better able to offer service in the Body of Christ. Ellie and Pastor Carson gathered a team for physical wellness and followed a process similar to that of the Spiritual Wellness Team at Faith Church.

> Ellie found volunteers who shared a passion to support an initiative for physical wellness: Terry, a personal fitness instructor, taught at the YMCA; Audrey had worked as a physical therapy assistant with adults and children; Holly, a nutritionist, was retiring from hospital employment; Eleanor was a homemaker and gardener who offered healthy meal alternatives for children's school lunches as a part-time job from her home. Jeff, a retired physician with a passion for preventing disease, offered to provide medical consultation to the group.
>
> Specific health issues within the congregation that emerged in the initial assessment phase of the group's work were cancer, stroke, heart disease, diabetes, and chronic lung and kidney problems. The group agreed on an initiative aimed at improving these health issues by looking at the contributing factors and root causes of these conditions.[3]
>
> This health ministry work group discovered these contributing factors: diet and exercise patterns, alcohol and substance abuse, tobacco use, illicit drug use, risky sexual behavior, infectious agents, and an unsafe environment involving motor vehicles, firearms, and pollutants. They decided to form task groups to explore how the faith community could make a positive impact on some of these contributing factors.
>
> Each group member offered to serve on one or more of the task groups, according to his or her health care experience and interest in the area. They would gather more workers to help assess the congregation and review public health literature. Then

achievable goals could be set and steps to achieve the goals could be planned and implemented.

At the end of the year, a number of positive outcomes had been achieved. Several exercise classes were being offered at the church twice a week—Yoga for Health and core-muscle-strengthening classes had been well attended. Healthy Cooking classes were offered, and all ages from teens to older adults had participated. Church coffee hour was now noted for the presence of heart-healthy snacks and the absence of donuts and other sweets. Blood pressure screening was offered twice a month by the FCN team, and numerous medical referrals for evaluation were made.

Awareness had been raised regarding impaired driving by collaborating with the motor vehicle department. As a result, several older drivers with vision loss had voluntarily returned their driver's licenses. These older adults were being helped to adapt to life without driving. Alcohol and substance abuse had been addressed with a seminar to raise awareness of patterns of substance use. Grace Church was now hosting Alcoholics Anonymous groups for teens (Alateen) and for women—groups who had been underserved in the community.

The next year, the team planned to address the subject of firearms in the home by collaborating with the local law enforcement prevention division. The topic was on everyone's mind after a local shooting had killed several citizens. To address healthy sexuality, in conjunction with the education ministry at Grace Church, a planned phased curriculum in sexuality would be introduced with parental involvement and clear theological integration. This vital part of children's education would be based on love, truth, and healthy boundaries. All teacher/parent teams were to be well trained to provide a phase of the Christian curriculum on healthy sexuality.

While Grace Church chose to focus on illness prevention to promote whole-person health, there was a continued effort to provide needed support to those who were already dealing with illness. The FCN continued to function in her role as integrator of faith and health. This meant that she listened and provided encouragement and information to those who consulted her about health issues. She helped people manage their illnesses and obtain needed care. Ellie conveyed that maintaining health care and self-care honored a person's body as a gift of God. Ellie respected the boundaries of her role as FCN—she did not provide direct physical care to members, with the exception of blood pressure monitoring. Her role was to be a health educator, promoter, advocate, counselor, and collaborator with health providers as a referral source. Her role was to integrate physical health with faith.

## EMOTIONAL WELLNESS

Emotional wellness encompasses how a person experiences and expresses feelings and emotions. This includes processing loss and grief, dealing with crisis, and seeking help when needed.

> Hope Church was experiencing a crisis in the community after a beloved member of the congregation had committed suicide. Members of the congregation whose lives were touched by the tragedy needed to grieve. Hope Church was called to minister to those who grieved such a deep loss. The suicide victim was a fifty-year-old man, Andrew, who had suffered with bipolar disorder. He had committed suicide the day after his divorce was final. Andrew had worked with the youth on retreats and was a musician. Hope Church's response was immediate. Pastor Pat called an emergency meeting of the Health as Wholeness (the congregation's health ministry) leadership team, which included Rich, a professional counselor; Julie, a part-time volunteer parish nurse; Ed, a retired school principal; and Tina, a high school student who aspired to a career in health. The group formed to minister to the emotional wellness needs of the congregation and the community. They never dreamed that they would be called into action before any planning or goals had been set!

The Emotional Wellness Team had a very personal connection with this tragedy in the faith community. Andrew had been a teacher at the high school where Ed had been the principal. Tina attended that same high school. Rich worked with the psychiatrist who had treated Andrew. Julie had been a friend of Andrew's ex-wife.

The members of the team first set out to process their own feelings about what had happened. They could not think carefully about any possible course of action until they each had acknowledged their own shock, grief, and pain. Pastor Pat listened with love and acceptance as each person talked about how he or she identified with Andrew, asking questions and expressing feelings. Pastor Pat asked each of them what they needed. The pastor assured them that they could call him anytime in the next week if they needed a listener.

All were charged with taking care of themselves with adequate rest, nutrition, prayer time, and activity, so that they would be equipped personally to help bear the burdens of those who were grieving while managing their own grief.

The group agreed that their primary ministry in this crisis would be to listen with love. Rich, a counselor, prepared them to hear expressions of anger, frustration, powerlessness, hopelessness, despair, and sorrow. They would see signs of stress—physical, emotional, and spiritual—as they listened. Ed reviewed with the group ways to listen actively, reflect feelings, and express empathy. Pastor Pat suggested that listeners ask what the grieving person needed, listen carefully to the response, and then pray with the person. The group wanted to reach out to the congregation.

> Pastor Pat was already turning over thoughts for Sunday's sermon that would provide a scriptural basis for a loving response to the loss and to deal with questions regarding faith.
>
> Julie was thinking about how this event could trigger feelings of fear and loss from the past or losses already occurring for many people. What response would be needed for them?
>
> Ed was wondering what could be done for students who had looked to Andrew as a role model.
>
> Tina felt mostly anger at the injustice and wanted to find answers. In her mind, she was asking God, "Why did You let this happen?"
>
> They decided to establish within the congregation a series of listening posts. They would find professionals and capable volunteers, such as Stephen Ministers, to staff the listening posts and provide support for the listeners as well as referral information for those who needed more help. They would maintain

self-care to prevent compassion fatigue from limiting their effectiveness.†

After the immediate crisis, the Emotional Wellness Team met to evaluate their ministerial response and form some long-term goals for promoting emotional wellness in their faith community. They decided to work on the following:

1. Education on personality disorders and bipolar disorder aimed at understanding and reducing the stigma of having an emotional disorder
2. Promoting acceptance of people with emotional disorders, identifying signs of increasing symptoms needing intervention and support, and knowing how to refer appropriately
3. Establishing a National Alliance on Mental Health support group at Hope Church in conjunction with the national organization to support individuals with mental illness in their families
4. Establishing a mentoring program for students in need of consistent, accepting, supportive contacts with a mature adult
5. Offering assertiveness and boundary-setting classes integrated with theology through the education ministry at Hope Church

A year later, the Emotional Wellness Team had grown to eight people. There was a deep appreciation for this health ministry that had developed out of a tragic loss in the congregation. The response reflected the name of Hope Church—a place of healing and hope in the faith community and beyond!

A faith community can establish an emotional health initiative based on the perceived needs both within the church and beyond. The energy that arises from such felt and expressed needs, such as in the example of Hope Church, can fuel activity in a direction of growth and positive change that can have far-reaching effects!

## Social and Relationship Wellness

Wellness in the realm of social life should encompass all relationships, including family, friends, and community. Since faith communities are in the relationship-building business, it makes sense to focus wellness initiatives on the human relationships that are a gift of God.

Fountain of Life Church (FoL) was blessed with a pastor, a director of education, and a leadership team that valued relationships and Christ's call to live and serve one another in love. They valued

---

† Many church judicatories have ministerial assistance programs with consultation services to assist in such situations with specific questions. If resources had not been readily available in the congregation, resources could be sought from programs such as these.

all of God's children, including those of every age group, gender, and race, regardless of social, emotional, or intellectual differences. In fact, they viewed differences among people as adding vitality and excitement to the community! The wellness initiative of FoL focused on building strong relationships.

The director of Christian education, John, had studied psychology and counseling. John understood that all live on a continuum of disorders sparked by spiritual DNA damage at various points in childhood. John wanted the relationship wellness emphasis to reflect acceptance, respect, and love for all persons. He hoped that this faith community could live out Christ's love by being a thriving relationship business: a group of loving, creative people who were a blessing to all as they shared Christ's love among themselves and in the larger community.

John and Pastor Bob knew that every business venture needs a plan, so they formed a Relationship Wellness Team. Its members included Tim and Elaine, who had been married for forty-five years and had parented four children to a healthy adulthood; Marty, a retired marriage and family therapist; Belle and Troy, high school students; and Anita, the activity leader in the older-adult ministry at FoL. This wellness team took a prayerful approach to their task, both privately and publicly. Members of the congregation were very aware that relationships mattered deeply at FoL, a church where intentional steps were being taken to nurture relationships with couples, families, friends, and groups.

The first step was to ensure that relationships among the wellness team were strong and loving. The team wanted to model a healthy We orientation to the congregation. When disagreements arose, loving confrontation was used to clear the air. When feelings were hurt or favoritism suspected, the group dealt with it openly. The team worked on their internal relationships in a spirit of love by addressing in every meeting how they were working together toward their goals. They practiced using good boundaries by saying no when necessary—"No, I am not able to take on another responsibility right now"; "No, Belle, I won't discuss your conflict with Troy unless he is present"; "No, I don't wish to discuss what someone says that others are saying about this wellness initiative. Let's invite them to come and speak for themselves."

The guiding principle of the team's work was that every person could be viewed as a gift to the Church, each with a passion for God's purposes. Family units were the building blocks of the congregation, so opportunities to strengthen couple, parent-child, and sibling relationships were valued. At all times there would be a Bible study group available that would focus on friendship or family relationship building. This concept of WE-oriented relationship building would form an alternative for families to counter the effects of a ME-oriented culture. The goal of all family-oriented activities would be to promote good internal boundaries, a healthy self-image, and concern for others.

The team decided to introduce intergenerational small groups at FoL as an antidote to the individualism and isolation present in the society. These groups would meet every two weeks and would consist of youth, young adults, older adults, and middle-agers. Younger children could be included with their own parents. The groups would rotate among each other's homes for meetings. With Christ as the Head of the Body, each person could show concern for one another and for the good of all. Teaching and learning, breaking bread, and prayer happened in the group time together.

Two of the groups' members were Cheryl and Joe, a couple in their late seventies. Cheryl was Joe's caregiver, as Joe's Parkinson's disease had progressed and he was becoming less able to move freely. Cheryl sang in the choir, and Joe had served his church by advising the financial team from the perspective of his many years of business experience. Cheryl and Joe became the "grandparents" of the group and contributed agape and wisdom to the younger members.

Helen, a widowed mother of two college students, worked from home. Being without the socialization of a work group, Helen appreciated the group meetings, where she could share a simple meal and also share her heart. She also appreciated a chance to converse with young people and to encourage parents of teens, especially those who parented a child with substance-abuse issues and needed extra support. Her own son had struggled with addiction in high school, and she had learned to practice love with boundaries to help him in his recovery.

Missy, a gifted high school student, was the eldest of her siblings, and her mother had suffered with chronic depression. Their mother's emotional disorder had created an isolated lifestyle for her daughters, especially as their father traveled with his work. Missy had learned to cope by finding support outside the family. She had only a few friends who could understand what it was like to live with a depressed mother. The group was a surrogate family for her, as it modeled mutual love and care with energy flowing upward and outward. Missy brought to the group insights about the youth culture and hopefulness for the possibilities in life.

Will, a divorced father, and his twelve-year-old son, Jason, attended the group together. Jason's parents had shared custody of him. He often experienced anxiety when it was time to move from one parent's home to the other. He didn't talk about it much, because he had friends with the same situation and it didn't seem to bother them. Jason liked meeting with Missy, who reminded him of his sister who was in college and had little time for Jason. Will was in recovery from alcohol abuse and attended AA meetings weekly. He wanted to rebuild trust with his ex-wife because he thought it would be good for Jason, as well as heal some of the pain of the broken marriage.

Tim, a married father of three, facilitated the group. Every third meeting, Pastor Bob visited the group and provided a pastoral model for this small group who were learning to give and receive agape, utilizing the model of the Early Church. The group had permeable boundaries, like a healthy family, and was open to incorporate new members. It was a safe, trusting space. Members were free to move in and out of the group if their lives changed; however, a commitment to love and serve one another remained intact.

A relationship wellness initiative such as the one at Fountain of Life Church builds committed, caring relationships. Having safe spaces to give and receive agape, practice honesty, and form healthy boundaries is a life-giving experience.

## Vocational and Financial Wellness

Every Christian has a *vocation*, a calling. Vocational wellness initiatives in the faith community can help each person to search the heart to find the passion God has already placed there. When opportunities to search out their passions are given, each of these gifts of God becomes a treasure. Some will find their passion in their career; others will find a sense of purpose in service outside of the workplace.

The Vocational Wellness Committee at St. Peter's Church noticed that much of the volunteer work within their faith community was done by a few. They noticed that capable volunteers were leaving their jobs after several months. They also were aware of a rising unemployment rate in the greater community that was affecting many of St. Peter's families.

The committee decided to focus on vocational and financial wellness in their health ministry. Pastor Pete and Liz, the volunteer coordinator, gathered some interested persons to brainstorm about needs and possible goals for building vocational and financial wellness at St. Peter's. The group consisted of Anne, a local banking employee; Judy, an independent financial adviser; Brian, a retired vocational counselor; Lisa, a social science major in her last year of graduate school; and Jack, who coordinated an older-adult lifelong-learning program at the local university.

This group understood the importance of a satisfying work life to overall health. They also knew that everyone does not have an opportunity to work at a job that provides a high level of purpose and meaning in their life. In the current economic climate, being unemployed could be considered a hazard to a family's health.

The team used Colossians 3:23–24 to guide their work: "Whatever you do, work heartily, as for the Lord. . . . You are serving the Lord Christ."

Anne was an instructor for Financial Peace University and taught a Christian financial management course. Many of the participants in her classes told her that it had significantly changed how they viewed money and its uses. Anne offered a class to St. Peter's families and would seek funds to assist with tuition for those who were unemployed.

Judy offered her skills and enlisted some of her colleagues to offer financial wellness checkups. Lisa was working on a class project to update a listing of social service agencies that offered financial and material assistance to families in the community. She offered to make information available to St. Peter's families.

Brian offered to facilitate a support group for those dealing with unemployment; he had maintained his referral network for employment assistance that could be a resource for families.

Jack knew that many people in the retirement community were helping out their younger family members who were financially stressed. He offered resources for this new family configuration (so-called "boomerang adult children").

Pastor Pete and Liz focused on providing a spiritual gifts inventory and a talent inventory to increase the volunteer corps at St. Peter's. They believed people needed to realize their worth through serving from their passion. They prayed that such awareness of each person's value would fuel energy to seek needed work that would flow from a healthy self-concept. They made plans for creative ways to lift up the work of the volunteers and formulate volunteer job descriptions that would attract capable, caring servants who could minister to one another.

Tending to career and financial wellness can have far-reaching effects toward building a healthy faith community. When people know that what they do makes a difference in building up the Body of Christ—whether at their workplace or as volunteers—energy flows up and outward and sustainable health changes are made possible in all areas of the Wellness Circle.

## NEED TO KNOW

**Wellness Circle:** This book utilizes a concept similar to the wellness wheel that the authors have worked with and used extensively in the many retreats for professional church workers and congregations organized by Grace Place Lutheran Wellness Ministries.[4] This chapter focuses on the areas of the Wellness Circle, giving specific suggestions as to how a faith community can organize its wellness emphasis.

## STRESS MASTERY AND SELF-CARE

Well-being requires the ability to manage and master stress in life. Stress mastery and self-care go hand-in-hand. Life stresses are inevitable and even necessary to spur one to action. Any life change produces stress because some adaptation to change is required. After a high level of stress is reached at any one time in a person's life, physical illness is imminent. In a similar way, emotional disorders are aggravated by stress.

Faith communities can become stress resistant. Each of the congregations described above found ways to build community and to promote the health of the whole person. Each wellness team gathers, prays, blesses, and walks with one another. They listen, respond, and are physically, emotionally, and spiritually present with one another.

Wellness teams build on strengths, accept the tension of disorders, and offer transformative change. They realize that change happens in stages. They respect that some are not interested. Others are thinking about making a change, some are ready for change, others will engage with change, and still others are maintaining positive change as a way of life. Individuals are accepted at their own point of readiness for change.

Wellness teams are willing to give sanctuary—a safe space with acceptance, blessing, hope, and accountability. As faith and health become aligned, faith communities can grow as healthy and healing communities.

# Caregiving, Motivated by Joy

## CHAPTER 9

## In This Chapter

- The joy of caregiving is examined.
- The authors contrast the joy of service with the sense of duty or obligation.
- Advice about avoiding resentment is shared.
- Keeping caregivers healthy is a priority.

God created humans to be in relationship with Him and with one another. God created His people to be intimate—to share and care. This is what brings joy to life. This is energy going outward and is an expression of agape in deeply personal contact.

Christ demonstrated this personal, caring contact in His many encounters with people in need. He would stop and look at the person, asking what he or she wanted Him to do. He would stop and talk, showing a deep interest and curiosity. He would reach out and touch. He showed deep involvement and was even moved to tears by the sorrow surrounding death. And He was joyful as His love flowed to others: "who for the joy that was set before Him endured the cross" (Hebrews 12:2).

When congregational members experience such intimacy, time seems to stand still. Joy comes through the process of caring. The moment of sharing and depth lingers and is transforming. Those who experience such moments of joy are moved from natural, self-centered emotions to concern for others. This experience is very attractive. This is the energizing Gospel motivation. This is enjoying the moment.

Jen was a young therapist who worked with persons with mental disorders. She often felt discouraged when she listened to their stories, and she sometimes could be heard talking about her clients in a disrespectful tone. Those who heard her wondered if she cared at all about the people for whom she provided care.

Jen lost her job as a result of company cutbacks. She was unemployed for a significant period of time and became involved as a volunteer with her church's soup kitchen. Jen began to sit with the people who came to the church for food. As she listened to the stories of loss and unemployment, Jen could relate to the people who came. She knew what it was like to be unable to find a job.

After a number of months, Jen was hired to provide therapy services to older adults who resided in nursing-care facilities. Jen began to see her new clients in a different light. She began to experience moments of joy in her intimate times with them.

One day, Jen met with a client who had stopped talking as her dementia disease process progressed. Jen offered to take her outside in her wheelchair to the courtyard while they met. When she wheeled her outside, the client breathed deeply and said, "Ah, cool breeze." It was a moment of enjoyment that stayed with Jen for a long time. It was as if the Holy Spirit had blown like a gentle breeze into her client's heart, giving her a moment of joy.

Jen could understand how lonely her clients felt so much of the time, being separated from family and friends. When Anna, the faith community nurse at her church, asked Jen how her work was going, she told her about the deep loneliness that her clients experienced. Anna wondered with Jen whether their church might expand their ministry into the nursing-care facilities by helping volunteers from the church to become comfortable in sitting with the loneliest of the clients.

## Intimacy and Joy in Caring for Children

It is natural to be intimate and personal when caring for children. From the moment of birth into a faith community through Baptism, the child's caregivers are parents, baptismal sponsors, family, and church members who minister to the family. This spiritual caregiving is sealed with a promise to nurture the child's faith. That promise is lived out as agape is given to the child.

Children experience honesty from their caregivers when they are genuinely affirmed for *being* (not just for *doing*). Children know when they are loved and are seen as a gift. This comes when the caring relationship is joyful and uplifting. A faith community can help with these relationships.

Some of the children's parents are single and struggling while others may be in troubled marital relationships. These families need support and guidance to develop healthy, caring relationships. Also, children who have suffered from spiritual DNA damage often behave negatively.

Adults working together to form a healthy WE-oriented atmosphere provide children with appropriate boundaries. This builds internal self-control. Caregivers of children can learn to function with respect, boundaries, and agape with the help of others in the faith community who know how to form healthy, caring relationships. For some of the parents, the church is where their most life-giving relationships are found.

> Tina wanted to affirm the dedication of the congregation Telephone Care Team, so one Sunday at coffee hour, she asked one of the team members how her telephone calling was going. The volunteer responded quickly, "Boy, my ear was filled last week on the phone with a Sunday School student's parent. There is some serious bullying going on in the classroom. Her child is a victim, and she is really upset." The volunteer had listened with love, but she felt upset at what she had heard. Tina encouraged the volunteer to talk with Julie, the care team coordinator, to decide how to approach the situation. Julie then talked with the Sunday School teacher and the pastor. They decided to form a WE-oriented team to discourage bullying behavior in the church.

> Julie felt passionate about protecting children. Remembering her own siblings' verbal abuse as a child ("You're stupid! You're dumb!" still rang in her ears at times), Julie's heart was touched by the situation. Julie knew how it hurt to be ridiculed, and she deeply wanted to be an instrument of healing for these

young girls, Eva and Emma, whom she knew were hurting. Julie believed Christ's promise "I am always with you," and she hoped to convey that promise to these girls.

An educational session for children and parents on bullying behavior was organized and offered to all families to create awareness of the issue. Participants prayed together to be instruments of healing.

As they invited Christ's presence, the team members were surprised by how naturally the solution occurred. Eva, who had been bullying the emotionally frail Emma, was helped to assess what her behavior was costing her and her parents. Julie pointed out what Eva would gain by ending the behavior, which was creating losses for her. Eva was disarmed by the genuine concern shown for her by the adults as they demonstrated active listening, respect, problem solving, and openness. The team decided that if Eva continued the behavior, a referral would be given for therapy. They understood how personal pain could often drive aggressive behavior, and Eva deserved a safe space to explore her feelings about herself so that she could make different choices.

How were the volunteer care caller, pastor, and teaching team able to respond out of such love to a hurtful young person? They had approached the situation prayerfully and guided by Scripture, remembering that the offender was a baptized child of God. Several of the group had been moved during the Scripture readings to share painful episodes they had experienced growing up. As they listened to one another, the group experienced a new sense of closeness and connection. They were honest in sharing with one another their feelings of hurt, anger, and frustration that one child of God was inflicting hurt on another.

The leaders prayed for Eva before they met with her and when they met with her and her parents. They reminded one another of the healing available with the Spirit's holy presence to guide the spirit. They had resources available to offer additional help and guidance for Eva. In their careful and prayerful approach, the leaders grew closer to one another in trust and appreciation. God's Spirit strengthened their teamwork relationships as they gave agape and boundaries to a young person in need.

The adult leaders spent time with Emma, who had been the target of Eva's bullying. They knew that bullied children are more likely to suffer with low self-esteem and emotional problems and often experience loneliness. The team affirmed Emma as a child of God, worthwhile and loved. They spoke with her parent who had vented to the telephone care volunteer, empathized, and assured her of God's love and care for the family. They listened respectfully to her concern. They explained that boundaries on bullying were being established in the classroom and that Eva would be held accountable for her behavior. The team modeled love, honesty, and truth to everyone involved. God's Spirit worked in the healing space as Eva was encouraged to apologize and ask Emma for forgiveness. Emma was allowed to explore what it meant to be forgiving, while still maintaining safe boundaries. This was a defining moment in Emma's spiritual DNA formation. She was lovingly held by God through her leaders as she forgave Eva.

The leaders did not abandon Eva and Emma after this episode. Surprised by the closeness they felt and sensing Christ's presence among them, they were moved individually to check in with both girls regularly. Eva's and Emma's faith walks took new directions, guided by Julie and her team.

## INTIMACY AND JOY IN CARING FOR YOUTH

Teens and preteens are often unsure and put on a front to keep from being embarrassed. There is usually no place in their life where they can be open with the more intimate struggles they are having. Yet the yearning for intimacy is there.

Stefan and Anna noticed a definite change in their sixteen-year-old son, Josef. He had not liked to attend the church youth group and would find excuses to be late or miss the meeting. But now, for the last several weeks, Josef had been ready on time and seemed eager to attend.

They sat down with Josef and commented on his change of attitude. "Yes, I do enjoy going to the meetings," he volunteered. "I get something out of them."

Stefan asked his son, "What changed? Why are you interested now?"

"Dad," Josef replied, "at school or when I am hanging out with friends, I have an image to keep up. I have to be careful about how I come across. This is the only place I can be real."

"What do you mean?" his mom asked.

Josef answered, "It is safe at the youth meeting. The leader has a Bible study, and then we sit around and share what has been going on in our lives. Several weeks ago, one of the girls in the group shared that she was afraid she was pregnant. She started crying when she talked about having to tell her parents. She felt so guilty. She was so afraid. We just gathered around her and prayed for her. It gave her the strength to face the situation."

"That must have been difficult," Stefan began.

But Josef cut his father off. "Dad, when we prayed for this girl and I saw how much this helped her, I felt so good. We really made a difference in her life. I have prayed for her every day since then. That's why I want to go back and continue with the youth group."

Church staff and volunteers who minister to teens and young adults recognize the developmental tasks of this age group: developing internal independence (learning to decide and draw one's own conclusions) and external independence (showing ability to act responsibly, showing respect and a positive attitude). Leaders develop relationships with youth using clear, honest communication. In a healing community, the youth will always know that they are loved and valued.

Living Water Church began a ministry to offer an intentional blessing to graduating high school seniors as they transitioned into a more independent phase of their lives. Some would leave home to go to college; others would expand their social and vocational networks as they worked in jobs and went to school part time. Many would be apart from the intimacy of the families in which they had grown up.

The ministry involved the entire congregation. A group of volunteer quilters made a "quillow"—a quilt that folded into a pillow—for each student. During the hours of sewing together, the quilters reflected together on their own "leaving home" stories. They prayed for the young people who would receive these quillows they were sewing. The quillows were presented to the graduating students in a special part of the worship service in May. An accompanying liturgy invited students to affirm their commitment to a life of faith in the Body of Christ, to offer their gifts to the world as a part of the Body of Christ, and to receive the support of a family of faith.

Parents gave blessings to their departing children as they laid their hands on them. The congregation voiced a promise to take an interest in their future, to be with them in their celebration as well as in sadness, and to welcome them whenever they return to Living Water Church. This ritual of "honoring and sending" acknowledged an important life transition for the students and assured them of God's love, embodied in the people of their faith community.

As the members of the congregation voiced their promises, many were transported back through the years to their own time of leaving home and that of their children. In those memories of the yearning to keep attachment while becoming one's own person, God's Spirit was working. A deep level of understanding began to move through the congregation, enfolding the senior students in agape. The community was bound together in the intimacy of that moment.

In such powerful communication of God's love and care—given and received—joy is evident. For those giving the blessing, a sense of commitment and connection binds them to those who receive the blessing. The sewers of the quillows are likely to keep the senior students in their prayers as they leave home. They may keep in touch in small but significant ways, providing a message of care and connection to the students as they face new life challenges. Members of the congregation who promised support may extend that agape to the families left behind, as they reorganize their family structure—sometimes a painful task. All are aware of the healing quality of the blessing and sending.

Those who use the new quillows in their dorm rooms or apartments will know they are loved and valued by their faith community. They will recall the touch of hands laid on in blessing when they received the quillows.

## INTIMACY AND JOY IN CARING FOR ADULTS

Adults in faith communities care for one another in a variety of ways. They realize that all have spiritual DNA injuries from childhood. As members of a healing community that is in the relationship business, they will show concern for one another and consider the good of all.

Healthy adults seek and yearn for intimacy, but many feel that yearning as an unfilled space within. God understands that yearning. He yearns for closeness with created beings. When adults experience a moment of intimacy with one another with Christ's love, it is a gift of the Spirit. Such moments motivate one to seek more genuine closeness. Rather than passively waiting for God to act, the seeker of intimacy reaches out without expectation and gives the gift of agape.

> As she spent time as a volunteer at her church with a group of patients with dementia, Jean focused on one person at a time. She offered her presence, just sitting quietly or engaging in an activity with the person. Jean began to experience a deep love for each person she sat with. She listened, laughed with, and held a hand. When the respite session was over, Jean felt physically tired and emotionally energized. Her spirits had been lifted by the close encounters and the love given and shared. The words "I love you, Jean. Good-bye" lingered in her soul.

Regular worship, study, and fellowship provide opportunities for individuals to receive strength to live in harmony with one another, care for one another, serve one another, bear one another's burdens, submit to one another, and forgive one another. This strength comes through the Holy Spirit in a variety of moments of intimate caring: the story shared in a pastor's sermon "meant just for me"; hymns carefully chosen and sung with words that strike a chord in one's heart; sitting together in Bible study, sharing one's response to Scripture when it touches the heart, and being really heard by those in the group; sharing a meal at church at a table of caring listeners and enjoying warm humor together; and sitting with a dementia patient who is totally "in the moment."

Adults need to receive love from other adults, practiced as described in Scripture—with genuineness, humility, mercy, and overcoming evil with good. Such practice of love builds community and creates healing space.

## Intimacy and Joy in Caring for Older Adults

Faith communities caring for older adults can experience a sense of meaning and purpose from ministering to those in later stages of life. Many faith communities are populated primarily by older adults caring for one another. Some younger adults are motivated to care for older congregational members by their love for their own parents and grandparents and the love they were given. Others are less capable because of their own fear of death and loss of capacity, and they may distance themselves from older adults. All can be offered opportunities to enjoy moments of closeness with those who have lived longer and experienced aspects of life unknown to younger people. Ministries that encourage older adults to tell stories and share memories offer such close moments and help them bring meaning to their view of their life as a whole. Reminiscing has also been shown to elevate one's mood when positive life events are remembered and reflected upon.

Aging adults experience losses and varying physical limitations. This can produce anger and frustration in some people; others show acceptance and even a sense of humor in the face of life changes. Aging persons who receive love, acceptance, honesty, and clear limits, like people of all ages, can cope with life changes with dignity.

Feelings of powerlessness, low self-esteem, emotional despair, and hopelessness are generally signs of depression, which is not a normal part of aging. A caring faith community recognizes the difference between challenges in coping and depression and will refer for treatment those who are depressed.

Some people in later stages of life may exhibit exaggerated patterns of coping with stress. A mildly depressive person may become profoundly depressed in advanced age. Someone who coped throughout life by keeping busy and occupied with activity may later in life have difficulty resting and feeling good *being* rather than *doing*. A lifelong collector may become a hoarder of objects, so that his or her living space becomes cluttered and unlivable. The person who defined himself by his work and productivity may begin to believe that life is meaningless without work.

Those in a healing community attempt to understand the reasons behind certain behaviors that may tend to separate older adults from the congregation. The problem of loneliness can be balanced with human contact in the form of phone calls (audio and video), visits, outings, notes, email, and text messages. There are many creative ways to prevent loneliness when living alone.

> Marty, a seventy-eight-year-old widow, lived alone in an elder-housing apartment. Unable to drive, she depended on friends to drive her to church, and she often offered them lunch at her

apartment after church. Her faith community was the center of her life.

Marty had chronic pain from a neurological disorder, and she had suffered through many episodes of depression. She was most happy around the Christmas season, when she would set up her Christmas village that had grown by leaps and bounds over the years to over a thousand pieces. Everyone in her apartment building knew that the village would be ready for viewing by Thanksgiving, and it would stay up until the end of January. Almost every day there would be a knock at the door, and a neighbor, young person, or even a teacher and young student group would ask to come in and see the village. Marty never tired of showing them the train, lights, bells, and whistles, and she loved to see the delight on their faces. She invited children to tell stories about what they saw in the village. She shared her faith story in a unique way as she pointed out the miniature churches with people, including a pastor baptizing a baby and a manger scene. She told the story of the first Christmas with an energy and glow about her that was caught by everyone who came into her apartment. Marty was truly a "village" missionary!

Marty's Christmas village was her legacy, and at her death, she had designated the village to be donated to her faith community, to be enjoyed for years to come. For those who had known Marty, her spirit was very present as the Christmas village was lovingly placed in the church gathering space each year. Her loving gift to those around her could be remembered in her favorite slogan: "I am too blessed to be stressed!"

## A Healing Community for Caregivers

In a healing community, there is support for those who want to give the gift of a nonanxious, healing presence to one another. This gift is reflected in every aspect of how members treat one another and themselves. As new persons in Christ, all members can strive to put others first while maintaining a balance of caring for self as God's precious gift.

Joan was a facilitator for a grief-sharing support group at her church. One Sunday, she commented to her friend Ann that she felt depleted after the group sessions from listening to so much pain and loss from group members who were grieving. Joan asked Ann if she would sit with her for an hour during the week between group sessions and listen to her share her feelings of hurt and compassion for her grieving group members.

Ann agreed to meet weekly with Joan while she was facilitating the group series. Ann's heart was touched by her friend honestly claiming her emotional limits in the ministry she was called to do. Ann felt with her as she remembered her career as a counselor and how hard it was at times to give to God the pain she was hearing. She offered her weekly ministry of listening to Joan in order to strengthen Joan for her task and to assist in her self-care—hopefully preventing compassion fatigue that might cause Joan to lose a connection with the group by tuning them out.

Joan found that Ann's listening presence helped to lighten the burden she was bearing for her grieving group. She shared with Ann that she experienced God's Spirit strengthening her for the task she was called to do. Ann experienced deep joy in giving of herself as a focused listener, and she imagined God's hand working through her to reach the grieving group members. Joan and Ann had found an intimacy with each other and with God.

Caregivers need strength and support to continue to provide agape, honesty, and clear boundaries when caring for an aging person. When a caregiver's needs for love, truth, and boundaries are met, their capacity to give those gifts of care to older adults will be expanded.

Peter, a seventy-five-year-old retired military officer, has been the primary caregiver at home for his wife, Linda, age 72, who had a stroke a year ago. The stroke limited her physical functioning. She has major depression, and her communication is limited. Care assistants come to their home four times a week to assist with bathing. Peter does the cooking and assists Linda with activities of daily living. Members of their church marvel at

Peter's caregiving ability as Peter pushes Linda's wheelchair to the pew. Most Sundays when people greet Peter and Linda and ask how they are doing, Peter replies, "Fine, fine."

On a recent Sunday, when the pastor greeted them at the door after the service, he noticed that Peter appeared sad and slightly unkempt. When Pastor Dick asked how they were, Peter shook his head slightly and said, "It's getting hard." Pastor Dick, moved by the deep sorrow he saw in Peter's eyes, made a mental note to schedule a visit.

At the home visit later that week, Pastor Dick noticed that the house was somewhat in disarray. He visited with Peter while Linda was sleeping. Pastor Dick listened as Peter described how exhausted he felt most of the time with no time for himself to even keep his own medical appointments. The couple's two adult children lived across the country and came to visit for short periods when they were able. "I promised Linda she could stay at home for the rest of her life. I want to keep my promise. I should be able to handle this," Peter tearfully said to the pastor.

Pastor Dick's heart was touched by Peter's devotion to his wife. He felt a deep wave of empathy for this strong man facing his vulnerability. He remembered his own parents' struggle to care for each other at home in their advanced age. Pastor Dick affirmed Peter's love for Linda and the good care he had given to her. He prayed with Peter for strength to make life-giving decisions for both Linda and himself. He reminded Peter of God's care, whether one is aging in his or her home or with the support of a caring staff in a nursing facility. He offered to schedule a visit by the faith community nurse on the church staff who would provide resources for assessment to help Peter in his decision-making. Pastor Dick knew that the nurse would bring a soothing presence for Peter and Linda, along with a wealth of resource information.

Peter experienced the love shown by his pastor and faith community nurse in their willingness to walk with him through a difficult life passage. Through that love, God's Spirit softened his attitude toward himself, and he accepted his limits in caregiving. He could then embrace the close moments with Linda as a blessing.

Peter was one of many older adult caregivers who needed support in determining the limits to their ability to provide care for loved ones. ("What am I able to do? What do I need help with?") Such discernment involves the body, mind, and spirit. Healing can occur without a cure. The residual effects of Linda's stroke would not be cured, but her related depression could heal with proper professional care, and she could come to enjoy the life that was hers. When no longer limited by the severity of her depression, Linda could participate in decisions about her future care. The healing community honored Linda as a worthwhile child of God. Maintaining contact with her and Peter demonstrated the agape that is so needed in their situation. Concrete assistance in the form of respite care, offering an occasional meal, and sharing resources honored Peter's needs for self-care. Listening with acceptance to Peter talk about his feelings of hurt, regret, loss, and frustration provided relief emotionally for him.

Adults who care for loved ones with emotional disorders need care themselves, but often they feel unable to take the time for self-care. Patterns of overfunctioning can easily develop in caregiving, leaving the caregiver exhausted and depleted. The stress of caring for someone with severe mood or behavior disorders can take a toll on the caregiver, who may neglect his or her own health and well-being. The loss of a reciprocal intimate couple relationship is painful for a caregiving spouse. It is important for those in a caring community to acknowledge such ambiguous loss that is not commonly recognized. Encouragement is often needed to change familiar caregiving behaviors and adopt more self-care measures, one small step at a time. Participating in reviewing a routine of care for a loved one can be an intimate experience. With prayerful attention, finding small steps to encourage self-care for the caregiver can be Spirit-led.

Faith communities with health ministries can offer support groups for family members and open the groups to the community. Keeping the caregiver in a communication loop, offering visits and prayers, and inviting caregivers to participate in the life of the congregation to the extent possible are all ways to be a healing community for caregivers.

Jane cares for her husband, who suffers with severe chronic depression. Her friend invited her to a monthly group for adults who desire to share on a deep level their understanding of

Scripture and how God's Word speaks to them. The group follows a format of *Lectio Divina*, which is a deliberate method of prayerfully and thoughtfully praying the Scriptures. The group begins with an update on what each person would like remembered in prayer. A selected Scripture is read three times, and after each reading, silence is observed. During the silence, members notice a word or phrase from the reading that they sense a connection with. They share the word or phrase with the group and spend time in silent meditation, considering how that word is speaking to them about something in their life today. There is time for sharing, then another reading, silence, and meditation on the question of what they are sensing a call to do or be during the coming week, related to the word or phrase from the reading.

This time together of praying the Scripture yields deepening awareness of God's presence in each person's life. Prayers are spoken at the end, remembering what each person has shared during the session.

Jane talked about how the *Lectio Divina* experience allows her to receive the love of others in the group as they listen to her and pray for her. She drew strength from the love and nurturing she received in focusing with others on God's Word in this manner. She has adopted the method of praying the Scriptures at home between group sessions, deepening her own relationship with God and finding strength for her caregiving tasks.

At one session, the group read together the first verse of Psalm 23. Jane focused on the word "Shepherd" in her meditation time. She was surprised by an image of Jesus, wearing an apron, working beside her in the kitchen as she cooked dinner for her husband. Jane felt herself being shepherded by a close Friend. Her loneliness vanished, and she imagined laughing together with her Friend as they cooked.

When she shared her image with her group, their hearts were touched to hear the depth of Jane's loneliness being filled with the presence of Jesus. Several were moved to spend time with her during the week between sessions, creating closer bonds of love and care as they witnessed her steady caring for her husband in his illness.

Compassion fatigue is real. Those who spend much of their time caring for others can forget that they, too, need to process their own emotions and care for their health. They need strengthening so that bearing another's burdens does not become a burden in itself. The healing community affirms, supports, and aids its caring members with spiritual, physical, and emotional feeding. Even the seemingly smallest act of kindness toward a caregiver can be strengthening to the person. Speaking the truth in love and saying no when needed give permission to avoid overfunctioning to a point of exhaustion. When boundaries are maintained with loving honesty, there is much freedom for love and intimacy within a defined space.

Caring for caregivers can bring purpose and meaning to routine days for those who reach out and for those who receive encouragement, respite, and support. The deep bond that develops between caregivers and their care receivers is a mysterious work of the Spirit. Caregivers who are cared for themselves are often surprised by the growth in their capacity to give. Like a wellspring within the person, their giving of self becomes life changing!

In addition to older adult caregivers, there is a "sandwich generation" of caregivers caring simultaneously for older parents and their own children.

Beth sought counseling from her pastor when she began to feel the stress of caring for her elderly parents who lived in another state. Although her father provided physical care to her mother, Beth could see that he was weary and becoming forgetful. Beth was married and worked at a full-time job five states away. Her only sibling was not involved in supporting their parents and instead wanted to depend on them. Beth called her parents daily and attempted to help manage their situation by phone as much as possible. She carried a constant dread that "the phone call will come" with news of the death of one or the other parent. She believed she could never do enough to help them, living so far away, and she felt guilty and sad.

Beth's congregation sponsored a caregiving support group, and she began to attend. She was surprised to learn that other adults also struggled with giving care from a distance. It helped her to share feelings and useful ideas that helped her cope. She had been so caught in her guilt that she had not been able to think of what might help. In the group and with pastoral counseling, Beth learned not to overfunction out of guilt and to allow herself to grieve the losses she was experiencing. She then had more energy to problem-solve issues that came up, seek out assistance, and enjoy moments with her parents without preoccupation with dread of the future.

The Spirit was present in those moments of enjoyment between Beth and her parents in their daily phone calls and periodic visits. Beth realized she was not alone, and she could rest in the intimate moments of remembering with her parents the times they had shared and the deep satisfaction they expressed about their family and life together. Those conversations became a gift to Beth and to her parents, which she cherished later for many years after they had died.

Every member of a congregation is a potential caregiver—of children, of older adults, of one another as adults, of self. The professional and volunteer ministry staff is charged with the "care of the soul" for a faith community. The congregation functions as a healing community for caregivers in so very many ways.

## A Healing Community for Ministry Caregivers

Ministry professionals (pastors, educators, musicians, youth leaders, parish nurses, and administrators) care for one another to strengthen each one's ministry. They also accept care from the faith community that supports and upholds them. In a healing community, ministry teams can function with a healthy We-oriented atmosphere to give love, share truth, and create safe boundaries for ministry.

When a minister operates outside of a safe boundary in the faith community, all involved will suffer. Sometimes, an individual is unable to see how vulnerable he or she is, and without a healthy We-oriented atmosphere to speak the truth in love, the temptation to serve Me can create disorder that can take years—and even generations—to repair.

Pastor Bill was a compassionate, caring minister. He served in a congregation for over thirty years and was loved and respected. He had sacrificed much in order to be available to those in need of care in his faith community. His own wife and children had become accustomed to having dinner many evenings without him. There were late-afternoon and evening meetings at church, pastoral visits, and community events to attend. Pastor Bill saw himself as essential to the well-being of so many who depended on him spiritually. He felt needed and loved by those he cared for, as they expressed over and over how much his ministering meant to them. His family was never as affirming of him; they just seemed to want more—more time, more attention. His wife gave all of her energy to the children and her job as she coped with his absence. They rarely had couple time alone anymore.

Pastor Bill spent more late evenings and Saturdays in his office alone, preparing for Sunday worship, reading, and surfing the Internet. He began to chat online, and he became involved with a woman who eventually asked to meet for lunch. He thought it would be fun—after all, he worked so much and could use a little downtime, he rationalized to himself. He really didn't think much but acted on impulse and met her for lunch. Soon they were meeting regularly, and Pastor Bill felt an attraction he had not experienced in years.

One day, Pastor Bill's wife noticed he had left his cell phone at home. She heard a text coming in and unlocked the phone to read it. She was shocked to read a personal message signed "Your sweetie." When he admitted to the emotional affair, his wife was angry and hurt. They decided to try to work on their marriage, and he promised to end the affair. When he told the woman, she became angry and threatened to "ruin" him. Within a week, Pastor Bill was approached by the president of the church council, who told him a woman had accused him of starting an affair with her while he was on the church computer. The church council had been notified, and a meeting had been called to confront Pastor Bill.

> How could this hurtful situation have been avoided? When a church professional shows signs of overwork, distancing from family life, having difficulty saying no, a healthy WE-oriented community can use honesty, speaking the truth in love, and confront the leader with their concern. Perhaps the leader has been distancing from his relationship with God as well as family, and there is a loss of intimacy. In addition, his relationship with himself has become unhealthy, marked by denial, avoidance, and lack of internal control. Loss of an intimate relationship with self can drive a person to seek relationships that are not life-giving but have a temporary appearance of closeness.
>
> In a healthy WE-oriented atmosphere, the leader is confronted: "We see that you are giving more time to ministry than to your own self-care and your family. You are living an imbalanced

life—you seem to have lost sight of what God intends to be an abundant life. We think that you are vulnerable because of this, and we want you to get help in rebalancing your life and ministry. We will support you in doing this. We will commit to making a plan with you and monitoring how it is working. We love and value you and your ministry with us, and we want you to be whole and healthy in service to God." Sometimes, even pastors and other church leaders need re-parenting in a healthy We-oriented atmosphere of love, honesty, and boundaries.

How can such a situation be resolved once it has happened? In some cases, a larger community with a healthier We (such as an enlightened judicatory or a congregational consulting team) can place its arms around the suffering community and encourage an open, honest, truthful approach with the establishment of safe boundaries and an opportunity to grieve the loss of trust. This is a long and complex healing process. Prevention is the best approach. Every faith community can establish a caring structure to protect boundaries. Any person in a faith community can initiate a conversation, speaking the truth in love, when concerned about a ministry leader.

## A Healing Community for Self-Care

Good self-care flows out of the new self that is a creation of God. Church leaders model what it means to value the gift of well-being. Sadly, many worn-out leaders model self-neglect rather than self-care. This is seen in patterns of overwork (doing "God's work"), isolation, neglect of health and fitness, imbalance of time and energy for family, self, God, and ministry. Ironically, attitudes that put self-care last and everything else first are symptoms of a Me-oriented focus ("It's all up to me").

When a leader takes care of self and strives for life balance, it reflects a We-oriented awareness, because the person is more capable of service to the whole Body of Christ when in good health and experiencing well-being. As this internal struggle—Me vs. We—is overcome by God's healing hand, self-aware adults take responsibility for creating a sense of well-being in their own body, mind, and spirit—forming a healthy We orientation within the self.

What is the responsibility of the Body of Christ to one another to stimulate awareness in regard to one's well-being? Sometimes, a healing process begins with a shared observation or concern: "I can see you are struggling with all that you are carrying right now at church—how are you taking care of yourself?" This can be followed with "What do you need? What can I do to help you care for yourself right now?" Such questions are invitations to intimate sharing of needs and risking trust that expressed needs will be met.

Two words that can be very difficult to say are "I need." Honoring one's own needs as the new self can motivate one to seek life-giving ways to meet those needs. When such vulnerability is expressed, others can be moved to reach out. There is no expectation of return, only joy in caring. And this is a very deep joy.

Those who wish to build a caring culture must withstand the pressures that would keep them from doing so. The ME-oriented culture says, "Don't get involved. Let the family help. It will take up too much of your time. It's not your problem." Such messages are not needed when godly boundaries are in place to protect the intimacy growing out of loving contact with another.

In a caring culture, all recognize the importance of personal boundaries around the use of time, energy, and physical and emotional presence. In such a caring culture, individuals honor their own limits and boundaries, and they respect those of one another. "Let your 'yes' be yes and your 'no' be no" (James 5:12). Besides being able to say a clear and unambiguous yes and no, those giving care can also say, "I need . . ." In this way, a rhythmic dance of caring—giving *and* receiving—takes place as God's creative hand moves through a caring community to bring healing and wholeness.

A true step of faith is taken when one pays attention to that "inner tugging" one feels to reach out when another's need is sensed. Motivated by the Gospel, each one reaches out, expecting nothing in return. When such agape is offered, transformation occurs, and a faith community becomes a place of healing for all.

# Partnering with Community Professionals

The authors share specific guidelines about when to refer.

Suggestions are offered on how to develop a referral system.

Finding the mental health professional that views the client's faith as an asset and is willing to work with the caring community of the congregation in the healing process is critical for referrals.

Congregations strengthen their ministries by forming relationships with professionals within the greater community. A beginning step is to connect with health education units at local hospitals for information about what educational offerings are available for the community. Hospitals and health professionals often present lectures and other learning experiences in the community, such as screening events that relate to health and healing. Local mental health associations, treatment facilities, colleges, and universities are other sources for mental health education that may supply speakers and workshops on topics related to mental health.

A key to successful partnering with community professionals is accessing and sharing information among church staff and members. Assessing the resources available in the community can be done by gathering a group of interested members and inviting any health professionals who are members of the church. This group can offer gifts of its own and share information to form a pool of resources that can aid the congregation in its effort to re-parent those in its midst who are in need.

## COMMUNITY PROFESSIONALS IN MENTAL HEALTH AREAS

Psychiatrists are physicians who have completed medical school and a three- to four-year residency in psychiatry. Some receive additional fellowship training in a subspecialty of psychiatry. Treatment requiring psychotropic medications is provided at the highest level of training by psychiatrists. In addition, when hospitalization is needed, psychiatrists provide inpatient care. Some psychiatrists provide psychotherapy as well as medication management.

Advanced-practice registered nurses have been educated in nursing and have a master's degree in a nursing specialty such as psychiatric–mental health nursing (adult or pediatric). In most states, advanced-practice nurses provide individual and family mental health diagnosis and treatment, either independently or in collaboration with a physician. They may provide psychotherapy as well as pharmacological treatment, depending on their specific training.

Family practice and other physician specialists may diagnose and prescribe psychotropic medication for disorders of depression, anxiety, and some other disorders. Referrals to a psychiatrist may be recommended when a course of treatment with medication is not successful. Newer treatments have begun to be initiated based on genetic testing for how patients respond to particular medications. Clinical psycho-pharmacologists are trained to consult with patients and their families and physicians for complex issues in treatment with psychotropic medications.

Psychologists have a master's or doctoral degree in psychology and provide assessment (often including psychological testing), diagnosis, and treatment for mental disorders. Psychologists use a range of therapy techniques, depending on their training and experience in using various therapies.

Professional counselors are licensed by the state in which they practice. They may be pastoral counselors (ordained clergy with advanced training in counseling and therapy), mental health counselors, or marriage and family therapists. Each of these is trained to assess, diagnose, and treat disorders with the application of therapeutic approaches. Some have advanced training in particular areas, such as post-traumatic stress disorder or attention-deficit/hyperactivity disorder.

"Christian counselor" is an unregulated term and can cover a wide range of theological ideas and levels of counseling skill. Counselors certified with the American Association of Pastoral Counselors (AAPC) are subject to a level of accountability established for pastoral counseling.[1]

Knowing firsthand who the providers are who advertise as Christian counselors in a given community will help in making wise referrals.

## ACCESSING APPROPRIATE PROFESSIONALS

There are many professionals who do not value faith, yet the majority of people seeking help do value their faith. One of the most critical aspects of partnering with a professional is to find those who not only value their clients' faith, but who will be willing to work with an individual's faith community as a support system for the client.

When making contact with a counselor or therapist, it is helpful to spend a few minutes talking over the potential role of the faith community in the person's therapy. Find out if a partnering relationship is possible—if the counselor is interested in collaboration with the church community.

Some questions to consider when interviewing potential partners include the following:

1. Do you value the faith of your client?
2. Would you be open to a partnership with our faith community for the welfare of your client?
3. How would you envision such a partnership?

Responses to these questions will yield information to help determine whether this professional is open to partnering with faith communities at any level of involvement. Some specific requests for collaboration could include the following:

1. Are you available to consult with Health and Wholeness Ministry leaders on questions pertaining to mental health and emotional disorders?
2. Can you provide any educational input for church members, including participating in a class session or workshop?
3. Will you accept referrals to treat persons with emotional disorders who want their faith community to be involved in their healing?

Licensed mental health professionals are accountable to laws protecting privacy of their patients and clients. They may view collaboration as inappropriate in regard to the person's privacy and their professional responsibility. For this reason, it is helpful to be clear and specific about what is meant by partnering or collaborating. This should not include sharing medical information such as diagnosis or medical treatment without the person's express written consent. Even when patients consent, many health professionals may be reluctant to communicate outside the therapy relationship, even with immediate family members. It is always the client's responsibility to initiate communication between his or her mental health provider and faith community.

# Mental Health Resources
# within Faith Communities

Resources exist within the ministries of many congregations. In addition to individual members who are health professionals, a congregation may already have an established "caring ministry," such as Stephen Ministry or Caring Community, which provides individual and family care during a crisis. This is an excellent place to begin to develop a deepening awareness of the complex needs of persons with symptoms of mental disorders, along with those of their families.

> The Caring Ministry Team of St. Michael's has an abiding respect for the whole person—body, mind, and spirit. This is demonstrated clearly in the priorities given to care of persons (and families) struggling with emotional pain, physical disorders affecting the whole person, and diagnosed mental health disorders such as depression, anxiety, and dementia. At times, the challenge to minister to all who are suffering seems overwhelming.
>
> The caring ministries have kept a clear focus. The congregation has partnered with a local pastoral counseling center to serve as a satellite office for licensed therapists, including certified pastoral counselors, providing professional counseling services on-site in a private church office.
>
> In addition to individual and family counseling, these professionals provide a variety of educational and support services within the congregation, including the following:
>
> Continuing education for Stephen Ministers is offered on specific topics such as Depression in the Religious Community and Anxiety Management Techniques. These topics are always integrated with faith and God's healing hand.
>
> Consultation is provided to existing support groups for caregivers, with discussion of topics such as Stress, Coping, and Resiliency.
>
> Parenting groups are provided for the parents of children within the congregation and school and are open to the entire community as well.

Many congregations have existing ministries that can be refocused on giving and receiving re-parenting within the context of faith. Brainstorming sessions with leaders can yield creative new connections within and outside the congregation.

A Faith Community Nurse can be a resource and a link to health and healing in the community beyond the congregation. One of the functions of a faith community nurse and/or a health ministry is to develop relationships in the community that support health and healing endeavors initiated by the church. For churches that do not have a developed health ministry, links to community professionals can be formed and nurtured by designated members and staff. This group can function as a Health and Wholeness Committee.

The healing power of a faith community is a significant benefit to those suffering with disorder. It can be a real blessing, when possible, to let this community be part of the process of healing along with whatever professional help the person may need.

The first line of defense is people who care and who know the person, including family and community connections that are an integral part of the person's life. A healthy faith community does this, especially when the pastor considers the role of *Seelsorger*—"caretaker of the soul"—as an important part of ministry. In this context, the re-parenting possibilities of the *new self* (described in previous chapters) are available through the process of confession and forgiveness.

## NEED TO KNOW

**Soul:** This term (*psyche* in Greek) describes the inner world of a person, one's private thoughts and feelings that make up personal consciousness; one's "home" inside, where things of personal significance are stored. For purposes of this book, three forces within the psyche are addressed, utilizing St. Paul's concepts of mind, body, and human spirit, seen in Romans 7–8

If a faith community lacks specific caring ministries, or is in a state of transition, and resources for healing are not readily available, it can be the mission of the congregation to ensure that every single person has at least one healing relationship that is life-giving.

## WHEN TO MAKE A REFERRAL FOR PROFESSIONAL CARE

The pastor and other church professionals are not trained to become psychiatrists or therapists. There is a definite need for help and referral when the person's disorder becomes more serious than the faith community can handle by itself. Knowing when and how to offer referrals for professional care can be a gift to persons suffering with disorders.

There are certain indicators that professional treatment is needed. Is the person showing physical signs of distress, such as loss of appetite, steady weight loss or gain, difficulty sleeping, or lack of energy for daily activities? Such symptoms may indicate a physical disorder or an emotional or mental disorder. A medical evaluation should be sought. Is the person having difficulty coping with daily life and/or withdrawing from social activities? Are there threats of violence, either to another or to self? Has the person threatened suicide? Is the person out of touch with reality? (Are visual or auditory hallucinations present?) Is the person in an abusive situation?

Situations of childhood abuse provide a good example of when to refer. In general, if a person was older when the abuse took place and always remembered it, the situation can be explored. In the context of a loving environment, the person will benefit from disclosing what happened. Since there was no detachment from the memory, going back and talking about it is usually helpful and can lead to healing and relief from the private distress that came from the secrecy.

But if the person was younger when the abuse took place and if the memory was repressed, or if the person detached from the memory, the necessity for referral increases. As the person talks through and remembers such abuse, the whole situation and the detached emotions come flooding back. Often the personality cannot handle such emotional power, and the person feels that he or she is back in the situation. The personality can start disintegrating as deep childhood anxieties rush through and flood the psyche.

The abused person may begin to show the signs described above in situations when events occur that remind the person of the abuse. These events (referred to as "trigger events") and their relationship to the earlier abuse may be out of the person's awareness, yet carry powerful stimulation and provoke a strong emotional reaction. A person's self-protective behavior (either withdrawal or striking out) may seem out of proportion to the immediate situation, indicating the deep anxiety that is rooted in childhood or later. Careful attention is needed in these situations to assure the person of his or her safety in the moment.

## Referral for Substance Abuse

Substance abuse is another situation when referring a person for professional care should be considered. Without treatment, drug or alcohol abuse and other addictive behaviors tend to worsen over time. These disorders are often brought to others' attention by family members rather than the person himself. The defense of denial is a primary issue with addictions. Persons with addictive disorders may have other coexisting emotional disorders such as depression. Referral to a mental health professional, preferably a certified addictions professional, in addition to Twelve Steps group work, will give the person an opportunity to heal from these coexisting disorders.

Referrals for family members are needed as well to help them cope with the addicted loved one and learn how to avoid being unintended participants in the disease process. Twelve Steps groups such as Al-Anon, Alateen, and Adult Children of Alcoholics (ACOA)[2] are appropriate referrals for family members and loved ones. These groups vary widely in composition. Visiting open meetings and becoming familiar with various groups would be a helpful way to establish a referral system for the congregation.

> Cory was active in her church women's prayer group. As the group members shared their concerns with one another for intercessory prayer, Cory developed a deep trust with her group. At one session, she shared with the group her concern for her husband, a retired military officer who had a chronic health condition that kept him isolated at home much of the time while Cory was at work. Lately, Cory realized that her husband was drinking alcohol more often than usual and in greater quantities. His mood was becoming more irritable, except when he was actively drinking.
>
> Cory asked the group to pray for her for strength to confront her husband, so that he might accept help. After the meeting, Cory's friend Grace took her aside and invited her to go with her to an Al-Anon meeting that met at the church weekly. At first, Cory was reluctant, as she thought her husband was the one with a problem. Then, with gentle, persistent encouragement from Grace, Cory decided to attend. At the group meeting, she learned that she was not alone, and she experienced God's love reaching out to her as she made a commitment to become involved and learn about addiction, its effect on her marriage, and the role she played in her husband's illness.

## REFERRAL FOR PSYCHIATRIC PROBLEMS

People who have a disorder affecting their perception of reality will typically benefit from psychiatric treatment at some point in their life. Many will need to take medication to help correct the misperception of reality, which can cause a variety of troubling symptoms such as auditory and visual hallucinations, fixed beliefs that are not rooted in reality (delusions), or the inability to tolerate being around people. These symptoms may interfere with people's ability to care for themselves or cause them to neglect or mistreat others.

Referral for psychiatric evaluation and treatment can help those with reality disorders of this nature to be more functional members of a community—particularly a caring faith community where members can support one another through life changes. This can decrease the effect of various stressors that may aggravate symptoms for a person with such a chronic mental disorder.

> John is a middle-age single man who worships most Sundays at his church and attends the midweek church dinner/activity time. He often sits alone, but sometimes another member will join him. He gives little response except a brief nod and may respond to direct questions with a very brief answer. He lives with an elderly parent and does yard work and other solitary activities.

> During Lent, the parish nurse noticed that John was not in attendance for midweek fellowship or on Sunday. After several weeks, she called his home to see if he might be in need. John's elderly mother answered the telephone and told the parish nurse that John was having one of his "spells" when he would not eat or speak and was staying in his room most of the day. He had stopped taking his prescribed medication several weeks ago and had accused his mother of trying to poison him.

> The nurse, along with a male volunteer from the care team, visited John at his home. They learned that John had received news of the sudden death of a neighbor who had befriended John and his mother. Without the capacity to process the loss, and as it reminded him of the traumatic death of his own father, John had begun to detach. He neglected his medical care, and his thinking had become fearful to an extreme.

> The church staff and volunteer were able to encourage John to return to the clinic where he received medical psychiatric care. They offered to drive him and stayed with him until he saw a medical provider. John was referred for day treatment at the

local community facility, where he could receive constant support and assistance in taking his medications for a period of time
until he was again able to manage for himself. He had regular
visits from the care team at his church; they prayed with him and
encouraged him in complying with his treatment.

## Referral for Abusive Situations

Another situation that requires referral is when abuse of any type is occurring.
Abuse can occur between spouses, with children, or with the elderly. Abuse
can involve body, mind, or spirit. Every local community has legal requirements for reporting abuse, and knowing those requirements and the process
for reporting is one essential first step. Immediate interventions may involve
legal action in order to contain the abusive behavior and protect the victims.
Current knowledge of mental health providers and available shelters for those
who need protection is important. Connecting congregants with these local
resources can be a way to demonstrate mutual love and care.

Annie brought her child to preschool at the local church. One
day she went to the restroom at the church and noticed a poster
that caught her attention. The poster depicted a woman who
was a victim of spousal abuse and read "You are not alone—
there is help if you are in need of protection." Attached to the
poster were cards with telephone numbers. Annie hesitantly
took a card and hid it in her purse. She knew that her husband
would have another violent outburst if he found the card. On
the card were the telephone numbers of a women's shelter and
of a person who volunteered as an advocate to walk with Annie
in her quest to find safety for herself and her child.

## Referrals for Depression

Depression is a disorder of body, mind, and spirit. It is similar to any other illness in that it may be mild, moderate, or severe and can progress in intensity.
The fatal outcome of untreated severe depression can be suicide. For this reason, early treatment is considered preventive and can be lifesaving.

A primary care medical provider can treat depression medically. Licensed
counselors and therapists have training in providing talk therapy for the treatment of depression. They can also monitor response to medication. Referrals
for persons at any point on the continuum of a depressive disorder can be life
giving for the person and his or her family. For example, children who live with

an untreated depressed parent are vulnerable to getting "stuck" at a developmental age without access to a healthy emotional climate in the home.

Susan, a married thirty-five-year-old mother of three children (ages 8 years, 4 years, and 2 months), sought a Stephen Minister at her church after she read a notice in the church newsletter about this ministry. Maybe, Susan thought, someone can help me—I know I feel terrible most of the time, and there is really no reason. When she met with her Stephen Minister for the first time, she explained why she had called. Soon, she was in tears as she described feeling listless and tired all the time. She was unable to hide her sadness, and she cried easily every day. Her two-month-old baby required so much time and attention, and her older children had started to ask, "Mommy, why are you so sad?" Susan's husband worked long hours for his company, and Susan performed most of the household responsibilities, including child care. She remembered that she had felt somewhat low for a period of time after the birth of each of her previous children, but she had eventually felt better. This time, however, her mood would not shift, and she felt she was sinking deeper into a pit of darkness.

## RESISTANCE TO REFERRALS

Fear is the primary source of resistance to treatment and can be explored and allowed healthy expression. Perhaps the person is afraid of being identified as a mental health patient. The older generations, in particular, tend to avoid seeking mental health care, fearing the stigma of needing such help. Others are fearful of change that might be required of them and do not feel capable of negotiating change in their lives. This resistance is not very different from the person with physical symptoms who resists going to see a doctor because he or she is fearful of receiving a bad diagnosis.

The best approach to take in order to gain the trust of a person who is resistant to referral or treatment is to provide consistent contact, exhibit concern for the person, and provide understanding of the help that is available. Making a commitment to walk with the person through the referral and treatment process is a powerful witness to the love of Christ.

Sometimes those who are in a position to refer are resistant to doing so. Having a dual relationship, such as that of pastor and friend, might result in a fear of embarrassing the person and jeopardizing the friendship, and might thus become a barrier to referring for care.

Pastor Tim had a close, friendly relationship with a young man, Brad, who was close to his age in the congregation. Brad taught the youth church-school class and was a fun-loving fellow. He and Pastor Tim played golf together once a week and often shared a beer after the game. One of the parents of a youth in Brad's class called Pastor Tim and expressed concern that her son reported unusual behavior from Brad in class Sunday morning. Brad had red eyes and seemed sluggish and scattered during the class. He joked to the class that he "really tied one on" the night before. Pastor Tim felt protective of Brad, his friend, and assured the mother that Brad was "a good guy" and everyone has "slips" now and then. He dismissed the incident and said nothing to Brad. Pastor Tim did not recognize that Brad's behavior was a warning sign that could indicate that alcohol abuse was a problem for him. He did not want to embarrass or aggravate Brad, his good friend, who was well liked by the youth.

## OVERCOMING NATURAL RESISTANCE WITH A HEALTHY WE ORIENTATION

Resistance to change is natural. Resistance must be overcome, both for the sake of the well-being of the person suffering with an emotional disorder and for the health of the faith community. A church leader or caregiver who is reluctant to make a referral should consult another trusted person. Forming a cohesive WE can reduce the risk and fear of being alone and create a situation in which love and concern with secure boundaries can be offered to the person in need. Making appropriate referrals to trusted professionals and walking with the person before, during, and after professional care is a mark of a caring and healthy community of faith.

# A Christian's Struggle with Mental Illness: One Journey

In this first-person account, a Christian woman describes her personal encounter with serious mental illness and the role of her faith and the Christian community in her journey. The reality of her struggle is presented just as it was written. She knows the struggle firsthand. She is living it!

I am damned.

I am condemned.

I have sensed this: that I walk a wickedly thin line as regards to my own salvation since early adolescence and possibly even from childhood, in the same way I sensed that I was somehow different from the rest of my peers.

I was sadder than other people; the thoughts in my head were often dark and ungrateful; I would cry for seemingly little or no reason; I couldn't sleep at night; I was painfully shy and socially awkward. I would adopt other people's pet tragedies like other kids my age were collecting pet rocks, and I would ruminate and brood on them; I raged and empathized along with other people's pain as if focusing on it would somehow explain the inexplicable turmoil and darkness that raged war within my own mind. For years, for decades in fact, I filled journal after endless journal with "Dear God" entries, which would all end in some variation of the sentences "Please God, let me die. Just let me die, Lord. I am so weary."

As I grew older and the unexplained darkness grew along with me, I began deliberately omitting the journal entry heading "Dear God" because I found I could not reconcile my faith in a God who professes to love us and promises never to give us more than we can bear with a God who either has created or allows or causes someone to suffer as I suffer. Truly, God has at times given me more than I can bear; maybe God is not for people like me after all.

In spite of my feelings of guilt and hesitancies, I continued to wrestle with God, but I did it more privately. I would cry too hard when I would attend church services, so I found it best to just avoid them entirely. I felt so damned for the automatic thoughts in my head when I would become clinically depressed, condemned for the suicidal impulses and rages, and the compulsive need to self-mutilate in order to calm my nerves, that I neglected my spiritual growth. Instead, I tested God. I laid it all out on the table and said, over and over and over again, "Lord, here is my life. I give it back; I do not want it. Unless You end this suffering or at least show me a sign that there is something meaningful that I can do with it that will help me to endure this hell on earth going on in my head, then I do not want to live. Let me die. Please, God, if You love me, just let me die!"

God didn't seem to answer me.

In fact, it appeared that God was taking away even more meaning from my life. Each subsequent cycle down into depression only resulted in fewer meaningful opportunities and whittled away at my life circumstances.

It took me eight years to get my college degree when it should have taken me only four, due to repeated hospitalizations for suicide attempts and medication adjustments. In the midst of the most chaotic part of it, I was banned from living in the college dormitories and almost got expelled from the university entirely. I lost jobs and, with them, all hopes of building a career; I lost friends, boyfriends, and I even at times lost my own family. Eventually, I lost my housing and nearly became homeless.

Even now, as I write this at age 32, I remain jobless, unmarried, and without children; I rent an apartment (with no white picket fence to gloat over); I depend on Social Security Disability payments and subsidized housing to keep a roof over my head, and I balance precariously on a complex stack of government "entitlement" programs and social welfare in order to stay alive and maintain access to the medical treatments and medications that help treat my mental illnesses. I am not self-sufficient; I am not earning my keep according to the social norm, and I feel stuck in this cycle of poverty and stagnation. I have been stricken, humbled, cursed, and humiliated, molded into exactly what I am at this very moment.

By God?

By God's grace?

By the sacrifice of His Son, Jesus?

By the Holy Spirit?

No, God did not answer me in my pain. I came back from hospitalization after hospitalization with only more questions than before and even fewer answers. Oh, what a cruel joke life can be. And You, God, proclaim that You wish to bless me with the gift of *eternal life*? No thanks, Lord. I can't even seem to appreciate this temporary one!

And from what I can see, it doesn't appear that You've given me much of an out, except to walk away from You entirely. What a cruel catch-22 . . .

And it all begs the question: *Did* God put me *here*? If so, why on earth would a loving God mold me into *this*?

God: why didn't You just let me be and allow me to become the child therapist I aspired to be? Why crush me so? Why test me like you tested Job? And not just once, not just twice, but over and over and over again, ad nauseam? Why, God, why???

My primary diagnosis is Major Depressive Disorder, Recurrent and Severe. At times, my psychiatrist, whom I have been seeing for eleven-plus years now, even adds the term "Treatment Resistant" to it because the medications and therapy treatments are so uncertain in their efficacy, and the side effects from the medications have at times been unbearable. In addition, I have Attention Deficit Disorder and Post-Traumatic Stress Disorder. Also, there is evidence of a traumatic brain injury on my scans, and I suffer from panic attacks that nearly paralyze me in certain situations. All of this adds up to proof that my brain really is trying to kill me. So again I ask God, Did You make *THIS*? What on earth *for*???

At various points in my cycling moods, I could feel God tapping on my shoulder, trying to get my attention; trying to make me remember, to open my eyes at least to the possibility of His perpetual presence. And at times, in my pain, I chose to ignore Him; at times I yelled at Him. I fell into bargaining with Him. I, too, like Job, demanded a fair trial. I wept, accused, tested, seethed, despaired, and made attempts to wrestle a blessing out of Him.

Many times I wrote:

Dear God,

This is ridiculous. You really MUST
give me *SOMETHING* as a sign.


Yours truly,

Stricken and trying to be
Your obedient servant, A.


I closed my ears to platitudes of all kinds, rolling my eyes sarcastically and rather viciously at the Christian ones in particular because I felt that they couldn't possibly apply to me any longer. After all, *real* Christians don't ponder suicide. Period.

Therefore, I am damned by my suicidal ideation; by my utter lack of gratitude; concerned by my pessimism and my flat affect; by the fact that I can't, on my own, reproduce the "feeling" that is so often associated with God and with faith; by my bitterness and my increasing neuroses/anxieties. I am surely damned by this illness.

One dark and gloomy day, with the sun shining bright-hot outside, I admitted myself to the psychiatric hospital once again. Upon settling into its bitterly familiar surroundings, I encountered a young woman, about my age, dressed in a hospital gown and slippers, perched on the piano bench in the dining room. She was singing softly while she played. She was singing of hope, of Jesus, of forgiveness, and of darkness. She was singing about love.

Over the next few days, I became friends with this fellow patient. I learned that her name is Mary; that she is a Christian minister by trade and calling and that she is here (this time) because she has tried to eat herself to death. Her demeanor and her girth and the pain visible just behind her eyes betrayed to me the truth of her struggle. But when she sang, I *saw* her faith; like a halo, it gathered around her, and its warmth drew others into her presence. And I knew then that I wanted to understand how it was that she had escaped the guilt and the shame and the self-condemnation that have plagued me and my personal relationship with God in *addition* to the symptoms of my Mental Illnesses.

While there, I witnessed her minister to fellow patients and staff alike; I saw the manner in which she somehow served as a great equalizer between our motley crew of drug addicts, schizophrenics, ex-cons, atheists, depressives, ne'er-do-wells, illiterates, professionals, pop culture Buddhists, sinners, the rich, the poor, with a kind of inspirational equanimity, even in the midst of her own personal and very severe breakdown. And I knew that I had seen God in her, in the same way that the prison guard and fellow inmates must have seen God in Paul in the Bible story retold in Acts 16:19–37.

I was released from the hospital and sent back home, into the same reality and mood cycles as before.

There was no real relief.

No joy.

No hope.

And no one to sing me songs about Jesus.

And yet I was different somehow, this time. God's persistent (and increasingly insistent) tapping on my shoulder could no longer be ignored. I found I had the courage to wrestle with God, to open myself up anew to His will, regardless of whether or not it made sense to me or to anybody else. After all, Mary's faith couldn't possibly have made any "rational" sense to her either, in light of her current circumstances.

I started going to church again—slowly, cautiously at first. At church, I found a community of believers, many of whom I could see were wrestling in their own ways. God peeled back the layers of blinders and cynicism that had formed on my eyes and allowed me to see what I now suspect was there all along, but I had somehow missed in my suffering.

I heard the pastors of the church pray, out loud and without hesitancy, in their services for those struggling not just with physical illnesses but also for those with mental illnesses and substance-abuse issues, for those mired in poverty, and the incarcerated as well. And in a moment of divine prodding, I accepted the helping hand extended to me by the pastor's wife, a woman who knew nothing about me except that I was new to the church but offered me a kind smile and an open invitation anyway. Upon hearing her husband, the church's associate pastor, speak compassionately to a Sunday School class about his work as an intern while studying for his dual degrees in divinity and social work/counseling, I opened my heart and allowed the Holy Spirit to guide me into his office and all but demanded spiritual counseling, from him or from somebody else ordained by God.

What an odd request for me to make, I thought at the time. After all, he's a *pastor*. Won't he just tell me to pray about it? Isn't he just going to tell me that suicide is an unforgiveable, mortal sin and then go home thinking himself superior to me because he doesn't have to fight such evil thoughts? Isn't he just going to tell me to read the Bible or get a job feeding the homeless to make myself feel better? O God, what have I just asked for???

So every Thursday afternoon, from one until two o'clock, I sat in the pastor's office and renewed my wrestling. I wrestled with God; I wrestled with the concept of justice; I questioned the eternal fate of individuals who commit suicide; I wrestled with the pastor himself in his role as my therapist, in his role as my pastor, his identification with the Christian faith, his role as a church leader, and his role as a mere mortal. And week after week, Thursday after Thursday, for nearly a year, he was there to do it all over again with me.

I cycled up: he was there. I cycled down: he was there.

In my downward cycle, I pushed him back a bit; my sense of self-worth and ability to hold a conversation failed me, as they always do in my Depression. But I continued going to worship services; I continued Disciple Bible Study classes. I kept my commitments to teach Sunday School and participated in the church's Diversity Inclusion Group. And when I cycled back up again, he was right where I left him. In fact, I still meet with him from time to time.

At this point in my life, I have been in treatment solidly for fourteen-plus years. Inclusive in this treatment has been almost every psychotropic medication currently available and many forms of secular therapy as well. I have been medicated, shocked, stuck with needles, and analyzed to the point of being utterly burnt out with the insufficient platitudes and limited nature of secular therapy. I have attended groups, educated myself, led groups, tried

155

alternative treatments, hospitalized myself repeatedly, and talked about everything under the sun.

*Except* God.

All of this only served to further confirm my conviction that all truly is vanity, as depicted in the Book of Ecclesiastes.

Now this is not at all to say that these treatments did not help me; therapy in particular has in fact been vital and lifesaving. I use the coping skills I have learned every single day.

But I maintain that something was missing. And it wasn't until I met Mary that I began to see precisely what that something was. Years of therapy and medications (and even a bachelor's degree in psychology) may have provided me with many of the puzzle pieces necessary to the successful management of my condition, but they still left me hanging with no real foothold or peace or a way to make it all fit together.

At the risk of sounding like the very presumptuous Christians who once alienated me with their certainty, I must say that now I know, I *KNOW* that the glue holding all of the pieces together is the very essence of the Trinity. That missing piece is God, forgiveness and love so big that it extends beyond the individual self to all people, no matter their current circumstances or station in life or their feelings or thoughts at this exact moment in time. And from the perspective of a year and a half since I resumed carrying the cross, I can state, with faith, that I KNOW that God was indeed there throughout it all; He was there, in the darkness and in the light.

God, however, did not work in any of the manners in which I had anticipated.

And because of this, I did not recognize Him.

He did not, nor has He thus far, given me answers to any divine mysteries nor revealed to me with any precision my exact purpose. Rather, instead, He has supported me through my journey by sending me many extraordinary people throughout my life who have exemplified persistence and Christian love. God has worked through the Sunday School teachers who planted the seeds of the Christian faith in my childhood; God was working through my parents when they made me go to church even when I raised Cain over the issue. God was with me through the doctors who brought me back from the dead, through the many teachers and pastors and counselors and friends and nurses who have taken the time not only to notice me but to believe in me as well. God was with me, and working through all of the people who stood by me, even when I made them uncomfortable because they did not know what to do to alleviate my pain. I see God in the people who are still here with me, in spite of my past and present struggles; through the growth and steadfast presence of my father, who once struggled so hard to understand but has now reached such a level of compassion that I consider him a rock of love and my very best friend. God proved His presence every time I found myself addressing my journal "Dear God," even when I did not want to acknowledge His existence. God walks with me through the medium of my psychiatrist; through the haphazard miracles of modern medicine; through the companionship of friends during a faux-competitive game of Mexican Train Dominoes; and through the silly giggles and hugs from the beloved children in my life.

Through many and myriad means, God is with me.

Yes, God has used many people as His instruments to remind me of His perpetual presence. And by His grace and through the forgiveness wrought by the painful sacrifice of His own Son, I am alive today. Still alive. Still cycling. Still wrestling. Still diagnosed. But with strength and a light that has no possible rational explanation other than proof of the power of a living and a loving God.

In this, I find a certain hint of the rest that I have so painstakingly sought my entire life, that rest we Christians call hope.

And I am finally, with a bit of confidence, able to hear God when He says, "My child, you are not damned. I will always love you."

# Part II

## Dealing with Specific Disorders

# Dealing with Specific Disorders

Part II presents groupings of specific mental and emotional disorders, with brief descriptions of tendencies toward these disorders along with examples. Insight is given into the nature of the disorder and how such a person can be helped, both professionally and within the support of a faith community.

Physical illness is real, affecting lives in powerful ways. Mental illness is real, also affecting lives in powerful ways. The examples given in this section are selected to represent the milder tendencies of the disorders. In such cases, professional help is generally not necessary. A healthy faith community often becomes the front line of defense for such people and can be instrumental in referral for those who need professional help. When more serious examples are given, the faith community is presented as working with a mental health professional who becomes the person's primary counselor.

Professional counseling and psychiatric help are available for these disorders and are not only very helpful but also essential as the disorder becomes serious and debilitating. For the purposes of this book, such help is not presented in detail, but is seen as a valuable resource for those suffering mental and emotional disorders. This book focuses primarily on the added benefit a person's faith and faith community can give to the healing process.

It is critical that church professionals who have not been clinically trained do not get involved in a therapeutic relationship. That is the expertise of those who have such training and background. The detail and examples presented in this section of the book are not meant to stand alone or to be construed as the way to do therapy with individuals suffering from such disorders.

This section of the book is written with the understanding that sustainable health changes can best be made in the context of family and community support. What are presented are insights and suggestions for the support that faith communities can give those who are struggling with mental and emotional disorders. This is additional help, not the primary therapeutic intervention for those with serious disorders.

It is helpful to remember that all are in this together. Everyone comes from a dysfunctional background, raised as a natural self with agape missing for the development of spiritual DNA. As a result, all suffer in various degrees from anxiety, depression, addictions, and so forth. A solid wellness community can be preventative, modeling and teaching healthy ways of handling situations to prevent the stress that brings on more serious dysfunction.

# Anxiety Tendencies

## CHAPTER 11

Anxiety-based problems are very common. About one in five—20 percent of our population—will suffer from an anxiety disorder in any given year.[1]

Anxiety often comes from viewing reality as dangerous and threatening. This is natural. In fact, life *is* dangerous without Christ's presence. A person has no choice but to protect self from physical harm, psychological damage, and emotional threats.

> Sofia knew it was not safe. Her father had that mood about him. As she scanned his face, her stomach tightened. She smiled, trying to create a better mood, but she knew that it was only a matter of time. Her mind raced as she tried to find a way to get out of the situation. As she started walking upstairs, she said, "I need to clean up my room."
>
> But Father stopped her with that tone of voice: "What is the matter? Don't you want to be with me?" The fear and guilt hit her stomach again as she stopped, not knowing what to do.

There are many situations in childhood similar to this one, such as being bullied at school or being made fun of by peers. Reality is dangerous, and the person learns to be vigilant and on guard. This is called *anxiety*. It is a natural result of not feeling safe—of having to protect self.

The *new self* is a nonanxious, loving presence. The presence of Christ takes away fear. But this does not mean that if a person has anxiety, he or she does not have enough faith. Rather, the presence of Christ has the power to change reality at its deepest level over a period of time. This is called *re-parenting*.

The new self is not a quick fix. Anxiety disorders have a long history. The human spirit has spent thousands of hours developing strategies to make life less anxious. In the process, the mind has overdeveloped and is often "stuck" at a young age, reacting like a fearful eight-year-old. These patterns of anxious behavior are deeply rooted in the personality.

Help for these disorders is found in the slow process of re-forming reality so that the need for heightened awareness and vigilance gradually diminishes. There are many ways that this is accomplished.

## Developmental View of Anxiety Disorders

Anxiety disorders can be viewed from a developmental perspective. An anxious person is often "stuck" at a younger age, viewing situations as too serious. Such a person may not have gone through an adequate teenage "rebellion" period that takes away much of the childhood anxiety with its "I don't care" attitude. Without this healthy counterbalance to childhood anxiety, the person is thus left with an overdeveloped mind. This is *spiritual DNA damage*.

In the developmental process, a healthy child will begin the process of developing an internal value system through the identification process at about age 6 or 7. A child will go through this serious period of life trying to get things right based on family values. Often right and wrong are seen as absolute during this stage, and the child starts feeling internal guilt when doing something wrong. This begins the shift from external control to internal boundaries.

The healthy child will start developing private internal thoughts and attitudes at about age 10 or 11, questioning the parents' authority and beginning the process of breaking away. As the youth moves into teenage years, an "I don't care" attitude develops. This becomes a healthy counterbalance to the anxious mind that developed its strength during the identification period (ages 7–10).

If the young person does not go through this adolescent stage, the mind overdevelops and life stays too serious. The mind believes it has to keep the person safe but becomes hypervigilant and anxious to do so.

## THE VALUE OF MEDICATION

Medication is a good start for serious anxiety struggles. The automated processes that underlie anxiety amplify perceived threat in situations. Antianxiety medication* diminishes the amplification process within neuronal circuits. It slows down the brain, allowing for new habits to form. It is fast acting, but it can become addictive.

Sometimes antidepressants† are used to reduce anxiety and panic attacks. These are slower, but they are nonaddictive. These seem to give an anxious person a different view of situations—they tend to foster an "I don't care" attitude.

In general, medication is valuable as a short-term therapy that gives other therapies a chance to make permanent changes in the person's anxious thoughts or perception. Medication by itself is usually not a long-term cure for anxiety.

## BEHAVIORAL AND COGNITIVE THERAPIES

These therapies are very helpful in extinguishing the hypervigilant behavior by retraining the person's reactions to potentially anxious stimulation. Exposure therapy pairs the anxious stimulus (like speaking in public) with a relaxation response, teaching a person to breathe differently and stay calm. Such "systematic desensitization" is slow, but it is effective with specific fears.

Cognitive therapy works with automatic thoughts that trigger anxiety, bringing the person more into adult reality that does not see the situation as fearful. The therapist listens closely to what the person is saying to self when in an anxious situation, like, "Everyone will be laughing at me when I speak." The client is then instructed to replace that thought with a more accurate one: "People will be interested in what I have to say."

Insight therapies do not seem as effective, though the process of bringing private thoughts out into the open (talking cure) does help reduce the debilitating effects of anxiety reactions. The safe setting of a caring therapist is in itself therapeutic and helps the client work through severe anxiety disorders.

## ADDED BENEFIT OF A SUPPORTIVE FAITH COMMUNITY

Anxiety is diminished in the context of healthy, caring relationships. Working with some form of medication and therapy, a supportive group structure can

---

\*    The benzodiazepines, such as Valium and Xanax, are GABA (neurotransmitter gamma-amino-butyric acid) enhancers, which have the effect of sedation and muscle relaxation.

†    The most common antidepressants, like Prozac or Effexor, are called SSRIs (Selective Serotonin Reuptake Inhibitors). These drugs work by blocking the cellular mechanisms that take back the accumulation of serotonin in the synapse, thus allowing for greater stimulation of specific neuronal pathways.

also be of help. In a Bible study support group, for example, specific teaching and modeling of the new self can retrain anxious thoughts and perceptions. In this re-parenting process, the person can learn from others who have some spiritual maturity about how to handle situations in a more nonanxious way.

In such a safe setting, the person can also be open with childhood memories of anxiety, putting Christ in the scene to connect His loving presence (agape) to the situation. Everyone can benefit from this re-parenting process.

## GENERALIZED ANXIETY TENDENCIES

Generalized anxiety is characterized by constant worry and apprehension. Sleep is often disturbed. The person has difficulty concentrating, finding it difficult to control anxious thoughts. Constantly on edge, such people worry about minor events, stressing over potential outcomes.

Unstable family situations when the person was growing up, especially during the critical time frame of ages 7–10, tend to produce such constant hypervigilance. Patterns of worry over a high-guilt environment or upsetting a violent parent often lead to attempts to control future situations by worrying.

Since *painter* personalities have a sensitizing defense that has them "flashing" all possible scenarios so as not to be surprised, they are more prone than *pointers* to such overactive worry about the future. Pointers tend to repress their anxiety and feel it as a constant, unsettling feeling in their stomach.

> Maitlan seemed on edge all the time. She could not get her mind to stop. They were going to her in-laws for a few days. She must have pictured the scene fifty times already. What if I look ridiculous in my jeans and white top? . . . What if they think I do not know how to dress? . . . What if I wear something better and they feel I am putting on airs? . . . Her thoughts just kept going and going, leaving her weak and dismayed. She did not know what to do.

> Maitlan can be helped to redirect her anxious mind. This learning cannot be done in isolation. Professional treatment and a supportive environment can help. The first person to reach out to Maitlan may be someone in her faith community or a friend who is a part of a faith community. Reaching out to Maitlan requires an understanding of what anxiety is about, so that Maitlan's anxiety does not create anxiety in those around her who want to help.

Just being able to name the anxiety is a good beginning. An ancient saying, "In order to tame a beast, you must first make it beautiful," can apply to anxiety. Viewing a person's anxiety as "the mind working hard to protect" can be a first step toward taming the "beast" of anxiety. Such a loving way to handle an overdeveloped mind can occur in the context of a supportive faith community.

## SOCIAL-ANXIETY TENDENCIES

Kendra never seemed at ease when talking to someone. She would agree quickly with whatever was said, fearful of getting the person upset. She would scan the person's face as she talked, and if she noticed the slightest disagreement, she would immediately back off from what she was about to say. She would stop midsentence and change her opinion to conform to what she perceived to be the person's attitude. She had considerable difficulty with confrontation and avoided conflict. She seemed to feel responsibility for everyone else's feelings and would prefer to do things herself rather than face upset and argument. She continually worried about potential future conflict, and if someone was upset with her, she would go to all lengths to make things better.

Kendra's spirit did not have much chance in the environment where she grew up. She lived with her divorced alcoholic mother. At age 4, Kendra was already fixing her own meals and cleaning up the house. Since her mother became verbally abusive when drunk, Kendra developed the habit of scanning her mother's face to avoid upsetting her.

When she came for counseling, Kendra only knew she was tired and had little desire to interact with her family. She had no capacity to experience anger and usually did not know how she felt about a situation.

When she talked about her situation, Kendra would scan the therapist's face to see if she was "doing it right." When the therapist looked puzzled, she would immediately apologize for being unclear. When he looked preoccupied, she would apologize for boring him. She was afraid to run beyond the allotted session and would ask every few minutes if she had time left. When he mentioned that a session was about over, she immediately apologized for keeping him too long.

Her therapist knew that Kendra valued her faith community and felt accepted there. With Kendra's permission, he contacted her pastor to see if they could work together. The pastor immediately thought of Hildegard as a spiritual mentor for Kendra. The three of them met with Kendra to talk over how she could best be helped.

Hildegard was compassionate, but she had worked through a difficult childhood herself. She had an immediate understanding of Kendra's anxiety. As they met together each week, when she sensed that Kendra was getting anxious, she would gently advise, "Stop for a moment and take a deep breath. As you exhale, feel yourself smile as you remember that God is with you. Then put that anxious thought into His care."

Hildegard also taught Kendra to acknowledge her own thoughts and feelings, rather than back down right away. She let Kendra know that God had given her good gifts in her thoughts and wanted her to express them.

A faith community that provides visitation to homebound persons can be a source of support for the agoraphobic person who cannot find the strength to leave the home. Such a depth of social anxiety can render a person unable to tolerate being in a crowd, such as a worship service. Making worship opportunities available through a ministry that distributes MP3 players with services recorded says to the person, "We want you to be a part of our worship community, even though it is hard for you to be physically present now. We trust that you will join us again when you are able." Such visits can also promote healthy, caring relationships that offer prayer and conversation as well as the Eucharist. If the agoraphobic person is not receiving treatment, a caring faith community visitor can offer to assist the person in finding help to treat the anxiety. Acceptance and interest convey agape to the anxious person who is filled with fear and worry.

## PANIC TENDENCIES

Panic attacks are very unsettling. The attack comes on quickly and is usually accompanied by powerful physical symptoms. The person often fears a heart attack is starting or that he or she will be unable to breathe. While there is no medical cause, the physical symptoms are very real. The person feels out of control. This is a horrible feeling.

Once a person has such an attack, there is always fear that another one will happen. The least amount of anxiety felt in the stomach will bring on this fear. Often the fear is so strong that the person will drastically inhibit his or her lifestyle, such as no longer driving for fear of a panic attack.

Panic disorders may result from a breakdown of trust in the relationship with self. The panicked feeling may be the mind trying to stop a person's emotional reactions. The body rebels at being detached and builds up more emotional strength. The person may be immobilized to the point that a simple action such as leaving the house cannot be undertaken. The mind is fearful of what the body may do, so it struggles for total control.

> Greg sought counseling to help him function better at work. He was getting increasingly anxious before work and during the workday. His job required rapid response to telephone callers. He worked under pressure to sell entertainment packages on the telephone. His salary depended on sales. Greg had always been a top producer in his work group, and the pressure to maintain his position over his co-workers was high.
>
> He had become increasingly anxious working in an emotionally abusive system that pitted workers against one another and changed the rules constantly, keeping workers on edge. No matter how hard he worked, he could not keep up with the ever-changing expectations imposed on him.
>
> His panic seemed to hit when he felt resentment toward his boss. He knew he was not being treated fairly, but he was afraid to say anything. He was afraid of his anger. He feared that if he expressed himself, he would be fired. So he just tried to work harder. But he had hit a wall. His body took his energy away.
>
> His therapist taught him to focus on his breathing when he felt panic develop. He was also learning about meditation in his

prayer group at church. One day as he practiced the breathing and meditation, Greg found himself breathing in and out with a prayer from his favorite psalm: "The LORD is my shepherd (*breathing in*); I shall not want" (*breathing out*). The repetition of this breath prayer brought Greg a deeper sense of calm.

He breathed his meditative prayer at night before sleep and found that his sleep improved. He breathed the prayer as he awoke and while preparing for work, as well as during the day when he noticed his stomach tightening before he became anxious. His feelings of anxiety and panic when his boss put pressure on him gradually diminished.

For those who suffer with anxiety disorders, or with any level of anxiety that is disturbing, there are spiritual disciplines that can bring peace and create a place for holding the anxiety. Practices that help the "too-serious eight-year-old" are those that remind the person of God's presence. A prayer group or a Bible study group adds to this awareness. Centering prayer done in a group may be more satisfying than when attempted alone. Spiritual disciplines that incorporate physical movement and body awareness can also help the constriction of anxiety.

## POST-TRAUMATIC STRESS TENDENCIES

PTSD is the acronym for the diagnosis Post-Traumatic Stress Disorder. PTSD was introduced into the mental health diagnostic manual largely from observations of veterans after Vietnam combat and their return to civilian life. It can develop after any traumatic event that is perceived as significantly threatening or disempowering.

PTSD can affect not only those who experience the trauma but also those who witness it or rescue workers who "pick up the pieces" after the event. Examples include life-endangering events such as combat, armed robbery, assaults, and sexual violations; vehicle accidents; natural disasters; and physical and emotional abuse.

What are considered normal reactions to abnormal stressors or events are different from PTSD in the prolonged length, intensity, and variety of the symptoms. PTSD symptoms include upsetting and recurring memories, sleep difficulties and nightmares, flashbacks, and strong physical reactions (e.g., nausea, digestive irregularities, increased pulse and blood pressure, sweating, tenseness, heightened vigilance, and concentration and memory difficulties). There can be avoidance of emotional attachment, edginess and irritability, numbing of feelings, loss of interest in previously pleasurable activities, and absence of a life-giving spirit.

A sense of purpose in life can be diminished. There can be the very real sense of guilt for having survived when others did not, or a nagging preoccupation with "not having done enough." A cloud of shame may descend; loneliness and isolation may increase, along with skewed perspectives that do not see any "silver linings" to life happenings. Self-medication behaviors (i.e., alcohol misuse or drug abuse) and addictive activities (i.e., gambling, pornography, or sexual acting out) often occur. Previously held values may seem discarded. Such behaviors are unsuccessful attempts to placate or soothe the hurt, pain, and fears that remain attached to the trauma.

Professional help is important through competent mental health providers who are respectful of a person's faith. A healthy faith community can be of significant help for PTSD. A caring, nonintrusive relationship can bring the face of Jesus to the person affected by trauma and its aftermath. This can offer a means of hope and recovery for the PTSD sufferer and the significant others who are also affected. When that caring relationship is connected to the church's ministry, the means of God's grace empower the hope and healing; in turn, the acceptance of the church community builds bridges to the lonely and isolated spirit. The PTSD symptoms become a means to respectfully connect to the person whose insides suffer. As the resurrected Jesus walked and listened on the path to Emmaus, the church's caregivers journey in the path of the healing spirit.

> Alice did not talk a lot, but one could always depend on her. When her National Guard unit was mobilized, she, a single mother, made arrangements for her parents to care for her two elementary-age children during the year of deployment. A mortar hit her compound. Although physically unhurt, she was a first responder. Several unit members were severely injured. Open wounds, screams of agony and distress, the fear of more attacks, not knowing who might die, and a paralyzing sense of "I need to do more" were pervasive as medics were on the way.

> Three months after Alice's return home, her parents, who were lifelong members of St. Mark's, contacted the pastor about their daughter's adjustments, her parenting, difficulties at work, and risk-taking behaviors. Although Alice had worshiped occasionally before deployment, she never did so after her return. "Pastor, please contact her. She needs help!" The pastor wisely responded

by having her parents ask Alice if it would be okay if he contacted her or, if she preferred, to have her contact him.

Subsequently, a connection occurred. "Thank you for your service in the military," the pastor began. "I'd like to know how you are doing." Not much happened at that meeting, and the pastor asked if they could stay in touch. Public places were chosen as meeting sites. He listened as she was able to describe her current struggle. He avoided any messages of judgment.

"I am surprised by how you listened," she said several meetings later. What then began to unfold was the beginning of many deep conversations as Alice shared those things she had kept private about the awful attack on her unit.

# Developmentally Based Overcontrol Tendencies

## CHAPTER 12

Overcontrol tendencies are based on one's mind trying to make an anxious environment safer. In the various developmental stages, anxiety can damage one's *spiritual DNA* by causing the mind to become hypervigilant to reduce the perceived danger. Specific physical and emotional threats can create defining moments for the child, resulting in lifelong strategies to handle anxiety that becomes dysfunctional.

## DEPENDENT TENDENCIES (AGES 0–3)

If a child experiences high anxiety or serious defining moments of anxiety during the first three years of life, dependency on others can develop as a way of reducing the anxiety. Explosions of anger that scare the child, fighting among parents or siblings, or a traumatic event, like the death of a loved one, can all lead to such excessive anxiety. The child's mind will try to make things safer by clinging to another person, trying to get that person to take care of the child. Such a child has formed a good attachment (unlike the borderline personality), but now is using that attachment to reduce anxiety and may get "stuck" at this young age with a strategy of dependency.

The basic trait of such a dependent personality is the excessive need to be taken care of by others. This constant need is usually associated with a fear of separation. The behavior could be described as clinging and submissive, but demanding. Such persons feel a strong need to be cared for, so they will urgently seek a replacement relationship if the one they are in comes to an end.

Such people will allow others to make decisions for them, even in important areas like employment, use of free time, and choice of friends. They may even volunteer for unpleasant tasks in hopes of building a dependent relationship with someone.

Those with a dependent personality actually see themselves as incapable of making decisions, so they feel they must rely on the advice and assistance of others. To maintain the dependent relationship, such people may even allow verbal or physical abuse, blaming themselves for causing it by not being attentive enough or by making the other person angry.

> Jacqueline volunteered for everything at church, but she always needed someone else to take the lead and tell her what to do. She was soft-spoken and generally liked by everyone, but she could not seem to stand up for herself. She would get others to fight her battles, presenting herself as helpless and vulnerable.
>
> Gradually, those who worked closely with her got tired of her constant need for reassurance and her hesitancy to make decisions. She began to feel unwanted, and her dependency seemed to get worse as she became even more "clingy" to those who would still work with her.
>
> Jan recognized that her friend's anxiety was getting worse. She felt for Jacqueline and decided to help her mature. She knew that Jacqueline was a very smart and capable person, but she was debilitated by her anxiety. Jan became a mentor for her and could begin the *re-parenting* process.
>
> Jan met with several other women who normally worked together and suggested that they no longer make decisions for Jacqueline. They would encourage her to be more independent. They then met with Jacqueline, and after praying together, they shared that being more like Christ was to be able to handle situations with confidence. They studied 2 Timothy 1:7 together: "For God gave us a *spirit not of fear* but of power and love and self-control" (emphasis added). "We believe in you," the group concluded, "and we will help you gain more confidence in your abilities."
>
> The very next week, Jacqueline was working with Jan on an upcoming celebration event for the congregation. Jacqueline

reverted to her usual helplessness when faced with how many people to prepare for. Instead of coming to her rescue with advice, Jan looked right at her and said, "Stop and give it some thought yourself. Your decision will be a good one, so go with it."

Hesitantly, Jacqueline walked away and actually sat down by herself to study the situation. Her whole demeanor changed as she came to her own conclusion. She had confidence in her voice as she announced, "Based on the previous year's attendance and accounting for the special emphasis we have for this year, let's plan on 150 people."

For Jacqueline, the spiritual disciplines of study, prayer, solitude, and a heart for service were stimulated and supported by a caring community of women. The practice of these disciplines offers the hope of a stronger attachment to God and a healthy dependency on a loving God, which can fulfill the need to be cared for while claiming one's own power, love, and self-discipline.

Jacqueline has benefited from seeing a spiritual director on a regular basis who offered support as she strengthened her relationship with God. For example, she practiced listening to God's words "I am with you always" as a reminder that she is cared for and will not be abandoned. In the company of her spiritual companion, she reflected on those words of comfort and explored what it means to feel the depth of those words and experience the power of God's strong attachment to her.

## Obsessive-Compulsive Tendencies (Ages 7–10)

Children entering grade school are beginning the identification process with the same-sex parent. This is the introjection period of value formation to form an internal guidance system. Up until this time, the child fears external punishment for things that go against the family's rules. During this period, the internal conscience develops so that the child is controlled by guilt rather than fear of punishment. Such internal control is a necessary step toward the child's becoming trustworthy without constant parental supervision.

There are many reasons that a child can get "stuck" at this period and thus manifest in later life such overcontrol disorders as Obsessive-Compulsive

Disorder (OCD), hypervigilance, and perfectionism. There could be a defining moment that produced high anxiety, such as alcoholism, divorce, or being picked on at school. The child could also find that a strategy of being good gets him or her high praise, so he or she gets "stuck" in this stage. There could also be a high-guilt environment when the parents control the child with excessive reminders of things that were not done right.

High-guilt environments produce hypervigilance. Instead of being free to react spontaneously to situations, the person is controlled by a fear of doing the wrong thing. Everything first must be cleared with the mind before being expressed. Anger seldom comes out directly, but is disguised in nonverbal passive-aggressive behavior. The person will not even be aware of anger, showing surprise when given such feedback.

> His father's reactions were predictable as Nolan was growing up. Whenever Nolan attempted anything, his father's first reaction would be critical. If nine out of ten things were right, his father would notice the one that could be improved. No matter how hard Nolan tried, it was never good enough. Somewhere deep down, Nolan decided he would show his father that he could be successful, proving he was good enough through his accomplishments. Thus began his perfectionistic, driven life that was so evident at his church.

> Nolan was the head of the building committee and was frustrating everyone else by his micromanaging style. He wanted this to be the ideal building, and he spent countless hours studying the church's needs and matching them against the proposed plans. Every day he came up with changes, angering the committee who were ready to begin the building process. They started referring to him as a "control freak" behind his back. He did not see himself as controlling, but only trying to do his best for the work of the Lord.

> The men's Bible study group was going through Philippians and focused on 4:4–7. One of the men asked Nolan about the joy in his life. That took him by surprise. "I never thought of that," he responded. Several men joined in to compliment Nolan on his excellent work, but then suggested that it was time to celebrate the project.

> Nolan objected, "But there are things we can do to make the plans better."
>
> But the group persisted. "You have worked hard, and now it is time to celebrate the gift this addition will be to our church."

As a spiritual discipline, celebration can be a challenge to the person on the obsessive-compulsive emotional spectrum. Celebration requires one to be carefree. How can one experience the joy of the Lord in the midst of incompleteness and imperfection?

Nolan's friends in the Bible study group had the right idea. Celebrating at each step in a process creates energy and joy to continue the journey. Celebration lifts the burden of over-responsibility for the outcome of the project and acknowledges God's hand guiding the process. Celebration gives God the glory and places one's own power and importance in proper perspective.

## AVOIDANT TENDENCIES (AGES 11–14)

When children move into preadolescence, they shift from developing their internal guidance system to moving toward independence of thinking. Along with the hormonal changes, they now begin to have an ability to think abstractly. They can now notice flaws in the family system, and they begin to disagree with their parents on the basis of these flaws.

You said that we should always be open with each other, but you kept your decision to move to another city from the rest of us, the twelve-year-old will think, but he will not have the power to face his father and confront him directly. The young man will realize that he has no power to do anything about it, but he can disagree internally.

If the child gets "stuck" at this age, he or she will develop a strategy of hiding feelings and thoughts. There will be surface compliance, but sometimes strong disagreement inside. Persons "stuck" at this age will avoid confrontation. But in a more passive-aggressive fashion, they will show their anger at what they consider is unfair.

> Zack was eleven years old. His family had just moved to a new neighborhood, and he wanted to connect with his peer group. All of his friends were going to buy fireworks, and he needed money. He knew his parents would disapprove, so Zack slipped into his father's study where he knew he kept his small change in a drawer. Zack stole some money, but as he was leaving the room, his father came up the steps. He raced to another room and hid behind the bed. His father came and found him. In the

defining moment that he remembers as if it were yesterday, Zack felt his stomach panic as he lay there motionless. He remembers his father giving a snort of disgust, shaking his head as he walked away.

Zack is now forty-five years old. He still feels panic when he is accused of doing something wrong, so he is hypervigilant in trying to please those close to him. He has trouble asserting himself and would rather give in than cause a conflict. He carries a free-floating anxiety about doing something wrong and comes across as helpless in his marriage and at work. His anxiety is sometimes debilitating as he tries to make a decision. But he also is very resistant to being told what to do. It is obvious that there is an edge of anger that goes with the feeling that he is being treated like a little boy.

Zack's marriage was falling apart. His wife had lost respect for him, and he was tired and resentful of the constant criticism. He was not used to sharing his life, but he had a good friend at church, Sergay, whom he trusted. In desperation, he stopped Sergay after choir practice and let him in on his marriage situation.

Sergay listened as Zack started his *litany*, describing his wife's controlling and critical nature. After about ten minutes, Sergay asked Zack how he reacted to her criticism. "I feel about eleven years old," Zack replied. "I feel powerless and just look away."

They met the next day for an early breakfast. Sergay began, "You really don't have to react like an eleven-year-old anymore. That is just your old self. Your new self can find a new way to react."

They got together many times with prayer and Bible study as Zack took seriously what the *new self* could do to change his marriage. At one point, he shared his memory of stealing money from his father when he was eleven years old. Sergay suggested that they bring the new self into that memory by putting Christ in it.

With Christ's presence, Zack gradually felt the anxiety of the memory go away, along with his stomach panic and helpless feeling. He even pictured a new ending to the scene: "I see myself, with Christ's help, getting up and looking my father in the face, asking for his forgiveness for what I had done."

Zack was definitely on the way to greater spiritual maturity and now had the power to change his half of the marriage relationship. Instead of turning away and feeling powerless when his wife was critical, he now could look her right in the eyes, thank her for her observation, and take charge of the conversation. This he could never do before, and it did change the course of their relationship.

In seeking out a fellow believer to listen to his pain, Zack engaged in the spiritual discipline of guidance. Trusting in God's guidance through the spirit of his friend Sergay, Zack was able to receive, through prayer and study with Sergay, a re-parenting experience in the Body of Christ.

## DEPRESSIVE TENDENCIES (AGES 15–18)

Much depressive thinking seems to originate during this age period. The adolescent's normal energy to break away from family to form identity is turned inward. Such internalized anger inhibits healthy expression of impulses. The adolescent gets "stuck" and immobilized as the normal rebelliousness is inhibited. Healthy energy for leaving the home is turned inward (*incurvatus in se*). Life seems to have no excitement.

The following chapter will look at depression in more detail.

# Depressive Tendencies

Depression is very common. All people experience periods of time in life when things are not going well and there is a lack of energy for getting things done. Often sleep disruption accompanies these periods of depression, amplifying the person's emotional state.

Most depressed moods are temporary and usually get better on their own. The cause is usually loss, serious disappointment, or a bad decision. Relationship problems often lead to depressed moods.

For some people, depression becomes more severe and long lasting. This is referred to as *clinical depression*. In order for a depressed mood to be considered clinical depression, it must persist for at least a two-week period and have certain features, such as loss of interest in one's surroundings and activities. There is a genetic predisposition to some forms of depression, as shown in family histories. Antidepressive medication is a real benefit to help such people function better.

## GENERAL DEPRESSIVE TENDENCIES

The World Health Organization considers depression to be the leading cause of disability worldwide.[1] Depression affects people of all ages, as well as their family members. There is a 19 percent lifetime rate of depression in the United

States. In any given year, 6.7 percent of the U.S. population experiences clinical depression. Women are 70 percent more likely than men to experience a depressive episode during their lifetime. Less than half of those with depression receive effective treatment.[2]

Depression can be viewed as the result of internalizing emotions, especially anger. In the developing adolescent, anger and rebellion are normal emotions that help identity formation and the process of breaking away from family and forming independence. If the anger is repressed by an overcontrolling mind, it can turn into an angry depression (internalized emotion). The healthy direction of the body's energy is outward. With an overdeveloped mind, the body is usually repressed, its expression inhibited. The result is a depression of energy as the person functions out of what "should" be done rather than including what the person might want to express.

Frequently, guilt and anxiety are underlying factors in depression. Guilt can turn anger inward. Anxiety, an emotion detached from its source, becomes diffused and experienced as enhanced vigilance. An overcontrolling mind will not allow free expression of emotion, thus blocking the normal outward expression of the body's energy.

When the *mind* (cognitive force) dominates over the *body* (emotional force), there is a heightened self-consciousness. The person often is afraid of making a mistake and can be indecisive or will think back over a past action again and again, trying to decide what should have been done.

> Craig was the perfect administrator. He never ruffled any feathers, was always agreeable, and was extremely responsible. He spent many hours double-checking things and making sure things went by the book. He would back down from any confrontation, giving in quickly to stop an argument. He just wanted things to be peaceful. His face usually had a worried look. You could see that Craig was efficient but not all that happy. Deep in his eyes, carefully concealed, you could see the little boy inside, depressed, watching, and wishing someday it would be his turn.

> The reason Craig could not express his nonverbal feelings was a twinge of anxiety he felt whenever he wanted something for himself or whenever his feelings were hurt and he became angry. The anxiety quickly dissipated the anger he felt, leaving his verbal side in complete control. This gave security, but not happiness.

Craig had no trouble feeling anger, but he felt it was wrong to express it. This was an attitude reinforced many times by his highly religious mother, who stopped any angry expression by saying, "Jesus would not like it." The mother, in turn, had been raised in a volatile, verbally abusive environment and was over-reacting to any expression of anger.

His Bible study group from church was studying Jesus' reaction to various situations He faced. Craig was struck with the direct-ness of Jesus' responses in confrontations. He realized that being able to confront things could be a blessing to the situation. But he needed practice.

As he shared his insight, one of those in the group volunteered to pretend to be one of his difficult employees. Craig responded with the usual sigh and compliance, looking down when faced with the "angry employee." With encouragement, he found the courage to look at the person next time, and he felt more energy in his eyes to face the situation. This started Craig on a spiri-tual-growth path to be more like Christ. He found strength in remembering that Christ was always with him. That helped him shift his energy from his stomach (where he felt like a little boy) to his chest (where Christ lives in his heart). This shift made it more possible for him to react with energy.

It took some time for Craig to get energy in his voice and to stand up to the co-worker. When he finally did it right, he felt something different. He observed, "It feels like a ton of weight falling off my chest!" This was the beginning. During the next months, there was a gradual but definite growth of Craig's spirit toward greater confidence in expressing himself. He no longer automatically backed down from conflict but could be appro-priately assertive.

## CHILDHOOD AND ADOLESCENT DEPRESSIVE TENDENCIES

Children can become depressed. Because normal childhood behaviors vary from one developmental stage to the next, it is sometimes difficult to determine whether a child has an emotional disorder. A depressed child may pretend to be sick, refuse to go to school, cling to parents, or worry about a parent dying. Older children may sulk, be grouchy and negative, feel misunderstood, and have trouble at school.

A child who is having problems across most of the settings in his or her life (school, home, peers, church), who has sleep or appetite problems, who withdraws from social contact, who seems fearful, who regresses to younger behavior for a long period of time, who is sad and tearful, who talks about death a lot, and/or who is self-destructive should be seen by a doctor. The child has serious depressive symptoms.

Families undergo many stressful life situations, such as illness, death, divorce, and natural disasters. If a child takes longer than a month to adapt to stress or loss or has an unusually severe reaction, medical assistance is needed. It is important to remember that untreated depression may affect the child's developing brain, so early treatment is beneficial. Helping children and their parents manage difficulties earlier in life may prevent the development of more severe emotional disorders later in life.

Teenagers are searching for identity and for a sense of self-worth. Those who have received a blessing from their parents in some form have an easier time feeling worthwhile. Those who feel that their parents are disappointed in them have a greater tendency toward depression.

Up to 13 percent of eighteen-year-olds have experienced a severe depressive disorder. Sometimes, depressed teens have been considered to be just moody or difficult. With medication, therapy, or a combination of both, most teens can be treated successfully for depression. If they are taking prescribed medication for depression, youth and young adults should be closely monitored. Suicidal thoughts and behavior can occur with depression even when a person is being treated, as they have more energy to act.

Suicide is the third leading cause of death in the 15–24 age group. Many adolescents who consider or have attempted suicide do not receive mental health services. Considering the chronic nature of depression, effective intervention early in life may help reduce future disability. Another reason for seeking early treatment is that having depression can increase the risk for heart disease, diabetes, and other diseases throughout life. The greatest antidote for suicide is a caring, knowledgeable relationship.

> At St. John Church, the Health and Wholeness Committee began an initiative to promote awareness about depression for the faith community. One of the teens in the youth group had attempted suicide earlier in the year. The Emotional Wellness Team decided to register with the National Depression Awareness organization to become a site for depression screening and education. The

Faith Community Nurse led the group in publicizing National Depression Screening Day, when sites across the country would offer the same education and screening event for their local communities.

Mental health professionals volunteered to screen and interview whoever came requesting screening. In this way, appropriate referrals could be given immediately to anyone whose screening indicated a need for full evaluation for depression. A pastoral counselor led the educational session, which included a PowerPoint presentation about signs and symptoms of depression as well as treatment options. Printed materials on depression were available for all ages. There was a large-print screening form for older adults and a Spanish-language form that could be used for the Spanish-speaking participants. One of the screeners was bilingual in Spanish and English, making the service user friendly for the community where it was offered.

When the Emotional Wellness Team evaluated the event at the close of the day, it was discovered that some who had come were concerned about a loved one being depressed; others had recognized their own symptoms and had been reluctant to see a doctor. Hearing the educational presentation that included testimonials, several accepted referrals and expressed gratitude for the assistance in locating providers in the community. All showed appreciation for the acceptance and assurance of confidentiality that was given. The team gave thanks for the opportunity to serve their community as well as their church members as part of a nationwide health initiative.

## GRIEF AND DEPRESSION

Loss is a natural part of life. Humans begin to experience loss in infancy when the mother is not constantly available on demand. Then, small and large losses accumulate over the course of life. The natural response to loss is grief—the process of accepting and coming to terms with the loss. With adequate support and a healthy spirit, most grief can be resolved. The faith community plays a large role in walking with people through periods of grief.

What is the relationship between grief and depression? Some of the same emotional experiences occur with a grief reaction and a depressive episode; the difference is in the intensity and duration of the mood change. When grieving, one can usually still experience a range of feelings, even though sadness washes over the person from time to time. In depression, the low or irritable mood is pervasive and unrelenting. There is loss of enjoyment of most of life.

Depending on what the particular loss means to the bereaved person, the grief process has a sense of movement from shock, denial, and anger, through sorrow and sadness, to awareness that life goes on and adaptation to a new way of being. Though these stages do not always proceed in order, they are experienced to some extent by most who grieve. Depression tends to persist and create deepening sadness and eventual detachment from life.

A caring community of healing and faith can provide a support system for the grieving person as he or she moves through the phases and experiences of bereavement. Those who have the gift of listening are valuable in helping to bear the burden of loss. Some who are grieving do not wish to participate in worship for a time, as being with people brings painful reminders of the loss. There is a wish to avoid the question "How are you?" and remain apart from the rituals that remind the bereaved person of time spent at church with the loved one.

Depression can develop during the grief process when the natural self closes itself off from expression of energy and dwells in guilt or shame related to the loss experience. For example, the suicide survivor often thinks, I should have known she wanted to harm herself. I should have paid closer attention to her. I could have stopped her from taking her life. Negative attitudes are formed toward the self, and the body responds with diminished energy, loss of appetite for nourishment, and loss of capacity for enjoyment. The mood is low and spirals lower with time. There is a loss of resilience for coping and sometimes a giving up on life itself.

When there is connection with the Body of Christ through relationships and faith, the downward spiral of depression does not have to progress to disability or death. As the Holy Spirit moves to strengthen the grieving spirit, whether in private prayer, silence, or meditating on nature or Scripture, there is often a gradual turning toward life. This is a time when the caring community becomes the face of Christ—offering self, patiently waiting, expressing caring while respecting boundaries, and sometimes speaking the truth in love when intervention is needed to halt the downward spiral of depression.

> Life for Angie had become constricted and stressful since the
> death of her husband and soul mate of forty years. In the months
> since Tom's death after a traumatic illness, Angie had closed

herself in her house, isolated herself from friends, and stopped going to church. She often thought, It's too painful for me when people ask how I am doing. I don't feel like going into it, but I don't want to be rude either.

She had previously been an active member of her faith community. When her pastor called, she told him she "just needed time." He was respectful and encouraged her to attend worship again when she felt ready to do so. She voiced her intention to return, but every Sunday morning she lacked the energy to get ready, or she slept through the morning hours. As the holiday season approached, she talked to her counselor about the day she anticipated would be most difficult for her—New Year's Eve, when she would not be able to enjoy her annual ritual with Tom as they welcomed a new year and made plans together for the future.

Angie and her counselor discussed how her isolation was helping her to sort out her feelings about living alone without Tom—they had known each other since elementary school—and what might help her to open herself to possible growth through the loss. Angie wanted to plan a new ritual for New Year's Eve so that she could honor her desire to have a future, even though she did not know what exactly it would be. She decided to have lunch in the cemetery near Tom's grave and then take her elderly widowed friend to supper. After New Year's, she decided to return to worship at her church, and she sat near the back, so she could slip out quietly if she felt the need. On that Sunday, she offered a sanctuary candle in Tom's memory.

Angie had begun to turn her energy outward, and she said she felt good spending time with her friend, who understood loss. She was taking small yet significant steps to reestablish her connection with her church while honoring the reality of her own loss and pain. She found herself smiling and laughing more often. She enjoyed talking about her life with Tom and how much she valued their life together. There were still times of sadness as she missed Tom. Angie felt accepted by her congregation members with the gentle invitations that were offered and the

willing listening to her reminiscing about Tom. She found herself being attentive to the pastor's sermons and listening anew
for words of hope.

## GERIATRIC DEPRESSIVE TENDENCIES

The risk of depression occurring in those over age 65 increases with the occurrence of other illnesses and a decreased ability to function fully. It is estimated
that five million people over age 65 have mild depression, putting them at risk
for developing major depression. Depressive Disorder is not a normal part
of aging. It is normal to have periods of sadness, grief, response to loss, and
temporary low moods. However, persistent depression that interferes with
functioning is not normal at any age.

It is important for older adults to receive treatment for depression, because
if untreated, it can delay recovery or worsen the outcome of other illnesses.
When older adults are treated for depression with medication combined with
talk therapy, 80 percent recover. In addition, there is a lower rate of recurring
depression than when treated with either modality alone.[3]

Not only health professionals, but also older adults themselves, have a
tendency to dismiss symptoms of depression as a part of normal aging. The
faith community can do much to increase awareness and advocate for help
for older adults suffering with depression.

> Beth was the activity leader for the Older Wiser Lutheran group
> (fondly known as "the OWLs") at her church. Beth interacted reg-
> ularly with all of the members of the group, who ranged from
> age 65 to 95. Beth had a special gift for working with this age
> group. She loved them unconditionally and could see beyond
> their physical changes and limitations to the beauty within each
> one. Beth appreciated how they showed love to one another,
> praying for one another and celebrating and grieving with one
> another. Beth could see in her beloved OWLs a spiritual depth
> that could be measured by how many of their moments they
> enjoyed—and there were a lot of them!
>
> Beth was interested in promoting whole-person health, and she
> attended seminars at the local faith-based hospital, which was
> sponsoring a campaign, "A Healthy 100," aimed at quality of life
> and longevity. At one of the seminars, she learned about recent
> research on depression and stress. She decided to implement

a program with the OWLs based on findings that physical exercise and positive psychosocial activity had a beneficial effect on "stress resilience" and reduced depressive behavior associated with uncontrolled stress.

At every gathering of the OWLs, a mild, low-impact exercise and stretching routine was offered as the group began. Some did chair exercises, and others worked on balance and strength. She offered them exercise DVDs that they could use at home. Beth believed that practicing spiritual disciplines produced positive psychosocial activity, and she led the group in exploring different forms of prayer, including prayer walks and visiting the stations of the cross in the sanctuary. She encouraged attendance at the healing prayer services at church once a month.

When one member of the group suffered a loss, Beth made sure to acknowledge the loss and invite prayers for the bereaved, as well as practical help and words of comfort. The group grew in closeness—beyond a monthly social activity group, it became a rich resource for healing and hope.

## SERIOUS DEPRESSIVE DISORDERS

Bipolar disorder causes unusual shifts in mood, energy, activity levels, and ability to perform daily tasks. The mood shifts are different from the normal ups and downs most people experience. The symptoms can cause damage to relationships, school and job performance, and even suicide. The disorder is a long-term illness that can develop early in life, before age 25. It requires management throughout life.

There are different types of bipolar disorder, with symptoms ranging from mild to severe. The person exhibits unusually intense emotional states that occur in episodes. An overly excited or joyful state is a manic state; an extremely sad or hopeless state is a depressive episode. Sometimes both types of symptoms occur, called a mixed state. A person can be irritable and explosive during a mood episode.

If a person experiences a number of manic or depressive symptoms for most of the day almost every day for one or two weeks, he may be experiencing a mood episode of bipolar disorder. In a manic episode, there can be a long period of feeling "high" or an overly happy or outgoing mood. There may be an extremely irritable mood, agitation, feeling "jumpy." In a depressive episode, there can be a long period of feeling worried or empty with a loss of interest in activities once enjoyed. All of the symptoms occur on a continuum from mild to moderate to severe.

Treatment is necessary for bipolar disorder because mild forms can become severe and a person's life can be severely affected. With proper treatment, most people with bipolar disorder gain better control of their mood swings and related symptoms. An effective maintenance plan includes medication and psychotherapy.

Keeping a consistent routine of sleep, meals, and activity helps prevent relapse. Education teaches people about the illness and its treatment and helps them recognize signs of relapse so they can seek treatment early.

> Anna came to see her pastor for help managing stress. "I have bipolar disorder," she said, looking down at the floor. She told the pastor that she had been diagnosed ten years before and had taken medication for most of that time. She appeared ashamed as she described the chaos in her life and how many different counselors she had seen. "I need to talk to someone who understands that I have faith in God, and that is very important to me." The pastor invited Anna to talk about her faith and how her relationship with God helped her as she faced her illness and attempted to manage it.

> Anna had stopped her medication because she was having side effects. She did not want to return to her doctor. Anna's pastor suggested that God wanted abundant life for her, even with bipolar disorder. Anna could do her part by seeking medical consultation to understand the need for continued treatment and by seeing a counselor to help her manage the stress in her life that triggered mood changes.

> Anna experienced the love of Christ being extended to her. She did not feel judged, but instead, accepted. She was able to hear the truth about her need for treatment, but she was afraid. After several sessions, experiencing her pastor's support, encouragement, understanding, and patience, she agreed to accept a referral from him to a psychiatrist whom the pastor could recommend as one who would honor Anna's desire to draw on her

faith in Jesus for strength to stay in treatment and learn more about how to care for herself.

Feeling the love and acceptance of her faith community, Anna could share that she had bipolar disorder. She could trust the honest observations and offers of support that others shared with her at times when her behavior signaled a mood shift.

## SUICIDAL TENDENCIES

Persons who think of harming themselves or who attempt to do so have lost the ability to see a purpose in life. This may be caused by severe depression, loss of contact with reality, or loss of impulse control, such as being under the influence of drugs or alcohol. Suicide is an increasing public health concern. Since 2009, the number of deaths from suicide has surpassed the number from motor vehicle crashes in the United States. There have been substantial increases in suicide rates among middle-aged persons (ages 35–64) over the last decade.[4] Many individuals who consider or have attempted suicide are not receiving mental health services. Anyone who hears a comment about self-harm should not ignore it. Expressing ideas about self-harm is often indicative of depression or other emotional disorder requiring treatment.

If a person in the faith community makes a direct statement of intent to harm self (or others), he or she should not be left alone. The situation should be reported to a health professional or to emergency medical services. This action forms a protective boundary that says, "We love you, and we value you. We will not stand by and see you harm yourself. We will help you to contain your feelings and actions by getting you the help you need."

Faith was a middle-age divorced woman who had attended St. Paul Church off and on over the years. Recently she had begun attending again. The director of Christian education, Tom, had noticed that Faith appeared agitated and overly talkative on Sunday during an adult class. She talked off the subject and stalked out of the class when Tom offered structure to her participation. After the church service, Tom went to the parking lot and noticed Faith standing by her car, shouting at people passing by. He went over to her and asked if she needed anything. She screamed at him, "You don't care about me! I'm going to get in my car and crash it. Nobody cares!" Tom listened, then asked Faith if she intended to hurt herself. Faith yelled back, "What do you care? I'll be dead tomorrow—then you can come to my funeral." Tom asked Faith to give him her keys. Then he took out his cell phone and called emergency. He asked the operator to send the mental health team. He waited with Faith until the team arrived and took her to the hospital. Later, Tom and the pastor visited Faith in the hospital mental health unit. Faith was angry and did not want to see them. Tom understood that Faith did not want to face her distress, but she needed protection with firm boundaries.

After Faith had a chance to process her hurt and anger with mental health professionals in the hospital, she gained perspective on what had happened. After a time, she was able to acknowledge that her thinking was distorted on that day at church, and though she did not want hospitalization, she acknowledged that it had helped her to receive the needed support.

As these examples illustrate, there is a significant role for a healthy faith community to fulfill in educating, screening, and supporting treatment for depression at every age in life.

# Developmentally Based Tendencies toward Poor Impulse Control

Impulse-control issues usually represent *spiritual DNA damage* suffered as the child was growing up. At critical ages, the child learned to manipulate situations to gain emotional satisfaction. Either critical emotional connections were missing, or the child had too much power to control the mood. Either way, the child got "stuck" at that age, and later in life, uses the manipulative strategies for emotional satisfaction. The problem manifests itself in a lack of internal self-control.

The person usually lacks insight into the immature behavior and considers the manipulative behavior justified and normal. A male who is abusing his wife, for example, is convinced that it is all her fault. Like a five-year-old throwing a temper tantrum, he believes that she caused him to be angry by her actions. His abusive anger is totally justified. If he is angry with her, the most important thing to him is expressing his emotions and feeling better by getting it out. He is completely unaware of the immature and self-centered nature of his behavior.

Trying to convince individuals with impulse-control problems that they should change their actions usually does not work. Since they do not have the capacity to control their own impulses, there will be surface agreement, but when the situation occurs again, the usual manipulative emotions will be expressed. *Re-parenting* is necessary.

What such individuals need are healthy boundaries that have automatic consequences. Such boundaries are most sustainable when they are part of a healthy family or community. If, for example, when the child was five, the family had healthy boundaries, the child would not have gotten by with the temper tantrum behavior. He would have grown up.

It is difficult for the family to handle these disorders. Usually, the immature personality has enough power to manipulate the mood, leaving the other family members feeling helpless. It is difficult for one parent, for example, to make such a drastic change since the spouse is part of the dysfunctional system and is usually participating in a codependent way.

Sustainable, healthy boundaries are possible within a faith community. Good boundaries are always set as WE-oriented boundaries. Thinking of the good of all concerned, leaders decide how the community operates and what behavior is appropriate. The boundaries are enforced with loving firmness: "We do not react this way as the Body of Christ, so this is not going to happen." Notice that the boundaries are the same as those of a healthy family unit: "This is not how we do things in our family, and so this is not going to happen."

Healthy WE-oriented boundaries gradually inhibit manipulative, impulsive behavior. Over time, the immature reactions diminish as these boundaries are internalized. The persons "stuck" at an immature age can gradually grow up. This is spiritual maturity as the *new self* takes more control over emotions and behavior, aided by the healthy boundaries of the faith community.

## ATTACHMENT-SEEKING TENDENCIES (AGES 0–3)

Picture a three-year-old child wanting to feel attached and belonging to someone. People "stuck" at this age with spiritual DNA damage are searching for a place to belong. At this young age, boundaries have not yet been established, so the person has nothing internal to help him or her stop crossing over the boundaries of others. It seems fine to become personally attached when that is not appropriate. When these tendencies become more pronounced and serious, the term *borderline personality* is sometimes used.

> Georgene always knew that her mother did not want her. Her father left the family soon after she was born. One of her earliest memories was chilling. "I don't know why I have to put up with you!" her mother shouted in her face, shaking her shoulders hard. "If you were not here," she continued, "my life would be so much easier!"

She never felt the security of a mother's love, and she learned early not to trust. She knew how to manipulate her father, who came around infrequently. She would crawl into his lap and make him promise to come back often. She knew how to make him feel guilty.

Her father would respond with lots of attention while he was there, but then he would disappear for weeks and months. When he left, her mother always got very angry with her as if it were Georgene's fault that he left.

Georgene had a history of failed relationships before she joined the church. She was divorced and had several young children. She started by making friends with the pastor's children, doing special things with them and taking them with her to have fun. As she got more connected to this family, she went to the pastor for help with her faith. She was very complimentary of his help, and she noticed that he liked her compliments.

She found excuses to stop by to talk, and she became more familiar, touching him subtly and moving closer to him as they talked. She also began to call more often at his house, needing his advice or wanting to tell him something. The pastor's wife voiced her objection about her familiarity, so finally the pastor told her not to come by anymore.

"But I thought you cared," she began with childlike tears. "No one has ever cared about me, and I thought you did." Filled with guilt, the pastor assured her that he did care.

As the contacts continued, the pastor and his wife started having arguments over this woman's intrusion into their time and his life. Finally, he told Georgene that he could never see her again, ushered her out of his office, and shut the door. Within a half hour, he got a call that she had tried to commit suicide. He felt a deep sickness in his stomach.

Those searching for attachment or a place to belong are not bad people. They desperately want to feel connected—to be a part of a family. They have no insight into the inappropriateness of their behavior. In many ways, they are like little children, using their emotions to manipulate the situation so they can get some attention.

These personalities are difficult to deal with alone, since they are very good and subtle at manipulation. Unless the potential counselor or friend is very good about setting personal boundaries up front, the borderline personality will find a way to attach to the individual's personal life or family life. Since the borderline does not trust, there will be endless ways that the counselor/friend has to prove that he or she cares. After expending so much energy, the counselor/friend has no choice but to break the relationship, leaving the borderline feeling abandoned once again.

## Handling This Disorder within a Healthy Faith Community

A healthy faith community can establish the boundaries necessary to help those with attachment problems to "grow up." The first step is to form a We with all concerned.

> After the suicide attempt, Georgene was placed under the care of a therapist who wanted to work with the church community for her care. He brought together the pastor and his wife along with a number of other leaders of the congregation who knew Georgene well. They all agreed on the boundaries that would be set and on how to handle Georgene's manipulation. Then Georgene was also brought in so that everyone could agree on how things would be handled for the good of all.

> Georgene stuck to her promise for the first several weeks and did not try to manipulate. But then she started calling Jenny, one of the women of the congregation, more and more often, trying to get her to respond. Jenny immediately got the We together again to decide how to handle things.

> The next day, Georgene was asked to meet with the group. "Remember, we all agreed that this would not happen," said one group member as the session began. "You have so much to offer, and we want you to be a part of our congregation. We respect each other's time. So you will not call Jenny every day, because she does not want you to."

With such constant enforcement of loving, healthy WE-oriented boundaries over a period of years, a borderline individual can be re-parented. The new self of such a person can respond to loving firmness and can gradually develop internal control, feeling an attachment to a community who cares.

Healthy boundaries can be established with an understanding of practicing *spiritual disciplines*. The faith community members are providing guidance as they lovingly offer boundaries with clear consequences to the person with attachment tendencies. Such re-parenting requires prayerful teamwork and consistency and is an act of service on the part of the members.

The person can be helped to see that the spiritual practice of *submission* means willingly giving up one's own rights for the good of others—giving up the right to demand that others return our love in the way we want. The practice of submission as a spiritual discipline involves *obedience*—accepting the limits others give to us. Georgene can be invited to submit herself to God, for example, by performing acts of unconditional love for others without expecting anything from them in return.

In terms of spiritual growth, a person like Georgene may be most in need of discovering her true self, with the identity God has given her as a person who can learn to control her impulses. The practice of *fasting*, not just from food but also from having one's own way in relationships, can provide a spiritual discipline for personal growth. A spiritual director or spiritually mature therapist with good personal boundaries would provide *guidance* to Georgene as she takes baby steps into a new way of being, framing her steps as spiritual practices leading to maturity.

## NARCISSISTIC TENDENCIES (AGES 4–6)

Every child goes through a very self-centered stage during ages 4–6 where the world revolves around the child. During this time, the child explores the full range of emotions, getting satisfaction and relief by immediate expression of feelings. If the child gets "stuck" at this age, such self-centered emotional expression will become part of the adult personality.

> There he goes again, Greg thought as Connor demanded the floor once again.
>
> "You are not listening to me," Connor almost shouted, frustrated that the meeting was not going his way. His voice became demanding as he continued, "You had better reconsider my involvement in youth ministry. I have to be there to keep an eye on my child."

> The group grew silent as Connor got louder. "I can't believe that you would limit the youth committee to only three people. You know I have always been interested in our youth. I demand to be on the committee." The rest of the people at the meeting looked uncomfortably at one another, letting Connor dominate the mood as he usually did.

Narcissistic personalities have little or no insight into the inappropriateness of their behavior. Like a five-year-old, they feel the right to express their emotions when they feel them, no matter what the situation. Their emotions are the most important thing at the moment.

Do not think of such personalities as bad people. They are just "stuck" at an immature age and did not go through the normal identification and internalization process that usually occurs between ages 7 and 10. As a result, they view the world through a four- to six-year-old's eyes and genuinely feel that everything revolves around what they feel.

When people like this are challenged or frustrated, they will not hesitate to go to great lengths to get their way. In fact, such individuals seem to thrive on emotional conflict.

> The pastor held firm to the board resolution that the youth committee be reduced to three people, thus eliminating Connor from consideration. He stormed out of the pastor's office, vowing that this would not be the end of things. He was tired of being treated as if he did not matter. He would make sure that he was on that youth team.

> He started a campaign to get people on his side. He met privately with all the parents of the youth, convincing them that the new policy would not be good for their children. He got the congregation stirred up when he sent out an email detailing the situation and calling for the pastor's resignation. In the email, he highlighted his value to the youth group again and again.

> When confronted by the pastor for sending out the email, he went into a rage. He demanded that the pastor resign on the spot or he would leave the congregation and take all the families with children with him. He snarled with contempt as he stormed out to let his friends know the latest news.

## Handling This Disorder within a Healthy Faith Community

Helping a person with narcissistic tendencies mature is a slow re-parenting process. Key to this process is a healthy community who sets firm yet loving WE-oriented boundaries. When such a person cannot manipulate the situation and does not get an emotional payoff, healthy internal control can begin.

Narcissistic personalities actually believe that they have the right to express their emotions whenever they feel them. Re-parenting occurs when this belief system begins to change. For the normal five-year-old who is throwing a temper tantrum, the belief system changes when healthy boundaries are in place. If the five-year-old ends up getting what he or she wants or ends up being able to control the mood, then the belief system does not change. The world will still revolve around this child, and self-centered behavior will persist. This is spiritual DNA damage in the 4–6 age range.

Such individuals often cannot be handled alone. They are too good at manipulation and controlling the mood. There is little concern for the feelings of others. Trying to be reasonable just does not work. That's like trying to talk a five-year-old out of a temper tantrum.

The leaders of the congregation must form a healthy WE. The WE is designed to include the narcissistic person, not to be formed as a power struggle against this person. The WE is first formed as leaders get together and ask, "How are we going to deal with this situation?" As good guidelines are formed, then the narcissistic personality is asked to join the WE.

> "We really do love your passion for our young people," the leader of the meeting began. "You are a true gift to our congregation, and we want to make sure what you have to offer is a blessing." After this genuine welcome to the disruptive person, the conversation immediately focused on the good of the youth program: "We want the best for our young people, and we are meeting to decide what is best for all concerned."

> "Don't give me that garbage," Connor attacked. "I know you are meeting to get me out of the youth program."

> He was raising his voice and was ready to say more when the others looked at one another and smiled, then looked back at Connor and stopped his outburst: "No, Connor, you will not react like that. We genuinely believe you are a gift to us and to this program. Your attack is inappropriate, and it is not going to happen.

> "Let's start with the gifts you bring to the youth program," the leader immediately continued. "We all know that you have a keen interest in keeping our youth in the church, isn't that right?"

> Taken by surprise, Connor settled down. A little puzzled, he said, "Yes, I do want them to stay interested in our program."

Just as with a five-year-old, healthy WE-oriented boundaries that include the narcissistic individual will start the maturation process. The re-parenting process takes a long time, with the narcissistic person repeatedly slipping into the old manipulative behavior. The healthy boundaries must be upheld repeatedly over a long period of time to be effective. The immature personality cannot be allowed to control the mood or manipulate things. There must be the constant re-forming of the WE by the leaders looking at one another, smiling, and reinforcing the appropriate behavior.

> About a week later, Connor got angry again since nothing had happened and he was still not part of the youth team. He sent out another scathing email to stir things up again. He was immediately asked to meet again with the group. He came prepared to fight. He started things with anger: "You said you valued me in the youth program, but nothing has changed. You lied."

> The group members looked at one another and smiled. "Your passion is a gift to our youth, but your anger is not appropriate, and neither was your email. This will not happen again. In this Christian congregation, we follow Christ's directive to speak to each other directly and not go behind people's backs." A group member went on to say, "We are in this together, and we will work together for the good of our youth. Certainly you will support that."

> When Connor saw that his anger was met with a loving, firm response, he immediately calmed down. The rest of the meeting was a good one, with Connor able to give many good ideas for the program.

Of course, this process will go on for years. Connor will still show his immaturity, but when it cannot manipulate the situation and he feels the loving, firm boundaries, there is a good chance that he will gradually mature. The re-parenting process in such a loving, firm way is slow, but it is real.

How can members of the faith community maintain their strength and resolve, forming a healthy WE consistently over such a long period of time? A variety of spiritual practices are involved in re-parenting those such as Connor who are "stuck" in disorders that challenge those in relationships with them. These practices include the following:

1. Pray for Connor at every contact with him, including when his emails arrive, and pray with one another for strength to practice love and boundaries for the good of all.
2. View the setting of boundaries as an act of service to Connor and to the entire faith community.
3. Study Scripture for God's Word to guide in the setting of limits; study teachings of inspired psychologists and behavioral specialists to learn techniques of limit setting.
4. Submit—that is, commit to God's care a narcissistic person who may choose to leave the faith community rather than accept the limits given.
5. Celebrate God's goodness when a narcissistic person shows signs of growth and remains in the faith community.

## EMOTIONAL MANIPULATIVE TENDENCIES (AGES 11–14)

As children get close to middle school, they start developing their own private world, often disagreeing with some parental restrictions. But they do not have the power to face their parents directly, so they detach somewhat from their emotions and fake their attitudes and feelings. In a sense, they "go underground" with their true feelings and can lie about what is really going on.

Such dynamics make it possible to be best friends one day and enemies the next. The person seems to have little depth and can put on a good show for effect. There can be rapidly shifting, shallow expressions of emotions (often manipulative) so that the person stays the center of attention. Sometimes such personalities are called "drama queens."

> Darcie was having another crisis. She was a staff member at church. She was hurt deeply. She had just seen a private email sent to another staff member criticizing her work as music director. She burst into tears as she sobbed, "I work so hard choosing the music, only to have this happen. I am so upset that I am going to turn in my resignation."
>
> Her friend tried to console her. "This is just one reaction to the choir piece you chose for last Sunday."

> But before she could continue, Darcie burst into tears again. "This is like a knife in the heart! I worked so hard on that piece. No one appreciates my talent. I just don't belong."

Darcie thrives on crises. Such persons seem to love drama and will tend to overreact to seemingly normal situations. The emotions seem to have little depth and can be switched on and off when needed. It is like the person is putting on a show for attention.

Those with emotionally manipulative tendencies are not bad people. Rather, they actually believe that this is a crisis and that they are the ones being unjustly hurt. They are using their ability to detach from their emotions and put on a front, or a persona. They are just trying out a way of reacting to see what it feels like. They are "stuck" in preadolescence and have not moved into healthy identity formation and the depth to personality that this process brings.

To some degree, using such a persona is less anxious than connecting to the real feelings involved. For Darcie, in her immature state and being unsure of herself, such criticism can be deeply unsettling to her identity formation. It is much easier to pretend that this was unjust and that she was deeply hurt by it. Keeping her emotions more surface and detached gets her attention and keeps her from having to face her deeper uncertainty over her adequacy.

## HANDLING THIS DISORDER WITHIN A HEALTHY FAITH COMMUNITY

Since this is an impulse-control disorder, firm, loving boundaries are also the way to deal with a person with emotional-manipulation tendencies. Such a person cannot be allowed to control the mood with his or her fluctuating emotions. But in addition, such a person must be led to a greater depth in looking at the situation in order to move toward the adolescent identity formation and away from the preadolescent detachment and facade.

> Her friend had a suggestion for Darcie: "Let's go and have a talk with the person who sent the email."
>
> "What?" Darcie exploded. "How can you even think of that? She will just hurt me more and lie about sending the email. How can you do this to me?"
>
> Her friend just smiled and said firmly, "No, this is the way we do things around here—this is the Christian way. I will call this person right now and see when we can go and meet face-to-face."

"What?" Darcie exploded again. "I will *never* do that! You are certainly not my friend to suggest that. I am sorry I even confided in you."

Her friend smiled calmly once again. "I am your best friend, and best friends take care of each other. It will really help your music ministry in this church to find out what is behind this, so we are going to meet with this person."

Darcie settled in resignation as her friend made the arrangements. She was more passive as they went to meet with the person who had been critical of her song.

There is good re-parenting material in face-to-face meetings, especially for a *histrionic personality* like Darcie's. This Christian way of dealing with conflict has the power to bring people out of their own immature understanding of things to a more shared reality. Challenging privately held attitudes is always healthy in talking through the issues directly with the other person. Such direct conversation is also good for the spirit of the congregation since it keeps hurt feelings from festering and building into hard feelings.

"Tell us more about your concern over the music in church last Sunday," Darcie's friend began as they sat facing the other person. "We want to use your insight to improve our music program."

Darcie and her friend looked at each other and smiled as Darcie continued, "Yes, I have a deep love for church music and need to know your reaction so I can better understand how others can benefit."

After that, there was a good, deep discussion over the need to keep more familiar music in the church service. The choir piece in question was a difficult one that had a less familiar tune. "I am just afraid that we will lose the old favorites that I grew up with" was the member's honest reaction. She then added, "But I appreciate the way you are challenging our choir."

After the meeting, Darcie admitted that she felt better about the situation since they all parted as friends. She agreed that this was a better way of handling things. She was showing some maturity.

The process of re-parenting with healthy boundaries is slow and needs repeated activity. Darcie will react again and again, but she can slowly grow though the firm guidance of her friend, whom she cannot manipulate.

Sitting down together to work through differences really involves the spiritual discipline of *study*—studying one another through listening and responding to what is heard. It also requires submission on the part of the person who just wants to be *reactive*—giving up one's own desire to receive attention through a display of dramatic emotion. The discipline of *guidance* is offered to structure the process in a Christlike way. *Prayer* undergirds the whole re-parenting effort.

Practiced together, these spiritual disciplines offer the hope of growth into maturity for those with impulse-control disorders and those who are in community with them.

## TENDENCIES TOWARD ADDICTIONS (AGES 15–18)

If an adolescent has a history of poor impulse control, when the normal energy for breaking away from family occurs, this energy can easily be misused for personal good feelings. Since there are many ways to get a quick fix for one's mood, the adolescent is vulnerable to addiction when experiencing such a mood-altering substance.

The following chapter will give more detail to the addiction problem.

# Tendencies toward Addictions and Other Impulse-Control Problems

Substance-abuse problems are very common. Close to 20 percent of the population significantly abuse some "drug" that alters the mood during their lifetime. Actual dependency rates are closer to 10 percent. Some common substances that are involved are alcohol, cocaine, opiates, methamphetamines, Valium, and barbiturates.

There are genetic predispositions to such behavior. Some people feel a powerful shift in mood and an alteration of personality when taking some substance. They have a greater danger of becoming addicted.

Substance abuse is a pattern of using mood-altering products that produces significant problems for the person during these periods of impairment. Excessive partying, binge drinking, driving while impaired, and alcoholic rage are just some of the examples. Even though there may not be a true craving for the substance, the person looks forward to the mood-altering experience.

For many such people there is a regular pattern of using a substance that causes impaired functioning and often seriously disrupts relationships. The person becomes dependent for daily living and often is unable to reduce or stop the use of the substance after trying unsuccessfully. Users have cravings for the drug and may spend considerable time and money acquiring, using, and recovering from the drug. They will experience withdrawal symptoms when they try to stop using.

The substance-dependent individual will continue to use the drug, knowing that persistent psychological, relational, or physical problems are being made worse. Often it seems like the person is self-medicating, trying to fix his or her mood.

## ADDICTIVE TENDENCIES

Addictions cause serious impairment to life. They start innocently as a way to fix one's mood, but gradually can begin to take over a person's life and become central to daily activity. In advanced stages, the person is controlled by the addiction, usually damaging physical health, relationships, and vocation.

The addictive personality usually has a history of poor impulse control and often a genetic predisposition to the addiction. As this person goes through preadolescence, there is a split in the personality between the mind and the body. The unhealthy preadolescent develops a private inner world and a facade for the outer world. The person, in essence, starts becoming two people. One force, the *mind*, pushes toward proper behavior, while the other force, the *body*, which gets progressively stronger as it stays private, pushes toward fixing one's mood. (It is interesting that men who get "stuck" in this stage are vulnerable to viewing pornography, a private way of getting enjoyment.)

If this stage is not resolved by the person's spirit moving to greater depth toward true identity formation, the adolescent (age 14–18) becomes vulnerable to more serious addictive behavior. As a stronger "I don't care" attitude develops, the split widens between the mind and the body. When the body takes over with the power of this rebellious attitude, the person will give in to the pleasurable behavior (sex, alcohol, drugs, etc.). Healthy boundaries for such destructive behavior seem to be missing.

## THE ADDICTIVE CYCLE

After the "high" wears off, the mind will then take charge and try to stop the behavior by using guilt. But the power of the mind has become weakened and does not last long. Thus begins the addictive cycle that can continue for the rest of the person's life.

The cycle starts when the impulse takes control of the personality with an "I don't care" attitude. This puts the person in an altered state of consciousness. A good term for this state is "La-La Land," a temporary state where the person really does not care and feels invulnerable.

Remember that the basic impulse is good, part of God's creation, and has a healthy base in the yearnings of the soul. It becomes destructive when the yearning seeks fulfillment immediately, without concern for one's value system, and takes this energy into the wrong direction. As described in the previous chapter, the body has become too strong as a result of pampering, not having to face consequences of actions, an indulgent parent, or making up for lack of love and affection.

When the impulse takes control of the whole person, inner conflict is automatically set in place. Such impulse-control disorders effectively split the person into two people, with the body winning and the mind regaining temporary control with a nagging guilt. In this sad, addictive cycle, the person's "conflicting thoughts accuse or even excuse them" (Romans 2:15). An ineffective spirit watches the impulse take over, without ability to take charge and restore self-control.

## ALCOHOL-ABUSE TENDENCIES

Alcoholism usually reflects such a bad internal relationship and widens the split between the two forces inside. Just ask anyone who has lived with an alcoholic to see if he or she doesn't recognize that the alcoholic seems to be two different people. When drinking, there is a powerful "I don't care" attitude, but then remorse usually follows.

> Ray was almost in tears as he pleaded, "I'm sorry. I won't do it again. Please give me another chance." His wife had threatened to leave him after his last drinking episode, and he was desperate.
>
> He was very attentive to her for the next several days and once again was the person she loved. "Maybe this time it's for real," she hoped to herself.
>
> But as the week went on, Ray became more agitated. He was irritable and finally started one of their usual fights on Friday night. He slammed the door and went out to get drunk. The other force inside had taken over, and he no longer cared about the marriage. As usual, he stayed drunk the whole weekend. On Sunday night, the remorseful Ray was back, pleading for another chance,

How could his wife get into such a pattern? Why would she give in again and again? The answer was simple: the remorseful Ray was real! This was not just a front, but at that moment, his mind had taken control, and Ray did not want to lose his family. He was genuinely sorry and literally punished himself for the pain he caused. He was angry with himself, and if his mind could stay in control, he would not get drunk again.

> Even though Ray was genuinely remorseful, it was only his mind talking. Once the body took over, he no longer cared, for he was a different person. He had built up enough resentment by punishing himself to have a "justified drink." The more times this cycle was repeated, the worse the relationship became within Ray. Inner peace was gone, replaced by the vicious battle between the mind and the body. Ray's spirit was in deep trouble, unable to take charge of the soul; therefore, Ray was not to be trusted. He would keep his word only as long as his mind stayed in charge. But as hard as he tried, the body would build up enough resentment to rebel again and again.

Ray's wife was an "enabler." Instead of helping to strengthen his spirit, she only wanted the mind back. So she aligned with Ray's "should" side against his impulse, only adding to the buildup of resentment. She added fuel to his internal conflict, making the drunken rebellion more certain.

The addictive nature of substance abuse is very difficult to break. Normally, the person cannot break the cycle without considerable help. Even with the firmest of resolve, the temptation of a mood shift just seconds away is too much for a weakened spirit to handle.

> Ray went to see a counselor after his wife filed for separation. He was angry, scared, and confused, blaming her for what had happened. But deep down, he knew he needed help, and he was open to insight into his inner spiritual problems. The counselor talked concretely about his inability to resist the "quick fix" to his mood. For the first time, he acknowledged that he could not stop his impulse to drink.

Admission of his alcoholism was the first step in the restoration of Ray's spirit. For the first time, he let someone see behind the mask of anger and blame. There was a scared little boy, ready for help.

> His counselor continued to see him, but immediately asked him to join an Alcoholics Anonymous group that met at his church. Several months into his treatment, he had a serious relapse. But he came back and went into a treatment center for additional help.

As he grew more open to his mentor from the AA group, he shared his private inner world in a way he had never done before. It was like re-parenting. He finally had a "best buddy" as most preadolescents have with whom to share all their secrets. As Ray and his wife struggled jointly to build a new spiritual foundation for their life together, Ray was on his road to recovery.

## FAITH COMMUNITY RESPONSE TO SUBSTANCE DEPENDENCE AND ABUSE

Faith community leaders need an understanding and acceptance of how the cycles of substance abuse and dependence affect the person and the family. Acceptance and the capacity to provide the love and boundaries (sometimes called "tough love" or "detaching with love") are helpful for healing to occur.

Because the use of substances affects the person's brain, logical thought and judgment are affected. Trying to talk a person out of using or abusing substances is generally not helpful. When sober, the substance-abusing person will agree with the logic of abstaining and promise to do so, or they will deny that their use is a problem.

Denial is the cardinal sign of dependence or abuse. The pleasure center in the brain has been so stimulated that one loses the ability to discriminate how that substance-induced pleasure creates anything *but* pleasure. Consequences are not considered. It is as if for a time, one's view of the world has become multicolored, and without the substance, the world appears to be black and white. The person's impulse is to color in the black and white by using a substance—how could that be a problem to anyone?

The faith community can offer an antidote to the culture that promotes substance use as recreation and a necessity for socializing. Alcohol- and drug-free social events, especially for youth, are a gift from the faith community. They provide opportunities to learn and relearn how to find enjoyment in the company of other people without altering one's mental status chemically. For example, the congregation that sponsors group laughter sessions has discovered that participants who overcome their initial self-consciousness can allow their brain's pleasure center to take over with the whole-person experience of "holy laughter."

The Twelve Step community exists within many faith communities as a source of healing and strength for those who are affected by substance abuse and dependence. Churches can sponsor groups by providing space for meetings, publicizing the presence of the groups, and linking with them in ways that make it easy for anyone to refer someone to a group.

The teaching and encouragement to practice *spiritual disciplines* in a faith community is another gift. Many who have struggled with the strong pull to use a substance will say that the discipline of *meditation* is a strong support in overcoming the urge to use. There are several reasons why the practice of meditation can be of help. With its focus on breathing, meditation brings the person's attention to his or her body in a positive way. The breath of life brings in oxygen and releases toxins; the breath can be seen as spirit, bringing one into the presence of God through the Holy Spirit. God's power is greater than any human power to resist the pull toward a chemical high. Meditation forms a powerful community with the Spirit.

Other spiritual disciplines can be practiced alone or with others. *Prayer* reminds the person that God is there. It is a discipline, because it does not always come naturally and must be voluntarily engaged in. But with practice, prayer can come as easily as breathing. In fact, breathing can become a kind of prayer. A Christian can breathe in on the words "My peace I give you" and breathe out on "Thanks be to God." The repetition of such a breath prayer can bring a calm spirit apart from the use of chemical substances, which provide only a temporary refuge. Prayer in the company of others provides a strong WE orientation that can connect a person with the true invulnerability of God's presence—a presence to break the self-destructive human cycle of giving in to a substance for immediate fulfillment.

When a person has reached the point of substance dependence that spirals down destructively, the faith community has a role to play. Some families will decide to create an intervention designed to show the person the destructiveness of his or her substance abuse. In this intervention, faith community leaders and members who have a place in the person's life may be asked to participate. Such interventions should be professionally led and executed with careful planning and strategy. The desired outcome is immediate transportation to a rehab facility for the person, based on the use of a "tough love" reality approach—the ultimate love with boundaries. The spiritual discipline of submission allows the person to accept the boundaries.

While the person's body recovers from the brain and nervous system being bathed in alcohol or other substances, there is an opportunity to learn new coping skills. There can be an opening of the mind at this point.

Engaging in *study* to learn these skills is another spiritual discipline. Encouragement from other believers during this painful but necessary process can maintain the connection with the Body of Christ.

Education for all in the faith community can center on the reality of human vulnerability to substance use and abuse. This means that no one is exempt—including the pastor and church leaders. Facing the reality of one's own pattern of substance use and one's attitudes toward use is essential to being able to educate others and maintain a healing environment. Knowing signs of substance dependence and what to do with what is observed is empowering to people of all ages.

The Church will continue to be challenged to stay aware of the cultural pressures to use drugs as recreation. Marijuana is readily available for legal medical use, and further legalization has already occurred in some states and continues to be a possibility in others. Business opportunities are present for legal distribution and sale of marijuana to the public. As is true of advertising for alcohol consumption, the culture will likely incorporate such advertising to idealize drug use. Young people and adults need fact-based education to make wise choices, and in the context of our faith story, the faith community can offer support and an honest appraisal of scientific knowledge pertaining to marijuana use.

## TENDENCIES TOWARD EATING DISORDERS

There is also a spiritual dimension to eating disorders. This is another disorder in which the impulse (body) is turned in the wrong direction and out of control. Again, without the spirit in charge, there is an internal battle, aptly described as "binge-purge." As the impulse takes control, the mind responds with guilt and anxiety over gaining weight.

Dieting is usually done out of anger at a feeling of disgust over the looks of one's body. Dieting comes from the mind and is an attempt to take control because it does not trust the body. Dieting seldom works since it just worsens the relationship between mind and body.

Many people wage a lifelong struggle with weight and body shape. The struggle usually gets worse after countless diets and little permanent effect. The person lives with the guilt over weighing too much and not exercising enough and then goes on crash diets and crash exercise programs to express the mind's anger. Then the body rebels, and the person goes through a period of not caring as the resentment takes over. With the impulse in control, the person feels that she or he deserves some pleasure. The weight goes right back on, making the mind even more distrustful and angry.

> Sheila could remember feeling fat as early as junior high school. She would eat when she felt lonely. Her family moved every few years, and she never felt like she belonged. Food seemed to bring her back to the secure feelings of childhood, before her mother died.

She became obsessed over her weight in high school, going on endless diets to become more attractive, but she still felt fat. After being dumped by her boyfriend, food became her source of comfort. This only made the internal war worse. She hated her body.

She finally told someone else about her internal struggle over eating. As she talked to a counselor, she admitted that she was out of control. She lived alone and at times would sit in the middle of her room, surrounded by junk food, and eat to feel better. She would punish herself the next day by not eating at all.

After a few counseling sessions, Sheila began to realize that she was mourning for her mother, who had died during her senior year in high school. Her intense desire to eat comfort food was a desperate attempt to feel better inside—to fill emptiness.

Her counselor realized that she needed more help for her poor body image. When Sheila mentioned that she was interested in a new class at her church that combined exercise with meditative prayer, her counselor encouraged her to attend.

In this class, Sheila began to appreciate her body in a completely new way. The instructor continually emphasized that one's body is where God lives. Sheila left the first class thinking, Wow, my body is the temple of the Holy Spirit.

During the next months, a new feeling about her body began to emerge through her faith with prayer and exercise. For the first time she looked into a mirror and actually liked what she saw. The deep knowledge that Christ lived within her body gave her a special feeling about her physical appearance.

The impulse to eat when she was stressed or lonely was still there, but the internal war had diminished to the point that Sheila felt a healthy self-control. In fact, she developed the habit of hugging her body when she felt the desire to eat comfort food, thanking it for letting her know that she was lonely and needed more social contact in her life. Very seldom did she feel out of control with her eating.

## TENDENCIES TOWARD SEXUAL PROMISCUITY

Devin was immature when he got married. He was still emotionally tied to his mother; thus it was somewhat inevitable that he would form a mother-son relationship with any woman he married. After twelve years of marriage, he found himself attracted to a woman at work. Something inside did not care that he was destroying his marriage and home. The feeling he got from being with the other woman was worth it.

Once he began a sexual relationship with her, he split into two different people and lost self-control as the spirit broke down. His body became bonded with the other woman, while his mind was still committed to spouse and family. Internally, there could be no peace.

When Devin was at home, his consciousness was filled with the good feelings from physical contact with the other woman. Depression took over, making him moody and irritable, and he tried to pick a fight so he could justify continuation of the affair.

When Devin was with the other woman, guilt would seep back as his mind tried to regain control by sending him images of the family and the "right" thing to do. Devin would think of home and everything that would be lost, and anxiety took over.

The two forces inside were locked in serious battle. Devin was "stuck," changing moods so often that others wondered who this person was whom they thought they once knew.

Affairs are normally resentment-based. A good barometer of the state of the marital spirit is the level of extramarital attraction and fantasy. When the spirit of the marriage breaks down, others become more attractive. As resentment builds up, the person becomes vulnerable to an affair. Finally, the sexual impulse gets out of control. The person can now justify the act on the basis of "deserving" it.

Much sexual acting out is rooted in immaturity. A male who has not matured often adopts a strategy to please his wife and often is attracted to a woman who will tend to control things. Often he is "stuck" in the preadolescent stage of hiding feelings and his wife is "stuck" in the 7–10-year-old age group that feels the compulsion to control things.

This produces a parent-child relationship that builds resentment. The man becomes resentful of being controlled, and the woman becomes resentful over having to take charge and do everything.

## FAITH COMMUNITY RESPONSE TO SEXUAL PROMISCUITY

The faith community has a role to play in the prevention of sexual acting out. Since the Church is in the relationship business, it can offer continuous marriage-building opportunities for couples. Learning to process emotions that lead to resentment when unexpressed is a gift to be offered by a mature, Christ-centered community. Couples at all stages of marriage can benefit from mentoring with older couples with healthy marital relationships that have stood the test of time and are Christ centered. Support groups and social groups can normalize differences and conflict as a real part of marriage and can offer models of conflict management to build closeness in couples.

When providing premarital and relationship counseling, pastors can pay attention to patterns of relating that are immature. They can educate couples on ways to examine and grow through such patterns of relating.

Couples prayer groups or couple prayer partners can open hearts of couples to practice prayer together. Spouses can pray for each other and for the relationship in each other's presence. The couple can establish a pattern of taking turns or otherwise sharing in the pattern of praying together.

Pastors can encourage couples to have conversations about their individual and joint prayer lives—what they like and appreciate and areas where they desire growth. Couples can ask for what they need in their shared prayer life. Couples can experiment and practice other spiritual disciplines together as well as prayer. They can try out different forms of prayer as a couple.

> Devin was in counseling for his sexual struggle. He and his wife, Marsha, were putting their marriage back together. Devin knew he needed help to break his sexual addiction to other women. He promised himself that he would tell his wife every time he started thinking about other women.
>
> They also met with their pastor and wanted to learn how to pray together to strengthen their commitment to each other. Their pastor suggested that they do a prayer walk each day. In the area

behind their church, some members had developed an outdoor prayer walk—a labyrinth.

This labyrinth was based on an ancient Christian form of prayer that was built into the floor of some cathedrals. It was designed to simulate the pilgrims' journey to the Holy Land, so that those who could not make an actual journey might experience the rhythm of walking while praying. The walkers would reach a point in the center of the labyrinth where they might pause, meditate on God's presence with them, and thank God for that presence. They would then resume their journey out of the labyrinth, praying along the way, listening for what God would say to them through this walk.

This was a new experience for Devin and Marsha, and they felt some resistance to beginning it. What if the other person was not engaged? Would it feel awkward? But they moved beyond their doubts, in faith that God would bless their walk together.

Devin and Marsha walked on the labyrinth prayer walk every day after work for a month, each at his or her own pace. When they reached the center, they joined hands and said a prayer of thanksgiving for their relationship and asked for God's blessing on a conflict they were experiencing. They asked God to open their hearts to each other and give them courage to be honest.

On the way out of the labyrinth, each prayed for the understanding of their partner and for honesty with self. They prayed that God would show what needed healing in their half of the marriage relationship. Through this discipline, Devin felt more control over his sexual immaturity. For the first time, he became aware of how deeply Marsha was hurt by his sexual behavior. He had never thought of that before. When he shared this with Marsha several months after they began their daily prayer together, they both knew that their marriage was on a healthy path of growth.

The prayer walk offered a combination of spiritual disciplines to Devin and Marsha: *submission* to a new way of *praying* together, *solitude* as they walked at their own pace, *confession* together when they reached the center and individually as they walked out. Each sought *guidance* as well.

When a relationship has shifted to the point of breakdown, as with an affair, individual prayer can be a centering discipline through the waves of anger, grief, shame, and uncertainty. Prayer that allows venting of emotions as well as listening for guidance can offer healing over time, along with therapeutic actions to rebuild the relationship. Journaling prayer can help those facing relationship decisions that can have far-reaching effects. Journaling prayer offers reflective time and an opening to God's gift of healing.

# Tendencies toward Behavioral Problems in Children

It is sad to see a child who is having a difficult time with life. Childhood is a time to develop healthy spiritual DNA with a positive outlook on life and healthy behavioral habits. But for so many children, life is a struggle.

The breakdown of the family unit contributes to childhood behavior issues. Without a loving, stable family, children learn to cope with often-dysfunctional strategies that carry on later in life.

Parenting styles in our current culture focus on giving the child every possible advantage so that they may be successful. This evolutionary-based logic actually is a good one if a person's happiness comes from winning or coming out on top. Parenting thus revolves around giving children choices and skills to function well in all situations. It is critical that the children are able to make their own choices and adapt to their environments to survive well.

Today's children are taught to stand up for themselves and for their rights. Modeling for children in countless cartoons and TV shows demonstrates how to stand up for self and win, even though you may damage a relationship. In many shows, disrespect is even modeled.

The value of Christianity in raising children comes from the basic belief that people are God-breathed, not naturally selected. One's identity is thus not based on *doing* things (accomplishments), but is a *being* concept. Identity is a gift of God, and the new self has nothing to prove. In this context, parenting can focus on helping children think of the good of the whole (WE), learn respect, care for others, and build healthy relationships.

## TENDENCIES TOWARD CONDUCT DISORDERS

When disrespect is modeled in family conflict, young people can easily develop habits of being defiant and oppositional. When there are repeated and persistent violations of rules, of the rights of others, and of social norms, the person has a *conduct disorder*. Often this takes the form of aggressive behavior and damage to property.

Much of the serious bullying and intimidating behavior fits into this category. The young person will initiate fights and can be physically cruel to both people and animals. Lying and other forms of dishonesty are often a part of this disorder, as are truancy from school and various forms of stealing.

The incidence of conduct disorder has increased in the past twenty years, especially among males, and is approaching 10 percent of the population. It tends to run in families and is associated with parental neglect, harsh discipline, abuse, alcoholism, and other family problems.

> Clay was referred for counseling by the school system for his conduct problems. The counselor met with Clay and his parents to begin training them in problem-solving approaches. At the first session, the counselor learned that the family was part of a local congregation, and the counselor received permission to meet with the pastor and staff to see if they could also help.
>
> The outcome of the meeting was helpful for all. The family life minister organized a series of parenting classes that he would co-teach with the counselor. Several other families in the congregation immediately showed an interest.
>
> After the eight class sessions, many members of the group decided to continue to meet to be mutually supportive of one another in the difficult task of parenting. As a result of the class and support group, the situation at Clay's house improved, and much of his defiant behavior diminished.

The discipline of *study* took place together with this group of parents who cared about their children's mental health. Parents willing to study and learn parenting skills in a Christian setting can *celebrate* together the progress and growth they are experiencing as families. *Prayers* offered for one another during group sessions and between meetings strengthened each family.

## TENDENCIES TOWARD AUTISTIC PROBLEMS

There is an apparent genetic factor in autism. One of the abnormalities in brain chemistry is higher serotonin levels, which may contribute to difficulty in organizing too many environmental stimuli. Autistic children find interaction with others distressing and thus prefer to pull back away from social stimulation. Any response will isolate one part of the environment in what is called *stimulus over-selectivity*.

Autistic children gradually develop an inner world of idiosyncratic speech and repetitive language that does not match the social or family environment. There will be a preoccupation with a restricted area of interest that is abnormal in its intensity. Often there will be distinctive rituals or repetitive movements.

> Wayne never wanted to be held as a child and, by age 3, preferred to be alone, seldom engaging in eye contact or spontaneous play with others. In fact, he seemed somewhat unaware of his surroundings. He would sit and rock for hours, amusing himself with a sunbeam coming through the window.
>
> As he grew older, Wayne was put on one of the newer antipsychotic drugs with some good effect. He seemed to be more open to interaction and would not engage in his repetitive behavior as much.
>
> His therapist wanted to do some intensive behavioral treatment that involved getting the parents to be the therapists in the natural environment of their home. When the parents wondered if their involvement in church could also be a part of the treatment, the therapist was very interested. She knew that the parents needed a lot of support to increase Wayne's communication and social interaction.
>
> The therapist met with the pastor, Sunday School teacher, youth director, and Wayne's parents, describing in detail the behavior-modification program that focused on getting Wayne to develop language usage and social skills. His parents were to use this program at home, but the church could also be a part of Wayne's training.

The next week, the Sunday School lesson was on the story of Jesus wanting the little children to come to Him. Wayne was sitting in his usual place, away from the others, rocking slightly and focusing on his fingernails. For the first time, the teacher focused on Wayne, moving closer to him and smiling as she said, "Wayne, did you hear that Jesus loves children?" Wayne ignored her and went on rocking. "Jesus wants you to talk to Him right now," the teacher said kindly. "Why don't you say, 'I love you, Jesus'?" After several gentle prompts, Wayne actually spoke in class for the first time.

Wayne was learning the beginning steps of how to pray. He talked to Jesus for the first time with kind encouragement from his Sunday School teacher. She used the discipline of *guidance* as she gently invited Wayne to speak to Jesus out loud. *Celebration* of each small step in communicating and interacting socially, giving thanks to God, would likely take place with the teacher, Wayne's parents, and with Wayne. God's Spirit moves in children with autism, just as in all children.

## TENDENCIES TOWARD ATTENTION DEFICIT AND HYPERACTIVITY

A common childhood tendency is attention deficit, sometimes coupled with hyperactivity. It is the leading source of referrals to some form of mental health care. Sometimes the diagnosis does not include hyperactivity, but there are always problems with the child's ability to focus attention for any length of time.

Many of the children who appear to have problems focusing on one thing are actually fairly normal but have the gift of noticing many things at once. These can be called *painters*, who communicate by giving lots of details, as contrasted with *pointers*, who think things through and start with the point.[1] Pointer children have no problem focusing on one thing.

When the child's inability to focus becomes a serious problem at school or within the family, then help is needed. Most are helped by stimulant medication. They seem to be able to focus better, listen to instruction, and in general, function better in following through. However, this seems to be a short-term benefit and can also stunt the growth of the child if used long term. The long-term use of stimulant medication for children is controversial and should be monitored closely.

The best approach is to work with the child using psychosocial interventions to see if that helps, before putting the child on medication. This means looking more carefully at the child's sleep patterns, use of asthma medication (which can stimulate hyperactivity), and parenting techniques that allow the child to ignore things.

Matthew was a difficult child at church. He was in constant motion, disrupting his class and generally not paying attention. The pastor met with his parents to see what could be done to help the situation.

Matthew's parents were not very receptive at first, blaming others who picked on their child and got him in trouble. They threatened to leave the church and find another one that would be more sensitive to their child.

The pastor persisted, calling another meeting and bringing Matthew's teacher in with one of the elders who also worked with troubled children at social services. After a warm prayer, the elder said, "We know how much you love your child, and we want to be on your side to watch Matthew grow up." His parents visibly warmed up when it was obvious that they were not going to be blamed for Matthew's disruptive behavior.

Together they developed a plan to handle any situation that Matthew would be involved in at church. They would work together so that when Matthew started to be disruptive, someone would pull him aside in a kind way, kneel down in front of him so that he looked at him or her, and explain that this type of behavior "is not what we do here."

After a few months and dozens of interventions, Matthew's behavior was different enough to be noticed. He was still disruptive at times and often was not paying attention, but he was no longer seen as the problem child at church.

Matthew's teachers and parents began to understand how difficult it was for him to focus, especially when faced with excessive stimulation, such as many choices, competing activities going on at the same time, or noisy surroundings. They paid attention to the environment, which could be over-stimulating, and made efforts to simplify the surroundings when possible. The adults began to accept the discipline of *simplicity* and to focus on seeking the kingdom of God above all else, clearing away some of the clutter of excessive stimulation in the children's learning environment.

The adults also helped Matthew practice solitude as a way of quieting the clamor of a stimulating environment. He could go to a quiet space in the classroom at church to concentrate without feeling different or bad. Quiet spaces became valued places for adults or children to retreat for a time to pray, think, or just relax. Even young children can practice centering prayer, paying attention to their breath, and meditatively repeating words from Scripture or simple prayerful words such as "Jesus loves me."

## Tendencies toward Eating Disorders

Eating disorders and obesity have become increasingly common in the younger generation of this culture. The prevalence of high-fructose drinks and high-calorie fast foods coupled with sedentary lifestyles has produced an alarming number of overweight children.

Especially for young girls, such eating styles pose a serious dilemma. Countless images of the perfect, almost anorexic female body show an ideal that most cannot attain. For many, an obsession over eating, weight, and body image is developed at an early age. In preadolescence, so many are constantly comparing their bodies to the others girls, yet they have a pattern of fixing their mood by comfort food.

### Tendencies toward Anorexia

Even though a low percentage of adolescent girls are actually diagnosed with anorexia, many more have some of its symptoms. The central feature of this disorder is a constant concern about weight and body image. Often there is a perception of being fat as they look in the mirror, even though their weight is below average. Food becomes a preoccupation as the anorexic is constantly on a diet, sometimes using pills to suppress appetite or as a laxative.

To some degree, it seems that serious anorexia is a way of coping with developing sexuality. In enmeshed family situations, this keeps the girl from developing sexually and thus having to break away from her parents. It is also a way to assert independence by having something she can control.

This is a difficult disorder to treat because the anorexic does not seem to care about losing more weight, even though close to death. The person's spirit seems to detach, leaving a strong "I don't care" feeling about the future. The person may have a lot of insight into the situation but does not seem to want to stop the starvation ritual. This is similar to other adolescent disorders where the natural "I don't care" attitude is used in the wrong way. Instead of leading to establishing independence, the feelings are "stuck" in a nonproductive, controlling way.

The power of this detachment and control is so great and so persistent that some of those diagnosed with anorexia end up dying from starvation. Medications, such as antidepressants that are widely prescribed for this disorder, have not shown much effectiveness. There has been recent success in working with parents to coach them on how to gain control over the adolescent's eating behavior. Healthy eating is associated with giving the adolescent more privileges and increasing autonomy.

In general, a faith community can be of help in teaching and modeling the new self as the "temple of the Holy Spirit" (1 Corinthians 6:19). One's body is seen as a gift of God. It becomes a privilege to care for the body. This message can be very helpful to counter the cultural obsession with external beauty that brings about fixation on weight.

Modeling these healthy attitudes toward the body may have a preventive effect. For the young person who suffers with distorted body image, the spiritual discipline of fasting should be taught in a broader context than just fasting from food, which could possibly exacerbate anorexia. Fasting from the habitual use of negative terms to describe one's body might be more beneficial.

A discipline of *guidance* in regard to teaching and learning healthy attitudes toward sexuality can have a powerful protective factor for youth in a faith community. Families with enmeshed dynamics that contribute to adolescents' attempts to control eating can benefit from guidance as well as study to learn how their family contributes to the disorder. In any case, professional referral is very important with anorexia tendencies.

## TENDENCIES TOWARD BULIMIA

This disorder is a little more common than anorexia, with close to 3 percent of females receiving this diagnosis. A much higher percentage of adolescent females engage in binge eating, often ingesting up to two thousand calories in private. There is an "out of control" feeling when the eating is taking place, as if another force takes over, desperate to fix one's mood. Then, after the person is uncomfortably full, most will purge to keep from gaining weight. Laxatives are also used.

The cause of bulimia is similar to that of anorexia. Cultural ideals of thinness are coupled with the cultural value of comfort foods.

This disorder is more treatable than anorexia. Antidepressant medications seem to help the person's mood so that fixing it with food is not as compelling. The best therapy is cognitive-behavioral that focuses on the self-talk and behavioral cues associated with binging.

> Kelley had a secret. She had been doing it for years. When she went away to college, it got worse. She lived alone in her apartment. Several times a week, she would get a "funny" feeling, and she knew what would happen next. She was out of control as she drove to the store, bought a dozen donuts, brownie mix, and a tub of ice cream. She would eat half the donuts on the way home, eat some of the brownie mix as she prepared it, then proceed to eat the rest of the donuts, all of the brownies, and most of the ice cream. Then she would purge.

She finally sought help from a Christian counselor. It was a big step for her to open up this intensely private part of her life. She felt better just talking about it.

As she described how she felt out of control when eating, then so guilty afterward as she was purging, the counselor realized that her internal conflict was a major part of her problem. Her mind and her body were at war (Romans 7:23). Her body would take control, and she would eat. Then her mind would take control and make her feel guilty, so she would purge.

After the session, Kelley's homework was simple. She was to keep in mind constantly that Christ lived in her heart and that she was the new self. She was to keep close to Christ in prayer during the next week.

Then when she felt that "funny" feeling and had the incredibly strong urge to binge, she had specific instructions: (1) Stop, keep yourself from reaching for your car keys, and sit down. (2) Pray and put your hands over your heart, feeling the warmth and presence of Christ. (3) Take a deep breath and remember that you are a child of God and a temple of the Holy Spirit. (4) Your hands are now Christ's hands, so hug your body and thank it for its impulse; then say to your body, "I know you are lonely and want to feel better, but we are not going to do it this way anymore."

But she also had other, very specific instructions. When she did lose control and binge and she heard her mind making her feel guilty and ashamed, she was to do the following: (1) Stop that guilt-inducing thought. (2) Pray and put your hands over your heart, feeling the warmth and presence of Christ. (3) Take a deep breath and remember that you are a child of God and a temple of the Holy Spirit. (4) Your hands are now Christ's hands, so hug your mind say, "I know you are trying to keep me from doing this again, but Christ and I are now in charge, so thanks for the information. You can go play now."

## SPIRITUAL DISCIPLINE TO HELP THE INTERNAL STRUGGLE

The person in recovery from bulimia is struggling to control impulses that lead to binging-purging for immediate fulfillment. Since the basic impulse has a healthy base in the yearnings of the soul, the recovering person is learning to tolerate the intensity of the yearning without quelling it with food. At this point, spiritual food is needed to deal with the stress, alter the mood, and move the person to a more-spiritual depth—keeping the mind and body in balance.

Spiritual disciplines that honor the mind and the body can be practiced. Any of the disciplines can be focused in such a way. For example, body *prayer* encompasses movement—such as dance, stretching, or even holding hands.

Experiencing the presence of God while maintaining body awareness can be a way to affirm one's body as a gift of God. As the whole person is engaged in interacting with God, neither mind nor body dominates the other.

# Developmentally Based Tendencies toward Poor Reality Organization

With faulty genetic inheritance or a confusing environmental background, a child's spirit has difficulty in organizing reality. Up to 10 percent of the population exhibits symptoms that fall into this category. Brain disorders that are either genetic or caused by damage after conception can make it difficult for the person to process information in a normal fashion. Fetal alcohol syndrome and its effect on the developing nervous system is an example of such damage.

Another cause for these disorders is the lack of good social feedback that helps a person develop a shared understanding of reality with others. Children are forced to rely on their own inner world if their environment is not trustworthy. Early in life, there can be disconnection from social interaction, leading to an increasing fantasy world and private communication styles.

## DISSOCIATIVE TENDENCIES (AGES 0–3)

Intense anxiety caused by an unstable, confusing environment at an early age can cause a child to dissociate (split off) certain experiences from the core sense of self. This can be a result of processing problems of the child's brain (faulty brain chemistry) or can result from an exceptionally sensitive child who feels unprotected. Of course, the family environment can also be dysfunctional and the child struggles to survive and understand mixed messages that are given. Studies of multiple personality disorders find that most carried a history of sexual abuse.

The memory started to come back with intense anxiety, so Jina sought professional help. First, she had flashes of a door opening and light coming in. As the repressed memory finally surfaced, Jina saw her father on her bed, fondling her. "Where are you?" the counselor asked.

"I am in that little crack in the ceiling," Jina answered.

At the young age of three, Jina found a way to deal with the horrible, confusing experience with her father. She focused on an external visual place and dissociated from her body and the feelings she was having. This detachment of her spirit was ingenious since it allowed her to repress the memory and live her childhood as if this did not happen.

Her counselor knew that when the memory came back, Jina would start reconnecting with this dissociated experience and would actually start feeling all of the weird things that had happened then. She would regress back to age 3, and her personality would show signs of disintegration. He knew that she would need a healthy support system that she would not get at home since she was divorced and lived alone. The counselor was careful that clear boundaries of "no hugging" were in place throughout his work with her.

With Jina's permission, the counselor met with her pastor and family life director. He asked if the small-group Bible study she was in would be willing to help her as she went through this process. The counselor then met with the Bible study group with Jina present and talked through the struggle Jina would be going through, emphasizing that she would need support to work through her abuse. He explained that she would experience the abuse and actually feel like a child again and would just need a safe environment that she could not manipulate. He also gave his phone number, cautioning that if she became unable to regain self-control, then he should be contacted so he could determine whether to have her hospitalized.

The group was her lifeline. She could share her struggle with them. During Bible study group sessions, she gradually could begin to show real emotion as she reconnected with some of the memories surfacing as the group studied about love and friendship. At one point, as she was shaking visibly and whimpering like a child, they gathered around her, touched her gently, and prayed.

"This was an astounding breakthrough," Jina reported to her counselor. "I felt like I was a little girl again, but surrounded by Christ's love and safety. For the first time, I felt anger toward my father."

To some degree, this process of detachment is similar to the Post-Traumatic Stress Disorder (PTSD), where the individual escapes the abusive situation by dissociating. The images and emotional distress caused by the disorder are like a shattered mirror with fragments of the memories coming back in dreams and in unsettling images or feelings when awake. Being able to reexperience the situation in a safe environment allows the reattachment of the spirit to the memories left behind. It's like the person is able to come back into his or her body and have more normal feelings. In the context of a healthy faith community, this is a re-parenting process that is slow, but of definite value in bringing the person to greater mental and emotional health. The help of a trained, faith-sensitive professional is critical when dealing with such deep disorders.

## Odd Behavior Tendencies (Ages 4–7)

There are many factors that result in children of this age group getting "stuck" in a private reality that increasingly does not match the normal perception and behavior of the preschool child. There may be a genetic vulnerability since this disorder tends to run in families, especially those that have some history of schizophrenia. There is also a personality predisposition that makes social interaction somewhat anxiety producing and distasteful. An abusive situation or an unstable family environment that does not allow for safe, loving interaction patterns may be additional issues.

Adults who are "stuck" in this stage are uncomfortable with social interaction that is more than a quick, formal greeting. If forced into a social situation, the person will stay alone and find a way to leave the situation as soon as possible. Though somewhat eccentric and unusual, such a person can be helped by a safe, stable environment with people who understand the difficulty this person has with social contact.

As a child goes through increasing isolation during this stage (ages 4–7), there is the development of a private world that is shared with no one. Reactions to normal social situations become increasingly inappropriate. The child prefers this private reality to social interaction.

> Daren was always an unusual child. He did not want to be touched when he was very young and did not have the normal social reaction to members of his family. He would make odd sounds and often seem oblivious to others. As he approached school age, he developed an imaginary friend. He would spend hours in his room, playing with his collection of cars, talking to his "friend," using a language that no one else could understand.

> He would sit by himself in his Sunday School class, not looking at anyone and obviously in his own world. Others in his class would avoid him, and he seemed fine with that. He never spoke out, even when the teacher asked him to respond.

> One of the grandparents of the congregation took an interest in Daren. He found that Daren loved cars, and he had a collection of old cars. He would drive different cars to church and take Daren outside to show him the car, opening up the hood and letting Daren start the car. Gradually, over several months, Daren started talking hesitantly to his "grandparent." He finally let someone into his world.

> Daren was still an unusual child, but the interest and love that this "grandparent" showed him brought him out more into the social environment. A breakthrough seemed to occur when another child started coming out to see the old cars with Daren. As these two started sharing their mutual interest, Daren had his first friend.

> The spiritual practice of *worship* can offer a person like Daren, who prefers isolation to social interaction, an opportunity to be a part of a community. He may choose to sit in the back row or on the edge of the group of worshipers for his own comfort. Participating in the liturgy and Eucharist provides a possible link to others in the Body of Christ without requiring painful social interaction.

At times, the sharing of peace could be scary and unwanted by Daren, not knowing how to respond to such open gestures. While Daren may not be comfortable in the ritual of sharing peace during a service, he can perhaps receive a smile or a nod with a greeting of "Peace be with you." Accepting Daren's need for personal space conveys love and respect, while inviting him into small steps out of his comfort zone. Members are communicating nonverbally to Daren, "We love you, and we want you to be a part of us. We understand that you need space to feel safe, and that is okay."

## INDIFFERENT TENDENCIES (AGES 7–10)

Children in this age category are developing their internal value system by identifying with the same-sex parent. If the identification process does not work, children will not form proper family identity, but will appear to be cold and aloof, not part of the family. The reasons for this are similar to the previous two categories, split between genetic predisposition and environmental dysfunction.

The child increasingly builds his or her private world and almost completely shuts out others. Detachment and flattened affect make it difficult to connect with such a child. Nothing seems to matter. The child does not want to be bothered. He or she has developed an increasingly complex private world that no one can enter.

Olson was a loner. He came to church because his family had always been members. He felt safe there. He generally talked to no one, and people found him detached and cold when they tried to speak to him. Over the years, he was left alone. That was fine with him.

He was a smart man and held down a good job working with computers. This allowed him to work alone, communicating only through electronic media. He was efficient and productive.

He lost his job when his company filed for bankruptcy. He withdrew even more and stopped coming to church. The pastor learned about his situation and talked with Charles, a Stephen Minister and a computer expert, about reaching out to Olson. He let Olson know that Charles would be contacting him.

Olson was not interested. He did not like the thought of having to talk to anyone. Charles persisted in a soft way. He wanted to know Olson's skills so he could help him find another job. He volunteered to show him some new skills so he would be more marketable. He prayed for him daily.

After months of being rebuffed, Charles still continued to contact Olson, not put off by his coldness. He felt led by Christ's Spirit to minister to this man. He knew there was a real person inside, but his disorder made it difficult for Olson to respond. Charles also knew that Olson needed his help.

"Thanks for the new lead on a job." For the first time, Olson actually called Charles with a hint of warmth and appreciation. "I have an interview tomorrow, and I wanted to thank you for being my friend."

Though seemingly minor, it was a huge breakthrough for Olson. He actually valued a friendship. He started coming back to church. He was still somewhat detached and cold, but he volunteered when the church needed to put in a new computer system. The change, though small, was evident.

Olson was able in his own way to *celebrate* having a friend by showing gratitude to Charles for his help. His gratitude drew him to offer *service* to the church by using his skill to help out. This was spiritual growth as well as emotional growth for Olson.

## DISTRUSTFUL TENDENCIES (AGES 11–14)

As a child gets older, lack of social interaction allows for the development of a private world that gets increasingly out of touch with shared reality. With the added touch of an oppositional attitude beginning to form with preadolescence, the person gets increasingly suspicious of others. The smallest incident can be construed as a major affront and can be woven into a fabric of distrust and paranoia toward that person. Gradually, the person becomes convinced that others are trying to control or harm him or her. Such delusions are usually not dangerous, but they push the person deeper into a private world.

This is an age when the child develops a private fantasy world. Fantasy games such as Dungeons and Dragons are popular. Books and movies that depict fantasy characters, like Harry Potter, are interesting.

Dawson did nothing but play with his elaborate soldier display. He was fourteen and had become increasingly isolated from his peers, choosing to spend his afternoons and evenings in the basement. His war games became increasingly real to him. He would spend all of his free time planning strategy; at school, he would often lapse into his internal world, eyes vacant as he planned another attack.

The best help for Dawson came from his tennis coach. Dawson was a good player. He always wanted to play singles and stayed by himself much of the time. His coach was also a youth leader at his church. He recognized the danger of Dawson's lack of interpersonal contact, so he started showing an interest in his collection of soldiers. It took months of patient interest, sometimes only a two-sentence exchange between them, but finally Dawson invited his coach to his sacred basement to see his elaborate display. The coach praised his careful work and wanted to know more about his strategies.

Almost a year later, Dawson had enough trust in his coach to let him bring a few kids from his youth group along with him. They let Dawson teach them how to develop good strategies. It was very slow, but gradually Dawson started to enjoy playing with others. He was still a loner in many ways, but for the first time in his adolescent life, he had friends that he was comfortable with. Almost two years after the coach first took an interest in him, he came to his first youth group meeting.

Adults who are "stuck" in this stage become increasingly distrustful of others and often build elaborate private realities that they actually believe to be true. Often the reality includes immature fantasies of grandeur, of being so important that others are out to harm. The person becomes dangerous as this belief system becomes rigid and the person becomes fascinated with guns or other weapons for protection.

Rango liked his name. It sounded powerful and seemed to protect him. He was a loner and lived in a house that was shut up all the time. As he became increasingly suspicious of his neighbors, he began to spy on them all the time. He became convinced that they were using some type of invisible ray to play with his mind. He put up a lead barrier and sat behind it much of the time so the rays would not penetrate his brain.

It is very difficult to change such a powerful belief system. Rango really, really believed that his neighbors were trying to harm him. If anyone tried to tell him different, he would automatically assume that they were part of the plot. He would work them into his delusional system.

Rango had been married for a short time and divorced when he was convinced his wife was trying to poison him. He was a life-long member of his church and would attend intermittently. He had a reputation for causing disruption, accusing members of trying to harm him. When he attended Bible class, he would use his angry voice and claim that the pastor was trying to poison everyone's minds by the false doctrine he was teaching.

The pastor sat down with several of his mature Christian men. Together they decided to deliberately show Rango that God loved him. They also would show a loving firmness in address-ing his strange beliefs about minds being poisoned.

One of the men, Jessie, started going to visit Rango. He approached him with respect and grew to realize how brilliant the man was. He enjoyed listening to his deep knowledge of the Bible. But when Rango would launch into his paranoid litany, Jessie would stop him kindly, let him know that his perception was not accurate, and then ask him for more detail in a Bible topic they were discussing.

While he was growing up, Rango had been beaten by his father. He finally shared this one day with Jessie. With tears in his eyes, Jessie said a prayer for healing. This touched Rango.

He was still often oppositional; with a loud voice, he would give his opinion. But the love and acceptance, plus the firmness that Jessie showed him, had a real effect on Rango. It was like he was re-parented by his heavenly Father and did not have to spend all his energy protecting himself.

When Rango shared that he had been abused, his opening of a shamed part of himself was like a *confession* to a trustworthy Christian friend. Rango experienced the power of love as Jessie *prayed* for him. Jessie's firmness was a form of *guidance* for Rango. These spiritual practices had a healing quality and conveyed to Rango, through his relationship with Jessie, that a loving God was present for him. In time, he may notice his energy flowing outward with a growing feeling of being safe.

## Irresponsible, Destructive Tendencies (Ages 15–18)

All of the disorders listed in this chapter utilize the incredible capacity of the human spirit to detach from reality in order to keep the person safe. If this detachment becomes severe and mixes with the adolescent rebellion attitude, tendencies toward *antisocial disorder* are the result.

What is frightening about these irresponsible, destructive tendencies is that such people can get so detached and angry that they are capable of harming others without remorse. Such people can become very manipulative, violating the rights of others without showing empathy for those who are hurt. There can be a surface charm to get others on their side, but the relationships will be exploited for their own benefit.

Franklin always won. He was brilliant. A new pastor was called to his congregation. In their very first meeting, the pastor opposed his ideas for change in congregational leadership. The pastor wanted to keep things the same, but Franklin wanted to form a more efficient organization that matched his successful work as a CEO of his company.

He did not take this opposition well and vowed he would take the pastor down. He met privately with council members, cleverly calling into question the pastor's leadership. He began circulating rumors about the pastor's drinking habits and his association with his secretary.

The president of the congregation saw what was happening. He met with the pastor and several of the long-standing, spiritually healthy leaders. Starting with prayer, he suggested they handle the situation as a W$_E$. They met with an objective counseling consultant for input and support as they made a plan.

They then met with Franklin and, in a disarmingly honest way, confronted what he was doing. Franklin denied everything and stormed out of the meeting.

The attitude of the group was "We want to continue to work with Franklin and one another in a Christlike way."

At the next council meeting, the president began with prayer. Then, with Franklin present, he laid the situation out on the table with genuine concern and disarming honesty. Franklin started to deny his role in disrupting the congregation, but others in the council spoke up: "We love your passion for leadership in the church, Franklin, but for the good of our congregation, we will not allow conversation behind people's backs."

With that, Franklin stormed out of the meeting, threatening to quit the church. Several days later, a few of the council members made a personal visit to Franklin. "We are sad that you are reacting this way," they began. "We value your contribution to our church."

With that, Franklin started tearing down the pastor again, trying to manipulate the situation. The members stopped him: "If you have anything to say about our pastor, you will say it to his face. This is how we believe God wants us to do things as a Christian congregation."

Franklin was difficult to work with. Because of the detachment, lack of empathy, and manipulative ability, there is little success in therapy for those with antisocial tendencies. In Franklin's case, the WE orientation of the congregation was able to establish good boundaries yet continue to reach out to him. He never did stop trying to degrade the pastor, but he did come back to worship on occasion.

The leaders practiced the discipline of *guidance* as they established good boundaries with Franklin. They had practiced the discipline of *study* by consulting with a mental health professional to learn how to set and maintain clear boundaries. With a prayerful practice of *service*, they continued to reach out to Franklin. The leaders practiced *submission*, submitting to God their need to intervene in Franklin's relationship with God. With God's guidance, they kept their focus on healthy behavior on their side of their relationships with Franklin.

# Tendencies toward Dementia and Psychotic Disorders

## CHAPTER 18

## Dementia Related to Alzheimer's

Alzheimer's disease (AD) is a progressive brain disease that occurs with increasing frequency as a person ages. One in three seniors dies with AD or another dementia. Currently, approximately five million Americans suffer from AD. As the aging population continues to grow, this number could increase by 40 percent by 2025.[1]

The onset of this disease is gradual, and the progression is slow. Three stages of Alzheimer's disease occur: Stage 1—Mild; Stage 2—Moderate; and Stage 3—Severe.

In the mild stage, the person may exhibit the following symptoms or behaviors:

- Forgets recent events, names of people, or things
- Begins to repeat the same thing over and over
- Forgets how to do simple tasks
- Gets lost easily, even in familiar places
- Is unusually irritable or quiet
- Has difficulty making decisions

In the moderate stage, the person may exhibit the following symptoms or behaviors:

- Paces back and forth or wander from home
- Has trouble recognizing family and friends
- Neglects bathing and grooming
- Has problems speaking and understanding
- Becomes anxious, agitated, or suspicious
- Has difficulty reading or writing

In the severe stage, the person may not be able to do the following:

- Speak or understand words
- Use muscles to walk or swallow
- Control bladder and bowel functions
- Recognize family or surroundings

It is important to recognize symptoms early and obtain an accurate diagnosis so that persons will have a greater chance to benefit from treatments and have more time with their families to plan for the future. While there is no cure for AD, treatment in the mild and moderate stages can help to manage cognitive losses and behavioral changes and may allow persons to sustain a higher level of memory and function.

While AD is the most common cause of dementia, other conditions that are treatable can also cause dementia. Medication-induced dementia is a common reason for cognitive impairment in older adults. The way that drugs are taken—how much; how often; with what other substances, such as alcohol, over-the-counter drugs, vitamins, supplements, and herbal preparations; and for what length of time—can provide clues as to whether a person's memory impairment may be drug related. Only a physician or pharmacologist can make this determination.

In an effort to educate members of the congregation about the potentially harmful effects of medication interactions, Susan, the Faith Community Nurse at St. Timothy Church, organized a health promotion event as part of the congregational health ministry. This event, "The Brown Bag Challenge," invited members and caregivers to bring a brown bag that contained all medications and over-the-counter remedies currently being used by each individual. The event was staffed by the nurse, volunteers, and Dr. Garfield, who was a community pharmacologist with special training in geriatric pharmacology and had a passion for educating older adults on the potential effects of medication interactions. After a group presentation on the subject, individuals met with Dr. Garfield. He inspected the brown bag contents and gave feedback to each person on any potential problems with medications and other substances brought in. As a result, several people were referred back to their doctors with written information from Dr. Garfield.

In reviewing the evaluations of the program, Susan learned that a majority of the participants saw the event as highly worthwhile. Several who were referred back to their prescribing medical professional expressed appreciation for the opportunity to learn how the combinations of medicines and the level of their compliance could actually be harmful instead of helpful. One family member later contacted Susan and expressed relief that her loved one did not have dementia as she had feared, but instead was taking medications inappropriately and had improved significantly as a result of the intervention. Such a carefully planned and delivered health promotion event is an example of a health ministry working effectively and the healing potential inherent in paying attention to the whole person—body, mind, and spirit.

In addition to medication interactions, other conditions that can cause dementia include strokes and alcohol addiction. In addition, vitamin deficiency, thyroid disease, and AIDS-related dementia can all cause symptoms similar to those of AD. These conditions can be differentiated from AD by medical evaluation.

There are various points during the progression of AD when spiritual and emotional support is needed. At the time of diagnosis, families and patients can feel devastated, isolated, and hopeless. They will be learning what the diagnosis means and what to expect as the disease progresses. Family members may feel anger, depression, and frustration. Medical providers guide families to a local chapter of the Alzheimer's Association for educational materials, support, and advice for planning for the future.[2] Family members and patients may be offered a Stephen Minister or another caring relationship in the faith community for ongoing support.

Today, more than half of people diagnosed with AD are cared for by families in the home. A person with AD is likely to live for eight to ten years from the time of onset of symptoms. That adds up to a lot of caregiving years. With an increasing senior population in faith communities today, those giving and receiving care are growing in numbers.

Family caregivers face a host of challenges. The many losses associated with caring for a loved one with dementia must be grieved. There is a loss of companionship, loss of future hope, and loss of social life and personal time. Most difficult is the feeling of pervasive helplessness to change or improve the condition of the loved one. Physical challenges include the physical energy required to care for an adult with increasing needs, lack of opportunity for rest and relaxation, and coping with aggressive or wandering behavior. Emotional challenges are significant, as the caregiver may become increasingly isolated when focused on providing care and may not have an opportunity to express feelings and emotions.

There is a high incidence of depression among caregivers that may go untreated. It is common for a caregiver to neglect his or her own mental, physical, and spiritual well-being when caring for a loved one. Some caregivers may have difficulty setting boundaries and may be reluctant to accept help. Spiritual challenges arise when caregiving becomes the primary life focus and personal spiritual growth is stifled.

A faith community has a vital role to play in providing a safe and nurturing place for persons with dementia and their caregivers.

> Victoria and Gus had been married for more than fifty years when Gus began showing signs of memory loss, periodic confusion, and social withdrawal. Victoria cared for Gus over the next ten years as his AD progressed. The couple lived in a continuing-care retirement center, where some support services were available. Victoria took Gus, a retired pastor, to church every Sunday. He usually appeared somewhat engaged, though quiet, during the worship service. This was an important time in their week, as worship had always been a central part of their lives. Victoria enjoyed seeing her friends and acquaintances at church, as she had little time during the week to visit. One Sunday, as the offering plates were being passed, Victoria placed an offering into the plate. Gus said in a loud voice, "You aren't going to give *them* money, are you?"

> Victoria felt embarrassed and fearful that other worshipers might be critical of her and of Gus. Later, she told her daughter that this was the last time she wanted to take Gus to church. "I can't

believe how many years your father worked patiently with stewardship programs in the church, trying to motivate people to give. How could he say such a thing?"

Victoria had lost sight of the fact that her husband no longer had the ability to discriminate and make judgments about issues that reflected his lifelong values. She was overcome by the realization that she could not control what he might say in public—especially at church—that expressed his altered cognitive function. As a pastor's wife, she had a fifty-year history of sensitivity to appropriate behavior and attitudes toward church. She could not tolerate the shame that she suffered when Gus made inappropriate comments. At the same time, she realized that she wanted to protect him from an environment that could stimulate emotional outbursts.

Victoria felt loss on many levels: loss of the mutuality of their marital relationship (for all their married life, they had tithed their income and budgeted together to raise their family); loss of the shared worship experience and being able to discuss the sermon after church; loss of the social stimulation in attending church services; loss of her role as a retired pastor's wife (her husband seemed to have forgotten that he had ever been a pastor).

Victoria gathered her sorrow and regrouped as a caregiver—her primary identity now. From now on, she would attend church services alone, as long as she could feel comfortable leaving Gus for one hour at home, or they would watch a service on TV—something she found happening more and more often.

How could Victoria and Gus's congregation offer support at this time of spiritual and emotional transition in their life? Perhaps their church organizational structure provided leaders who would shepherd a group of families through various life changes. This is what the shepherding might look like for Victoria and Gus:

The leader, Tom, contacted all the members in his "flock" regularly, either by talking with them personally at church or phoning them during the week. Tom asked how the families were and listened to concerns they expressed. He was aware if they were missing at worship services. He would make contact to let them know they were missed and determine if there were needs that the church could meet.

Tom checked in with Victoria to learn how she and Gus were doing, how she was managing caregiving, and if there were unmet needs. Tom was guided by his understanding of Christ's command: "Inasmuch as you have done it unto the least of these, you have done it unto Me." He viewed his service to this family and others as an opportunity to live out his faith.

As a shepherd, Tom paid attention to what spiritual needs might be unmet. In the process, he learned that Victoria did not feel able to attend worship services anymore due to Gus's changing condition. He inquired how St. Michael's Church might best support her. What was she experiencing with loss of church participation? Would she consider respite care for Gus on Sunday morning? Would she prefer to attend services on another day or at a different time that was available? Would she consider visiting a support group for caregivers? Would she like to speak with a Stephen Minister? Did she desire a visit from the pastor? Tom made sure that the lines of communication were open and that Victoria had access to caregiver care.

Tom did not ignore Gus. He talked to him and offered to pray with him as well as with Victoria, who knew that she was not alone with the challenges of caregiving.

## Spiritual Needs of Those with Dementia and Their Caregivers

Church leaders can be the face of Christ when offering specific and consistent support to aid the spiritual and emotional growth of caregivers and persons with dementia. Such acts can include the following:

1. Envisioning both the person with dementia and the caregiver as children of God, worthy of care
2. Regular telephone, email, or texting contact with the caregiver
3. Providing respite care during worship service hours so that care-

givers can worship and draw strength for their serving

4. Bible study groups, prayer groups, and other small groups, such as caregiving support groups

5. Encouragement to attend whole-person healing services in the church or community

6. Awareness of community resources available to caregivers, such as services provided by the Alzheimer's Association or local aging services organizations

7. Counseling services that are older-adult friendly

8. Other respite care alternatives, such as a church-sponsored day respite program or individual volunteers for in-home respite

9. Retreats for caregivers with respite care provided for the care receiver

10. Concern for the whole person of the caregiver and the person with dementia—body, mind, and spirit

## DEMENTIA

Spiritual care for the person with dementia is guided by the call to help one another find meaning in life and a greater connection to a loving, accepting God. Caring communities are called to view a person with dementia as a child of God—forgiven and redeemed by Christ.

> Julia had been diagnosed with early stage dementia. She had been a member of the choir at St. James Church for many years. The choir had become her extended family. She attended choir rehearsals and Sunday services faithfully. Julia was becoming more and more forgetful. Her friend Anna picked her up at home and drove her to church. To help her remember to be ready, Anna would call a half hour ahead and remind her that she was coming. Anna had marked Julia's calendar and put it in a prominent place as well. With prompting, Julia was able to get ready and be on time most days.
>
> The choir members were aware of Julia's diagnosis, and they knew that she would need more care as time went on. They noticed that Julia continued to sing in a clear, sweet voice, and they valued her as a choir member. As her "family," they accepted her and loved her. Some Sundays, Julia would arrive at church with Anna and express surprise: "Oh, we are singing today?" More and more, she was living in the moment. Yet, Julia could

relish the moments in worship with familiar music and rhythms of liturgy. She always left the service with a sense of joy and wholeness.

Healthy church communities can view the person with dementia as having purpose (though it is not always easy to discern) and as being in need of continued development of a healthy soul. Because cognitive impairment alters the ability to communicate verbally, special attentiveness to nonverbal communication is needed. How does the person show the fruit of the Spirit: love? joy? peace? kindness? gentleness? faithfulness? goodness? patience? self-control? A close look with careful attention can reveal many of these qualities. *Prayer* and *worship*, especially with music, can be offered as spiritual disciplines to the person with dementia. Remembering that the person primarily lives in the moment, prayer that focuses on immediacy can be meaningful. Gentle touch, voice tones, facial expressions, and a calm presence communicate deeply to the person with dementia. It matters less that there is recognition of individuals than that there is a sense of God's presence in the now.

Spiritual growth and health may be measured by how many moments are enjoyed in any given time. Someone with dementia—unencumbered with thoughts or anxieties about the past or future—can enjoy many moments in the present as the new self!

Visiting, listening, accepting, and offering assistance are ways of putting the presence of Christ into a caregiving situation. These actions from the new self of the person caring for the caregiver can shift the reality in the situation from hopeless and despairing to hopeful and interested. The power of the new self is absolutely awesome!

> Peace Lutheran Church began an initiative, Share the Care, to give care to caregivers in the congregation when the church leaders recognized the needs of this group in the congregation and community. A group consisting of a health ministry team, a nurse, a musician, an artist, a social worker, and a spiritual director met to determine the needs observed within the congregation for assisting caregiving members. Each person in the group had some understanding of the needs of this group. Some had been caregivers for family or friends; others had worked professionally with persons with dementia; several had been caregivers from a distance and understood the pain, lost dreams, and fears of family caregivers. Everyone in the group had a desire to serve God through serving those in need.

As the team prayerfully explored its own experience and passions for this ministry, a sense of hope and possibility emerged. The team decided to form listening posts to hear from caregivers what they needed. Communication would be in person when possible, and also by telephone and email when needed.

Out of this initiative, starting with targeted, achievable goals, the team built a network of support for caregivers that touched every existing ministry in the congregation, including worship, education, fellowship, shepherding, and youth ministries. One outcome was a quarterly event in which the ministry of caregiving was lifted up in worship with naming those in the congregation who were family caregivers, including those who gave care from a distance. Music, prayers, readings, and sermon themes centered on bearing one another's burdens, the common bonds of caregiving, and putting the presence of Christ into caregiving situations. A fellowship event honoring caregivers was held. Special gifts encouraging self-care were given. Youth in the congregation were matched with caregivers and challenged to develop creative ways to connect on a regular basis. Emphasis was on building relationships. Eventually, this initiative grew into collaboration with a community agency to house a weekly respite care program at the church and involve volunteers committed to being the face of Christ for persons with dementia and their caregivers.

Caregivers share common bonds: the stress of not having enough leisure or personal time, the emotional pain of loss and fear, and often the severe depression that many suffer. With the support of an educated and caring faith community, a caregiver may be given the opportunity to spend time in Christ's presence, experience agape, and feel the protection of that love of God. Being "made new" in the spirit, the person may then put on the new self and face the challenges of caregiving in a much healthier manner. As this transformation takes place, the caregiver begins to recognize his or her inner strength, self-worth, and self-respect. He or she uses that inner strength to get through difficult caregiving days, to take better care of self, and to experience the beauty of being a caregiver.

> After Gus died, Victoria commented to her family that she often felt strong during the years of caregiving. She knew that she was called to her special role. She learned to trust her instincts, to accept help, and to be good to herself in small ways that added up to self-care. She had come to know herself and her capabilities in a new way. She had often experienced the love of Christ through those who ministered to her and to Gus. She loved her husband deeply and felt a sense of accomplishment in caring for him. Ten years later, Victoria volunteers in her church's Alzheimer's Respite Program once a week. She states, "I love it. I know how to be with our patients, and we have fun together. When the day is over, I can come home and put my feet up and watch my favorite TV show." She participated with joy in an art exhibit by the respite care patients that was open to the community to raise funds for the program.

Being able to be humbly grateful and empowered as a caregiver is a gift of God. Caregiving as a spiritual discipline embodies *service, prayer, simplicity,* and *submission.* Completion of caregiving is a cause for celebration!

## PSYCHOTIC DISORDERS

Psychotic disorders are debilitating. There is something wrong with basic perceptual and thought processes. The person cannot interact with the environment in a normal fashion. Brain disorder is usually associated with such serious problems. Speech, social interaction, and even basic hygiene are negatively affected. The person is in danger of social isolation and lack of caring human contact. Often such people live out their lives alone, sometime becoming homeless and without support.

Having such sickness is not a sign of moral weakness, but of being afflicted. The brain can be sick, but that does not mean that the soul has to be dysfunctional. The brain is not the soul.

People with psychotic disorders do not have to be isolated. They can feel love and can love in return. They have a longing for God. They yearn to be productive and helpful to others. A faith community can help with this.

Even though many psychotic symptoms may remain and become amplified at times, a faith community can provide the acceptance and love that is good for the person's soul. The example of Christ hits right to this point. He did not shrink back from those in distress, but was up close and personal. He touched those who were diseased and confronted their demons. His love was intimate and personal. He empowered them to reach out and love others.

Members of a faith community can have this regard for such people. Rather than isolating them and making them feel unwelcome, normal interaction is the best way of handling even disruptive behavior. Personal contact that has good boundaries treats such situations in a matter-of-fact way. The person is accepted and guided into more appropriate behavior but is not shunned and stared at.

## SCHIZOPHRENIA

Schizophrenia can be considered one of the most serious of mental disorders. There are many types of schizophrenia, divided roughly into *process* and *reactive*. The reactive type usually refers to a schizophrenic episode that is induced by a stressful situation. It usually has a shorter duration and a good prognosis.

> Talitia was twenty-one years old and living on her own. Her father left the family when she was ten, and her mother leaned on her for emotional support. She finished several years of college and was an A student, obsessing over her homework and staying up late to get everything perfect.

> She had to interrupt her college career to get a job. She worked in the hotel business and quickly advanced because of her good work ethic. She could handle anything. She gradually took on more and more responsibility.

> She had a boyfriend, but she was taking care of him also. She would drive for hours to meet up with him for a weekend and then drive back just in time to go to work. She was exhausted much of the time. She was also taking a class two evenings a week and would lose sleep trying to keep up with her studies.

> Her mother contracted breast cancer and started pressuring her to spend more time with her. She felt pulled at from all ends. Her mind started obsessing over everything she had to do.

> One day, after another sleepless night, she stopped everything at work. She just sat and stared into space. Her boss tried to interact with her and then became alarmed when she had no reaction at all. She was in a full-blown catatonic state.

Talitia was hospitalized and given powerful drugs and shock treatment to get her out of the catatonic state. She only got worse and seemed to be headed toward a life in a mental institution.

Her father, Frank, was in a men's Bible study group when he shared his agony over his estranged daughter. He explained that he left the marriage partly to keep the daughter from witnessing the endless fights, but then his ex-wife would not let him see his daughter. She convinced her that he did not love her.

"I have thought of her every day since then," Frank admitted with tears flowing down. "I pray for her constantly."

One of the men challenged Frank: "You do love her, but she does not know it. Let's go together and visit her."

Frank was reluctant. "That will just make it worse," he began.

But his friend was insistent. "She will never know your love unless you show it to her."

They went together at first, and then Frank went alone almost every day to see her. He talked to her and told her how often he thought of her, even though she was totally nonresponsive. Two weeks later, when Frank brought along a teddy bear that she had had as a child, she had the first spark in her eyes. It was as if she finally believed that he was for real, and she reconnected to his love. She was on her way to recovery.

*Process* schizophrenia usually has a long history of poor functioning. It can show serious disorganization of speech and behavior, often more infantile in affect. The person has had such inappropriate reactions much of his or her life. The thought process is usually highly personal, showing up in a "word salad" when communicating.

Drug therapy is a true gift for such people. There is serious disruption in brain function, leaving the person unable to organize a baffling world of perceptual and thought fragments. Antipsychotic drugs work by stopping some of the excessive functioning of dopamine receptors. This seems to help the overstimulation of the brain that makes it difficult for the person to organize thought and perception into a manageable unity.

Members of a faith community who want to be of help to such persons must work closely with a psychiatrist or other professionals to make sure medicines are monitored. Help is also needed to decide when more serious intervention is needed, such as hospitalization. The greatest help of the faith community is the acceptance of such people, welcoming them and seeing them as gifts to the community.

# Tendencies toward Marital Relationship Problems

The most common personal problems are relationship disorders. Starting with dysfunction in the family of origin, everyone struggles with relationships throughout life. In fact, in today's ME-oriented culture, families are hurting. Family breakups, bad moods within existing families, and poor parent-child relationships are the norm.

Family relationship problems are related to most of the other diagnostic categories. To a large degree, mental and emotional problems are helped by improving these relationships.

Faith communities are in the relationship business, helping people with their relationships with God, with one another, and with self. Strengthening family relationships is part of this ministry. To do this, the community models healthy relationships and mentors family relationships.

To some degree, the family is the new mission field for the Church. A healthy faith community can be a true healing force for family relationships. The Church can become an attractive oasis for family struggles, modeling healthy relationships and teaching essential ingredients for developing good interaction styles.

## Problems with the Marriage Relationship

Relationships grow as people share their thoughts and feelings and feel understood. Communication is critical for relationship growth. Misunderstanding is the cause of most marital problems.

The couple usually begin their relationship with the exciting process of getting to know each other. Often there are long, sometimes all-night conversations in which they hang on every word. The cadence of communication is a slow back-and-forth. One person shares deeply while the other listens intently. Then the other shares and also feels understood.

A few years after marriage, it is normal for the two to spend more time defending self and correcting the other person than really listening. The conversation normally goes from "soul-searching" to "but" interactions. The cadence changes dramatically. The slow, deep-listening conversation is replaced by defensive reactions. Before the first person can finish a sentence, the other is now reacting. This creates a pattern of interaction that leaves both people frustrated.

### Painters and Pointers

The fastest way to change a relationship pattern is to focus on listening. This brings the relationship back to its beginning, when the couple spent hours exploring each other's souls.

Listening differently is especially important in "painter/pointer" conversations[1] to keep misunderstanding from occurring. In most marriages, one is a painter and one is a pointer. This difference is attractive, but it causes endless annoyance and miscommunication.

About 25 percent of males are painters and 75 percent are pointers. The opposite is true of females: about 25 percent are pointers and 75 percent are painters. In 85 percent of couples, one is a painter and one is a pointer. This difference seems to be very attractive.

|  | PAINTER | POINTER |
|---|---|---|
| **COMMUNICATION** | Paints a picture | Sticks to the point |
| **PERCEPTION** | Notices everything | Notices task at hand |
| **CONSCIOUSNESS** | Keeps many things in mind | Focuses on one thing |
| **DEFENSE OF SELF** | Vigilant, so no surprises | Puts things in perspective |

Long-standing listening habits are very difficult to change. People automatically listen based on how they communicate. This causes endless misunderstanding and hurt feelings.

### What Pointers Can Learn

Since pointers think through things inside before talking, they will naturally focus on the first word or phrase and assume that it is the point. This works when they are talking to other pointers. The conversation goes very well as "points" are shared and easily understood.

But when listening to painters, this natural strategy does not work. Painters cannot think through things before they talk since they are processing out loud. The first sentence is just the first brushstroke of a picture they are going to paint. They actually need to paint the whole picture before they know what they are trying to say.

When pointers focus on the first sentence, assuming that it is the point, they miss the whole picture and often misunderstand what the painter is trying to say. The typical reaction of the pointer is to get defensive, correct the painter's reality, offer a solution, or assume the painter has made up his or her mind and just walk away.

Pointers can change the way they listen, but it is counterintuitive and takes effort and awareness to make the change. Key to the change is the belief that painters, no matter how definite they sound, are processing out loud and just need a chance to paint the whole picture.

### For Pointers When Listening

1. Sit back and watch a picture being painted.
2. Do not focus on the first statement as the point.
3. Become fascinated with the colorful detail.
4. Do not try to solve anything.
5. After listening for a while, summarize to see if you are getting the whole picture.
6. Remember that a painter must express things and is processing out loud.

### What Painters Can Learn

Since painters use emotional color and detail to paint their pictures, they are not tuned into the logical words of pointers. They think that pointers are not telling them anything, so they have to dig for the details. Painters really do not understand what is being said unless they can get to detail and emotion. Then it will make sense.

The detail and emotion painters need is imbedded in the first word or sentence. Pointers think through enormous amounts of detail and emotion and pull it together into a single point. Painters, however, do not even hear this word since they are looking for detail and emotion. The pointer's word does not sound interesting, and it certainly does not sound important. Since pointers do not have to talk to process, they have no need to elaborate on the point, assuming that it was heard.

Painters then start asking rapid-fire questions to dig for detail and emotion. Pointers become very frustrated with this process, since they have to jump from file to file inside, summarize, and then give another point. Painters do not get to the details and emotion because they force pointers to come up with new summaries for each question.

Painters can change the way they listen, but it is counterintuitive and takes effort and awareness to make the change. Key to the change is the belief that pointers, no matter how unemotional they sound, are giving a logical summarization that contains all the detail and emotion that the painter would need to understand the pointer's soul. Painters need to unpackage the point to get the detail needed to understand.

### For Painters When Listening

1. Listen closely to the first words spoken—this will be the point, even though it does not sound important.
2. Carefully note the exact word.
3. Take one of these words and ask, "Tell me more about
   _____." This is similar to "double-clicking" on an underlined word on the Internet. Use the exact word.
4. Make it safe for the pointer to talk. Don't make any fast reactions until you have unpacked the point.
5. Remember that it will take three or four unfolding questions to get to the interesting details and then several more "double-clicks" to get to emotion.
6. Remember that a pointer cannot talk when too much emotion gets stirred up.

## MISUNDERSTANDING LEADS TO DISTRUST

The function of a person's spirit is to organize reality, producing a belief system that develops specific attitudes toward individuals in that person's life. This involves listening to another person and matching what is being expressed with one's own reality. Distrust occurs when things do not match, leading to the conclusion that the other person is being manipulative and is not telling the truth. This creates considerable damage to relationships and is hard to overcome.

Much of the time, this is a false conclusion when painters and pointers are involved. Both are being honest when expressing their thoughts and emotions, but they have vastly different ways of defining truth!

## LEARNING THAT THERE IS TRUTH FROM DIFFERENT PERSPECTIVES

### Painter's Truth

1. Painters will react according to the feeling of the moment and will express their thoughts and feelings in very definite ways.
2. Those feelings cannot be put into perspective, or their expression will not be valid.
3. The words that painters use are not logical entities, but valid expressions of their feelings at the moment.
4. Once expressed and processed, painters can then flow to other emotions with their mood shifting often, depending on the situation.

### Pointer's Distrust

1. The painter will say "always" and "never" to share the emotion.
2. The pointer will notice that the strong feeling is only temporary.
3. The pointer will think, I won't trust what you say next time. You just make a big thing out of nothing and then forget it.
4. But the painter is being honest with what is going on at the moment!

> Kirsten was visibly upset. "You always do this to me. You never stop to check with me before you buy something."
>
> Arthur listened and shook his head. Here she goes again, he thought, blowing things out of proportion and blaming me for everything.
>
> After several more outbursts, Kirsten's mood shifted. She was now excited about the trip they were planning. Watching the mood shift, Arthur was now certain that Kirsten had been trying to manipulate him and make him feel bad. She was so upset just a few minutes ago, he thought to himself with some resentment, and now she is fine. He concluded, "I don't trust her emotional outbursts."

### Pointer's Truth

1. Pointers will react by summarizing feelings over time.
2. These feelings will be put into a broader perspective.
3. Pointers can be angry but still validly say, "I love you."

4. Those words are valid logical entities, not feelings of the moment.

### Painter's Distrust

1. The painter will pick up nonverbal feelings.
2. When the pointer gives the summary, it will not match the feeling.
3. So the painter will say, "I don't trust what you say—you are not being honest."
4. But the pointer is being honest in the summary.

> "You know that I love you and care about you," Arthur said flatly in the midst of an argument.
>
> How can he say that? Kirsten thought. She had just observed Arthur's anger and disgusted expression and now he was saying he loves her? He is still angry with me, she continued to think; I do not believe what he is saying. Kirsten did not feel any warmth in his statement and concluded with some disgust, "He is just saying that to appease me. He does not mean it."

Trust is a function of the relationship. Long-standing attitudes toward another person represent reality. It takes a change in one's belief system to change attitudes. Much of this distrust goes away with the awareness of these differences that leads to belief that the other person is being honest.

> Arthur and Kirsten attended a marriage seminar at their church that taught them about painters and pointers. On the way home, Kirsten was excited. "I never knew that you have to summarize your feelings. I thought you were like me and could just express what you feel," she said.
>
> Arthur was also excited about his new insight. "I thought you were like me. When you expressed your feelings, I did not realize you were focusing only on what you felt at the moment."
>
> They looked at each other with a new appreciation of their differences. Their conversations would be better now. Some of the old resentment was disappearing.

# Powerful Spiritual Forces Build
## within Relationships

Imagine being in the presence of a good friend. Look at the words that describe the atmosphere between the two of you: *caring, friendly, open, honest,* and *free.* You are a good person and fun to be with. You walk away from this atmosphere with your spirit uplifted.

Now imagine being in the presence of someone you never want to see again in your life. Look at the words that describe the atmosphere now: *cold, distant, hostile, closed,* and *dishonest.* You have changed and are no longer a good person; you are negative and resentful. You walk away from this atmosphere with your spirit upset.

The next time you see that person, can you, with an act of your own mind and will, genuinely give that person a hug and say, "Good to see you," and mean it? That is humanly impossible. You cannot change the spirit of this relationship by willing it to be so.

Powerful spiritual forces reside in relationships, causing interesting mood shifts. These are some of the most powerful forces on earth, either bringing deep joy and fulfillment or leading to lifelong resentment and bitterness. The atmosphere of any relationship is controlled by these forces that swirl invisibly between people as they interact.

# Relationships Cause Feelings

Relationships are patterns of interaction. These patterns become automated and are somewhat predictable. Often each person knows how the interaction will end when it starts. But both seem unable to stop the pattern, and they end up blaming the other person for the mood shift that just occurred.

> The phone rang. It was Mother. Jarad had a twenty-second conversation with her. He hung up the phone and started out the door.
>
> Grace stepped in front of him and blocked the door. "What did she want you to do this time?" she challenged with a hint of sarcasm in her voice.
>
> Jarad looked down and sighed, "Nothing, really."
>
> "Then why are you rushing out the door to go do something for her?" she questioned, her voice getting louder. Jarad continued to look down and tried to step around her, wanting to get out as

quickly as possible. "I asked you a question," Grace demanded, getting more upset by being ignored.

"Why can't you get along with my mother?" Jarad said quietly, still trying to escape. "She has always been nice to you."

With this, Grace could not take it any longer. "You jump anytime she calls. You treat her so much better than you treat me."

Jarad pushed her aside and headed out the door, shoulders squared in anger. Why does she have to react like that? he thought, resentment growing in his stomach. She knows my mother is old and needs help. As his mood slipped into sullen anger, he concluded, "She just wants to control everything I do."

Still catching her balance from being pushed, Grace felt her own mood grow bitter. His mother has him wrapped around her finger. She does this deliberately to ruin our evening together, and he lets her keep interrupting us. She was very angry as she concluded, "I don't really matter to him."

This same pattern of interaction had occurred hundreds of times in their marriage. It always ended the same way, with both building resentment. These patterns are predictable and play out again and again when the same situation comes up. And both people blame the other person for the pattern, not realizing that any relationship pattern is created by automated mood sequences by both people.

A relationship pattern is made up of two persons who are interacting. One person will say or do something. The other will react. Then there is a reaction to the reaction. This goes on and on. Both are reacting in an automated way as the mood shifts downward. Both are to blame for the bad pattern!

Yet both want a better relationship. Both want to feel close and intimate, and both use considerable energy in trying to make the relationship better. But this energy is misplaced and does no good. The focus is on trying to change the other person. This just leads to more conflict.

There is an unused source of power for change. One person has power to change a relationship. Picture a relationship as made up of two halves. If one half of the interaction pattern changes, the whole relationship will change. The automated mood sequences cannot exist if one person does not react in the predictable fashion.

The only way negative feelings toward another person will genuinely change is if the relationship is changed. And the good news is that with Christ's help, a person can always change his or her half of the relationship! With this change, the new relationship patterns are formed.

> Rachel was getting more and more frustrated with her husband. Every time she tried to start a conversation, he would turn away and grow silent. "He just does not care about our relationship," she concluded with obvious resentment growing.
>
> She shared her frustration in her women's Bible study group, expecting a show of support for her dilemma. Instead, one of the women (who was also a painter) challenged her conclusion: "Perhaps you are starting the conversation in a way that is not helpful."
>
> Rachel started getting defensive. "No, it's my husband. He just does not want to talk to me."
>
> In a kind voice, the woman went on, "I did the same thing. I assumed that it was my husband's fault for not responding when I started something. Then I realized that I was 'painting on his face' in my frustration to get some response. I would challenge him, and he would immediately withdraw or get defensive."
>
> Rachel was puzzled. "Then it's his problem for withdrawing," she offered. "No," the woman continued, "it was a *relationship* problem . . . it was *our* problem." She went on to explain that this was a pattern of interaction they had developed, leaving both of them frustrated. "I found that I could break the pattern by a totally different approach."
>
> "But why do I have to do all the work?" Rachel complained.
>
> "Look at it totally differently," the woman advised. "You helped develop this pattern, so you have the power to change it."
>
> "So what did you do?" Rachel asked, getting more interested.
>
> "I actually took someone else's advice," the woman replied. "I found out that if I 'painted' on the wall instead of on his face, he

was able to listen and respond to the conversation."

"How do you do that?" Rachel wanted to know.

"It is actually pretty simple, but certainly is still not natural for me," the woman explained. "When I want to start a conversation, I now start out by saying, 'I need your help. I have things going on inside me and just need a chance to sort them out.'"

"But doesn't he still get defensive and take it personally?" Rachel wondered.

The woman explained further: "After making the two of us allies by that first statement, then I 'paint on the wall' by letting him know that this is how I feel and that he can feel differently. It's a disarmingly honest way of talking. I make my observations and share my feelings without any hidden motives."

"I am beginning to understand," said Rachel. "I make it clear that we are just sharing our ideas and feelings. We are getting to know each other better, not trying to convince each other to agree."

## MARRIAGE: TWO SPIRITUAL HISTORIES COMBINING

"Therefore a man shall leave his father and mother and hold fast to his wife, and the two shall become *one flesh*." (Ephesians 5:31, emphasis added)

Marriage is a sacred union. Two separate lives are organized to form a new *spiritual entity*. To put it in simple terms, a WE is formed from two ME's. The word *spiritual* is a good term to use since the marriage relationship is not visible, yet contains some of the most powerful forces on earth.

The human spirit is the creative force that is constantly involved in organizing one's life, from infancy to death. Two individual spirits, each with a deep history of organizing consciousness, come together to form this new relationship.

## SPIRITUAL DNA COMBINING TO FORM A "ONE FLESH" UNION

DNA strands combine to form the beginning of a baby's life. Spiritual DNA strands combine to form the beginning of the new entity: the marriage relationship. Physical DNA represents the genetic heritage of each person. Spiritual DNA represents the relational history of each person.

There are many flaws in the physical DNA strands. When they combine to form a zygote, the healthy strand usually prevails if one is damaged. Genetic problems normally occur when DNA strands from both parents are damaged at the same location.

This concept can be applied to spiritual DNA. When two spirits join to form a spiritual entity, they become *one flesh*. When both spirits are healthy within a specific area of interaction, the mood will be good. These are the healthy areas of the marriage.

## DEFINING MOMENTS

Healthy segments of spiritual DNA are developed when the family atmosphere is loving and secure with good, consistent boundaries. The child develops a healthy view of life and of identity with good capacity to love and be sensitive to others.

Damage to the child's spiritual DNA occurs when the child experiences distress or is not given good boundaries. This usually occurs when the WE orientation of the family unit breaks down, forcing family members to look out for themselves (ME-oriented situations). The child realizes that he or she is on her own and develops a private strategy for handling the situation.

Such spiritual strategies are age specific and are utilized throughout life whenever the person encounters similar situations. The specific situation remains in the consciousness as a vivid image. These are *defining moments*. These images represent basic organizational structures of the psyche and contain automated mood sequencing.

Since this organizing moment is a private strategy and usually not shared, it remains immature, "stuck" at the age when the intense anxiety occurred. This can be viewed as a damaged place in a person's spiritual DNA. These damaged places are very powerful.

## AUTOMATED MOOD SEQUENCES

When encountering a similar emotionally threatening situation later in life, an *automated mood sequence* becomes activated in a self-protective way. This sequence is powerful in changing the mood of the person, and it brings the person back to childhood feelings.

These automated mood sequences control the mood of the individual by controlling perceived reality. When activated later in life, this is what the person now believes to be true. These are immature attitudes, "stuck" at a particular age. It is like a seven-year-old takes control in a marital conflict, even though the person is thirty-five.

Damaged spiritual DNA is invisible to the person. Since the damage represents the ways the person has dealt with situations throughout life, the immature reaction seems normal to him or her. This is why each person in a marital conflict will blame the other for the bad mood between them. One's own dysfunction is invisible, but the other's immaturity is clearly apparent!

Listening to voice tone or watching body language is the best indicator of such damaged spiritual DNA. Is there the whine of a three-year-old or the "worrywart" of a seven-year-old? Does the person act like a five-year-old bully? Does the person look helpless or even lie like an eleven-year-old? Is there a sense that marriage takes the fun out of life and the person is rebelling against responsibility like a fifteen-year-old?

## TWO "OINKEYS" TOUCHING

Where a person's spirit is damaged, his or her mood will shift during a specific area of interaction, revealing a childhood distress or anxiety. If the spouse reacts to this mood shift in a healthy way, the mood of the relationship will not shift. The love of the spouse will prevail and help the immature reaction grow up.

Marital problems occur where two damaged DNA sequences are activated at the same time. Both feel hurt and distress when two immature areas touch. The mood of the relationship now shifts, and the WE orientation breaks down.

A good term for the immature, negative shift in a person's mood is an *oinkey*. When feelings are hurt, the stomach feels energy going downward and the internal mood shifts. This automated mood sequence is very common. A damaged place in the person's spiritual DNA has been activated. Now the person shows the internal shift in mood by becoming oinkey in the relationship.

Pointers become oinkey by pulling away and pouting. In the interaction, the pointer feels hurt or disrespected. What the other person did or said was not deserved. Things are now out of balance. Becoming oinkey is a way of getting even in the relationship. The loss of energy (pout) will last twenty minutes, one hour, even two days. The process of getting even can be pictured as *units of ignoring*, measured in ten-minute increments. Depending on the severity of the feeling of disrespect, the withdrawal of energy by the pointer may require three units of ignoring (thirty-minute pout) or even twelve units (two-hour pout).

Painters become oinkey by showing their hurt feelings verbally. The process of getting even can be pictured as *units of annoying*. The painter will feel the need to point out things that are wrong with the other person, like, "You forgot to call again, didn't you?" Depending on the severity of the feeling of disrespect, there may be four annoying comments or even fifteen units of annoying. An hour's pout by the pointer is about equal to six annoying comments by the painter!

The mood of the relationship shifts when two oinkeys touch. This represents two immature spiritual DNA segments combining and being activated at the same time. With such mood shift, the couple can no longer talk things through. Both are hurt and are blaming the other person. Further talking usually leads to escalation of anger and bad feelings. This is why the "sun goes down" while the couple is still angry, giving the devil opportunity to build a base of operations (Ephesians 4:26–27).

## Mood Particles Build Up

In the marriage relationship, areas of spiritual DNA damage that have combined allow resentment to build, causing the powerful spiritual forces that end up destroying the marriage. These forces build as *mood particles* accumulate in an area of the couple's interaction. Mood particles are remnants of previous unresolved moods that leave behind hurt feelings and resentment.[2]

If the same dysfunctional interaction occurs hundreds of times in an area of the marriage relationship, the accumulation of these spiritual particles can produce a powerful, mood-altering force. Trust breaks down, leading to a negative spiral of the mood.

When the mood shifts early in the marriage, there is no accumulation of mood particles in that area, so it is relatively easy to get the WE orientation back. But after hundreds of mood particles have accumulated, mood shifts last for days, even weeks. The couple begins to lose hope that they can become allies again. That is when thoughts of divorce begin to surface. In other words, the couple does not "fall out of love"; rather, they lose hope that they can get the mood back and become close and intimate again.

## The Role of Confession

The reality is universal. When there is a bad interaction in the marriage relationship and the mood shifts, each will blame the other. This is natural. The mood shifted, feelings are hurt, and each person knows privately that he or she did not want this to happen. Since the relationship is invisible, the blame will always go to the other person.

In fact, hundreds of hours are spent privately trying to understand why the other person reacted in such a hurtful way. The person's spirit will gradually solidify what is wrong in the relationship. This becomes the person's reality. It is a *litany* that is carefully rehearsed and backed up by hundreds of examples. This is a hardened heart.

Confession is critical in order to heal the pattern. As long as the couple is focused on changing the other person and defending his or her own litany, the relationship will just get worse. When one person, in confession, is open to taking a look at his or her own half of the relationship, growth can occur. Confession means looking at one's own oinkey instead of endlessly blaming the other person for the hurt feeling and mood shift. Instead of the natural shift to one's litany of blame, confession is the unnatural process of searching for the source of the oinkey in one's own spiritual history.

## UTILIZING FAITH IN HEALING RELATIONSHIPS

Relationships work when concern for the good of the whole (the WE) is more important than personal advantage. That is the insight of Ephesians 5:21: "[Submit] to one another out of reverence for Christ."

Christian faith produces a new self by creating new spiritual DNA with the missing agape back in place. The new self (*pneuma*) is the combination of Christ's perfect DNA with a person's flawed spiritual DNA. This is the only relationship anyone will ever have where the mood of the relationship will never shift because one person will never get oinkey. Christ's loving presence (agape) will never change. It will grow a person's spirit up, healing past damage. Another term for healing this spiritual DNA damage (oinkeys) is *spiritual growth*. The person becomes more like Christ, able to break free from self-centered living to concern for the good of the whole.

The person's faith can be of help in working on his or her half of the marriage relationship. This healthy process brings the anxiety-reducing presence of Christ into the vivid images that created the damaged spiritual DNA, thus letting agape repair the DNA. Such a process can also be utilized in the automated mood sequences of a relationship problem to break the downward mood spiral.

> The pattern had been there since the beginning of the relationship. Becky (a painter) looked at her husband, obviously upset. "Why do you always leave me when I need you?" she asked. Wayne sighed, looked down, and did not say anything. "Talk to me," Becky demanded, getting more upset. By the time Wayne sighed again and walked away, a bad mood was set between them.
>
> Of course, Becky blamed her husband for the bad mood. He just did not care about her feelings and was emotionally unavailable when she needed him. Wayne, on the other hand, was blaming

his wife. I can never do anything right, he thought to himself with deep resentment. She thinks the whole world revolves around her feelings.

It was in a marriage class at church that a breakthrough occurred. Wayne sat up and took notice when the teacher said, "Christ can help break the mood with His presence." Wayne thought back to the last time he and Becky were in a bad mood. He looked at himself and realized he felt like a twelve-year-old who was being blamed. "That's when I need Christ," he realized, "because I cannot get out of the mood myself."

He was able to break his part of the pattern over the next several months. Every time he felt like a twelve-year-old and looked away with resentment building in his stomach, he stopped with this freeing thought: With Christ's help, I do not have to feel this anymore. This is just my old self.

As he prayed, he could feel the knot of resentment in his stomach move upward toward his heart, where Christ lived. With a deep breath, he felt the change of heart. Confidence replaced resentment. He was now free to pray for his wife and her struggle with the mood. He changed his automated reaction, and that began to change the patterns of the relationship itself.

## SPIRITUAL DISCIPLINE FOR COUPLES

When the breakthrough for Wayne occurred, helping him to look at his part in his marital conflict, it was in a marriage class at his church. Faith communities can offer ongoing learning opportunities through classes and seminars for relationships as a part of the education ministry. Many faith-based books and DVD series available for marriage education and support can be used in Sunday classes or small groups that meet in homes. The spiritual discipline of *study* can bring God's Word into marriages.

One congregation has a monthly "Marriage Matters" night out for couples at a local restaurant. A speaker and discussion are provided to explore various relationship topics of interest to couples. Free babysitting at the church attracts younger couples and encourages them to take time to focus on building a healthy WE orientation for their marriage.

*Prayer* for healing marriages can be offered corporately in worship services on a regular basis; individual prayer can be encouraged for marital partners (both for themselves and for each other) through prayer groups, prayer partners, healing services, and anytime two Christians gather and share their hearts. Learning how to pray for one's partner (besides "Please let him change and be more like me") and pray for the marriage can be a powerful means of asking and trusting the Holy Spirit to shift the mood and process the accumulated mood particles.

*Meditating* on one's marriage as a gift of God can help to soften a hardened heart. This may help a partner move away from automatic reactions and change negative relationship patterns. Faith communities can support the practice of meditation with quiet times before and during worship services, setting apart space for individual or couple prayer and meditation, such as a small chapel or room.

During certain times in the liturgical year when fasting is encouraged, such as during Lent, couples can be invited to *fast* from blaming. When awareness grows through shifting the focus in a relationship, there is room for growth.

A couple may decide to adopt the spiritual practice of *simplicity*. This could involve decluttering their lives from excess activity and creating space for simple time together of listening and responding. Free from distractions and multitasking, a couple can then devote a slice of time every day to a simple, clear focus on each other and the relationship. Such attention can have a powerful effect on the spirit, especially when accompanied by prayer, both individually and together.

The discipline of *submission* of one's own needs as having to always come first underlies many of the other spiritual practices related to marriage. It is actually the first step and is done "out of reverence to Christ."

*Celebration* of the gift of one's marriage (even though imperfect) and God's presence in the relationship as it grows and matures is an expression of the joy God intends for couples. Simple appreciation shared with each other is as significant as a large party to celebrate a wedding anniversary. This is the discipline of gratitude.

# Tendencies toward Parent-Child Relationship Problems

Children are born curious, eager to explore and understand the new world. They watch their parents' every move. They know every facial expression. They know when parents are serious and when they will give in. In fact, their spirit quickly organizes their world, developing strategies as to how to interact . . . especially with family!

> Corie discovered early on that a piercing scream would get her brother in trouble. She also found that if she defied her mother, her mother would look at Dad angrily, expecting him to discipline his daughter. When he didn't, the two parents would get into an argument. She has found power that can shift the mood—and she'll use it again and again.

## THE POWER OF WE

The key to good parent-child relationships is a healthy, loving WE. It is the parents' job to form the WE and bring the child into it. To do this, the parents must value the good of the family over their own personal power or agenda. In other words, the parents must have a spiritual maturity of their own.

Children will not rebel against a healthy, loving WE. They feel the security of a family working together and know they are an important part of the WE. Such security is central to a child's development and leads to spiritual maturity.

Parents form the initial WE by focusing on an issue with the intent of working together as a family to resolve it. One starts by raising the issue and then using the word *we*. Then the child is brought into the WE so that everyone is in agreement as to what would be best for the family.

> Katelyn was six years old. She did not like to go to bed. She wanted to be where the action was. Her parents would put her to bed, but then she would come out of her room with some question or in need of a drink of water. Often, it took more than an hour to get her to stay in bed.
>
> Her father addressed the issue with her mother. "We need to find a better solution to Katelyn's bedtime," he began. They talked over Katelyn's need for enough sleep and also her interest in being part of the family in the evening.
>
> Then they brought Katelyn into the discussion. With the child sitting across from them, the first thing they did was look at each other and smile. This controlled the mood to make the discussion a healthy one. Then they looked back at Katelyn, and her father said, "We need to talk about your bedtime. You are getting to be a young girl, and we want you to have more freedom and make your own decisions. We want to treat you like a six-year-old."
>
> They raised the issue of going to bed. "What time do you think should be your bedtime?" Mother asked. "We know you are growing up and perhaps you can stay up later, but you need enough sleep so you can get up in time for school." Katelyn liked the discussion, and they all agreed that her bedtime could be a half hour later.
>
> "That means that you will be in charge of going to bed at that time," Father continued. "This will show us that you are acting like a six-year-old, and we can treat you that way. But if you choose not to go to bed at that time, or if you get up after you go to

bed, then you are acting like a three-year-old, and we will have to treat you that way."

They looked at each other again and smiled. Then Mother asked, "To help you with your decision, what do you think should happen if you do not go to bed on time?"

Katelyn thought for a while and then offered, "Maybe I should not be allowed to watch TV the next day?" They all agreed on that.

Of course, the very next night, Katelyn did not want to go to bed. "I am not sleepy," she whined. Her parents looked at each other and chuckled. "You are making an interesting decision," Father said. "That means that we have to treat you like a three-year-old and you cannot watch TV tomorrow. We are sad about that because we know how much you like your favorite program, but that is your choice."

It did not take long for Katelyn to shift her mood, once she found that she could not manipulate the situation. Bedtime was much different after that.[1]

What just happened was the development of healthy WE-oriented boundaries for Katelyn that considered the best for all concerned. Boundaries help children grow up. As Katelyn grows, she will internalize these loving yet firm boundaries. They will become the basis for healthy self-control when she begins to function outside the sphere of parental influence. This internal sense of a WE orientation will lead her in making good life decisions. Without such boundaries (or boundaries that are too rigid), Katelyn will find it difficult to handle situations later in life. She will give in to impulse and then regret it later. There will be a constant internal struggle between what she *wants* to do and what she feels she *should* do.

## WHAT GIVES CHILDREN POWER TO CONTROL THE MOOD?

Children are born with radar. They quickly find their parents' damaged spiritual DNA. They watch every guilty expression, every frustration, and every hint of anger. They also watch when their parents disagree.

This is a real blessing to parents. The child will spot the damaged DNA and the parents can fix it, with Christ's help. But often parents do not see this as a blessing. Instead, they blame the child for their bad mood.

Children get inappropriate power from their parents' immaturity. When they can activate a parent's damaged spiritual DNA sequence, the authority of the parent breaks down and the child does not have to obey. The parent ceases to be the adult who has the good of the family at heart and, instead, reverts to an automated sequence of immature anger, guilt, or frustration. The child can manipulate the mood by activating that sequence.

> Jeremy stood there, defiant. "You'd better get moving, young man, before I take a belt to you," his father hissed, barely able to control his anger. Jeremy did not move a muscle, but just looked at his father with a defiant smirk on his face. With that, his father lost it and started yelling—which brought his mother in to intervene. His father stomped away, fuming with anger. He had felt the same frustration and anger growing up. His father would react with a sarcastic smirk when he tried to have a conversation with him. His anger was an automated reaction to that sarcastic look. Jeremy's radar had found this sequence, and he could not help but activate it and manipulate the mood.

Whenever children control the mood, everyone suffers. Power struggles erupt. Parents regain control using their natural authority in immature ways. Children get over-focused on the struggle. They will throw temper tantrums, get whiney, argue endlessly, or look sad and dejected. They know all the automated sequences to make their parents feel guilty, frustrated, angry, or overwhelmed!

Parent-child relationships get "stuck" with the same patterns occurring over and over again. When the WE orientation of the family unit breaks down in this manner, the child gets "stuck" emotionally at that age. That is why a twelve-year-old will whine like a three-year-old. Or a seventeen-year-old will still be telling lies and hiding things like an eleven-year-old.

Parents are also "stuck." They instinctively treat their seventeen-year-old like he's still eleven, checking up on him, not trusting what he says, and feeling the same frustration that was there seven years earlier!

Parents will blame their children for not growing up. They will call a child lazy, self-centered, unrealistic, or even sneaky. This continues the dysfunctional relationship, for the root of the problem is the relationship. The WE orientation of the family unit has broken down into individual ME's, and the inevitable power struggle has taken over.

## HEALING SPIRITUAL DNA OF PARENTS

Better parent-child relationships develop when parents stop blaming their children and look at their own damaged DNA sequences. When parents get upset and angry at their children, most of the time it is not the children's fault. They are just doing their job in finding the immature spiritual DNA of the parent and the automated mood sequence that goes with it. It is the parent's job to use this information to heal the DNA and spiritually grow up!

Sherie was so frustrated she could scream. She was a single parent, and her six-year-old daughter would not obey her. Everything she asked her to do was met with opposition. "That's not fair! You don't make my brother do that!" was the usual defiant remark. Sherie would argue with her to no avail and end up so frustrated that she would do it herself.

She finally brought her child to a counselor, expecting him to diagnose her child as having something like an oppositional defiant disorder. To her surprise, the counselor wanted to talk to her alone. "What do you feel like inside when your child talks back to you?" the counselor wanted to know.

"Children are supposed to obey," Sherie started, but the counselor stopped her and repeated the question. Her voice tone shifted as Sherie thought for a moment and then replied, "I feel so frustrated, so helpless, and I feel like giving up."

"Do you remember feeling like that when you were growing up?" the counselor gently asked.

As Sherie thought back, she had a sudden insight: "Why, that is just how I felt when I would try to tell my mom something. She would never let me finish, but would argue back with me until I just gave up."

"Think of a vivid scene when this happened with your mom," the counselor instructed. "Where are you standing or sitting when you remember trying to talk to your mom?"

Sherie thought for a moment. "I can see it like it was yesterday," she began. "I wanted to spend the night with my friend. I found Mom in the kitchen, and I was standing next to the stove when she started arguing with me."

"How old are you as you remember this scene?" the counselor asked. Sherie responded without much hesitation: "I am in fifth grade, and this was my very best friend who I wanted to be with. We had planned the evening together at school. Mom just would not listen to me."

"You feel powerless with your daughter like you did with your mother when you were eleven years old, don't you?" the counselor suggested.

With that, Sherie suddenly brightened up. "I get it!" she exclaimed. "I fell back into an old pattern with my child. She is so smart! She found that reaction in me. Wow!"

Sherie was open to discovering her damaged spiritual DNA and was able to focus on her own growth instead of blaming her child for her frustration. Her counselor led her into putting Christ into her memory with her mother. That had an amazing effect. For the first time, she felt her mother's concern for her safety in that scene. Her frustration started to diminish. With Christ's re-parenting (agape), she felt herself slowly growing up.

She also realized that she felt the same frustration when talking with one of her good friends from church. They got along well, but anytime Sherie disagreed with something, she felt she was not heard. She fell into the same pattern of feeling frustrated and giving up with this woman.

Her homework from her counselor was to bring this good friend into her confidence to help her break the eleven-year-old pattern of feeling helpless and giving up. With the friend's persistent help, she was able to start standing up for what she believed without giving up so easily. With this newfound strength, she was able begin a change in the relationship with her daughter.

Such DNA damage is invisible and feels normal, so the parents' natural response is to blame their children for the bad relationship. A faith community can be of help by emphasizing the freeing power of confession—of looking at one's own half of any relationship rather than blaming the other person for one's bad feelings. This is one of the spiritual disciplines that can be taught as part of the culture of a congregation.

## INTERESTING REACTION OF CHILDREN TO DIVORCE

Children find much of their security in the marital relationship. Even though part of their job is to find the damaged places of this relationship and manipulate them, ultimately they want the relationship to stay together.

When divorce occurs, the children want the original WE back, so they cannot warm up to a new spouse without feeling disloyal and insecure. Their natural reaction is to try to break the new relationship apart so that the old one can come back.

In an interesting attempt to keep some of the security of the original WE, one of the children will develop the same relationship with the parent as the ex-spouse had. Often the parent feels like he or she did before the divorce, with the same frustration and bad relationship—only this time, with one of the children.

> "I am so frustrated with my fifteen-year-old son," Corrie began in her women's Bible study group. "He is so rebellious and lies to me all the time. I am so afraid he will turn out to be just like his father."
>
> "Does he see his father much?" Penny asked.
>
> "He sees him once a week since we have been divorced," Corrie continued. "He seems a lot worse after that visit."
>
> "How do you feel when your son reacts that way?" Penny questioned.
>
> "I feel frustrated and angry," Corrie answered.
>
> "Isn't that the way you felt with your ex-husband when the two of you interacted?" Penny observed.
>
> Corrie stopped and thought for a long time and then brightened up. "Wow," she said, "I feel just the same. It's like having my husband back."
>
> The Bible study group then had a long discussion about the effect of divorce on children. Corrie seemed to have a deep new insight as she said, "I guess that my son wants the marriage back, so he feels he has to react to me just as his father did."
>
> Penny added, "But you do not have to continue that bad relationship with your son. You can find a different way of reacting to his behavior."
>
> The group ended with prayer, asking God to give Corrie the strength to react with greater love to her son when they got into the usual pattern.

A good way of describing this situation is that the son has a "spell" cast on him and without knowing it, feels compelled to continue this old marital relationship by behaving just like his father did. This feels familiar and gives some sense of security.

It is the parent's job to break this pattern. Again, the parent can change his or her half of the relationship with the child through spiritual growth. The parent does not have to continue the pattern. The starting point is to stop blaming the child and, in confession, search for one's own automated mood sequence (oinkey) that the child is activating.

Of course, if there is divorce, the best thing for the child is that the original parents form a WE for the sake of the child and even bring the new spouses into the WE. This is highly unnatural since the WE orientation broke down to cause the divorce in the first place.

However, after the divorce, when the parents no longer have to contend with the powerful forces that were present in the marital relationship, their mutual love for the child can come to the front and help them form a WE for the sake of the child. This brings the child powerful security in the midst of the chaos of divorce and also sets appropriate boundaries for the child so the child will not get "stuck" at that age with serious spiritual DNA damage.

> Katalena attended St. John's Preschool and was becoming more difficult to handle. Her parents had divorced, and her behavior deteriorated even further when her father remarried. Her teacher asked both parents and the new spouse to come in together for a conference.
>
> The mood was tense when they all gathered. After introducing the new wife to Katalena's mother, the teacher began, "I know it is difficult for the three of you to be in this room together, so thanks for coming. I know you all love Katalena, and that is why you are here."
>
> They all nodded in agreement, but the tension was still evident as the teacher continued, "I know there are hard feelings between you, but for your child's sake, we are going to work through this. We will need help, so let's begin with prayer: God, You know the struggles we have, and You know the powerful forces involved in this situation. Let Your Spirit be with us as we talk things over so that hard hearts are softened and Your will be done."

With some of the tension relieved by the prayer, the teacher challenged both parents: "Are you willing to work together for the sake of your child? She needs you to be a united front so that she can feel secure and be a child again."

As the session continued, both parents and the new spouse began to see the high importance of working together to form a WE for the sake of the child. There was complete agreement by the end that anytime Katalena showed behavior problems, they would come back together and decide on a plan of action together. It did not take long for Katalena's behavior to improve with the new WE that was formed.

## CHILDREN GET POWER WHEN THE WE BREAKS DOWN

Children get inappropriate power when the WE between two parents breaks down. Without a united front, the child can ally with one of the parents to form a WE against the other parent. In this way a child starts controlling the mood.

In most families, one of the parents becomes the disciplinarian, or "policeman," who is concerned that the child obeys and that there is follow-through with discipline. The other parent is more the "friend," concerned that the child is happy and loves being part of the family. Like painters and pointers, these two styles attract each other. In most two-parent situations, one is the policeman and the other is the friend.

Children gain control over the mood when they find that they can manipulate these two styles and break down the WE. The child will disobey the policeman and watch. The policeman will react and try to get the child to obey, frustrated that the other parent will not back up him or her or get upset with the child. The friend will get upset with the harshness of the other parent and will give signals to the child (often behind the other parent's back) that she is loved.

The situation gets worse as the policeman has to come down harder to compensate for the way his or her authority has been undermined. The friend has to be more protective to compensate for the harsh way their child is being treated. Of course, the child knows exactly how to manipulate the situation. The child will let the policeman know that he or she does not have to obey by his or her defiance. The child will let the friend know how scared he or she is or how much he or she has been hurt.

"Brad laughed at me again," Adeline began with tears in her eyes, running up to her father.

What happened next was disaster. Dad picked Adeline up in his arms and yelled at his son, "Brad, get in here!"

Mom looked away in disgust, knowing he would blame Brad again. He is too harsh with his son, she thought in anger.

As the four gathered in the den, Mom and Dad did not look at each other. Dad directed his words at his son: "I told you never to tease your sister again," he threatened, his anger barely under control.

Brad remained silent during the tongue-lashing, infuriated by the smug smile of his sister, who was safe in Dad's arms. The scene ended as Brad stomped out of the room and Mom gave Dad an angry look. The mood had shifted.

Such interaction will occur again and again, breeding more anger and upset. Mom will act as the friend and go behind Dad's back to comfort Brad, since she feels he was unjustly criticized. Dad will act as the policeman and come down even more harshly next time because his authority had been undermined.

There is no reason that these two styles of parenting cannot work well together! The policeman will notice what needs to be addressed. The friend can address the issue without a power struggle.

When these two styles form a WE, there are good boundaries and healthy follow-through without a power struggle. The child knows the parents are loving by their tone of voice, but he or she also knows they are serious by the firmness of the boundaries. Blending these two styles allows the child to internalize good, loving, yet firm boundaries.

In a parenting class at church, Brad's parents learned how to form a united front and blend their two styles of parenting. It took some time to accomplish this. The scene was quite different six months later.

Adeline was upset. Her brother had teased her, and she came running to her parents. "Brad laughed at me again," she began with tears in her eyes.

What happened next almost seemed like a well-rehearsed

sequence of events. Mom and Dad looked at each other with a knowing smile. Mom called out to Brad, "Would you come here, please? We would like to talk to you."

As the four gathered in the den, Mom and Dad looked at each other again and smiled. Dad began, "We want the two of you to get along." Mom picked up the same idea and added, "So let's talk this over so we can learn from what just happened." In the next few minutes, the truth came out, and both children admitted doing things to the other to escalate the situation.

With peace restored, Brad and Adeline went back to what they had been doing. Mom and Dad smiled as their eyes met, obviously a team when it came to raising their children!

Later in life, both Adeline and Brad will be aware of their impulses and not dismiss them. And they will also be aware that acting out the impulse in an immature way would not be healthy. Healthy WE-oriented boundaries build the internal WE so that the child does not have to struggle with internal conflict.

## FAMILY CONFLICT IS VALUABLE

Conflict, especially between siblings, is healthy and good. After all, it provides a lot of ground for learning. The conflict itself is not the problem. How the family handles conflict is the important thing.

One of the core teachings of a healthy faith community is that conflict is always handled face-to-face with all parties present. When something upsetting happens, there is good energy available in the frustration involved. Such frustration is anger energy that can be used to clear the air. This is the meaning of Ephesians 4:26: "Be angry and do not sin; do not let the sun go down on your anger."

Dealing with conflict in this manner allows disclosure of private thoughts and feelings. In this way, people get to know each other better and can clear up the usual misunderstanding that was the cause of the conflict in the beginning.

Part of a healthy family culture is handling conflict in this face-to-face fashion. Parents create this culture when they stop the conflict and sit down together to talk. The parents start by looking at each other and smiling (to control the mood) and then say, "We will talk this through so we can understand each other better."

Tattling is usually a part of the dynamics of family conflict. When one of the children starts to tattle, the parent should stop the child midsentence and call the other child in. Then hold a face-to-face discussion, having each one tell what happened. It is amazing how the story changes when the other person is present.

The object of the conversation is not to prove that one is right and the other wrong, but to teach children a positive model for handling conflict. Deeper understanding of one another builds a stronger family. A healthy family has good, healthy relationships.

In order to model healthy relationships for families, members of a faith community are called to treat conflict in the congregation in the same manner as just described. When tattling occurs, the complainer is stopped. The involved parties are invited to sit down together and discuss what has happened.

Faith community members do not carry their anger into the sunset; rather, they process the feelings and come to resolution. As in families, there is much to be learned from situations where a person is hooked by another's behavior or attitude. More spiritually mature members have a great deal to offer those who are in need of growth. Such treasured members can practice guidance as a spiritual discipline as they point out areas for growth and support to fellow members, such as those struggling with parenting their children. For example, sharing the perspective that family conflict is valuable—and why that is so—can be of help to families who are caught in repetitive cycles and are fearful for their family well-being. In this way, parents can receive re-parenting for themselves.

## HEALTHY BOUNDARIES AND AUTOMATIC CONSEQUENCES

Healthy child development goes through a gradual shift from external to internal control. During the first five years of life, children react to external boundaries. During the critical identification stage (starting at about age 6), they begin the process of internalizing boundaries, leading to good internal self-control. When this process is healthy, the young adult is ready to move out of the home environment, having developed a good internal guidance system.

In order to develop these internal boundaries, children need to have choices and automatic consequences for these choices, helping them more clearly understand how their choices affect both self and others.*

---

* The scene described here is similar to an earlier scene with a single parent, but the concept of letting the automatic consequence be based on the child's choice is so important that it is presented again here with a two-parent family.

Tara woke up in a bad mood. She refused to dress for preschool. She was a stubborn five-year-old and would not come out of her room. Her mother came up three times to get her to dress herself, but she ended up lying on the floor, throwing a temper tantrum. "I hate school!" she yelled. "Nobody likes me there."

Her mother then got angry with Dad for not doing anything. He reacted by stomping upstairs. In anger, he jerked her up off the floor and started putting her socks on. She screamed and fought as he held her tight and finally got her dressed. He physically carried Tara out to the car and threatened her as he put her in the backseat. The mood of the house was not good. Everyone was late and upset.

Healthy boundaries are always We-oriented boundaries. The parents form the initial We by shifting from focusing on their own feelings or need to "get the child to obey" to thinking about the good of the family. They talk together about how to deal with this situation.

Then both parents and child talk together and agree on automatic consequences if the child does not follow through. When all agree that this is not good for the family and the automatic consequence will be the loss of some privilege, then the We-oriented boundaries are set and there need not be a power struggle.

Her parents sat down with Tara that evening. They had formed a We. They were not angry, but they were determined to change things. They looked at each other and smiled and then looked back at Tara. "You are growing up, and we are proud of you," Dad said. We want to treat you like a young lady and give you more privileges. But when you act like a two-year-old, like you did this morning, then we cannot treat you like a young lady."

Tara was happy to be a part of the We and admitted that she did not like acting like she had that morning. "I will act more like a five-year-old," she said proudly.

Mom and Dad looked at each other again and smiled. "We like to hear you say that," Dad began.

Then her mom finished the sentence: "And what should happen if you forget and throw a temper tantrum again?"

Tara suggested that she not be able to go to her friend's house after school the next day. They all agreed to this.

That lasted one day. Tara got upset two days later and was on the floor, kicking and screaming again. But this time, her parents reacted very differently. Both of them came into the room, looked at each other and smiled, even chuckling a little. Her mother said, "You know that it is not good for our family when you react that way."

Her father continued, "Remember, we talked about this, and if you choose to continue, you have just chosen not to go to your friend's house tomorrow. This is your choice, and we are sad, but we cannot do anything about it since we all agreed."

Her mother added, "We really do hope you go to your friend's house, since we know how much you enjoy her, but it is your choice."

Parents do not have to use anger; the mood does not have to shift. The consequences are automatic. The consequences become the child's choice. Setting boundaries and following through in this manner helps the child to grow up.

## Single Parents Can Use the We Also

The WE orientation is effective for the single parent or if the spouse is absent or uncooperative. Now the radar of the child will find the parent's "hot buttons." Guilt, resentment, anxiety, inadequacy . . . the child will manipulate these emotions!

The single parent can form a WE with God as the new self finds strength in the Holy Spirit. This oneness with Christ is a new set of thoughts and emotions that will allow the single parent to say, "It is not good for our family for you to be disrespectful, so we will not allow that." This is much more powerful than threatening or getting angry, for it includes the child in the WE orientation and takes away the child's desire to rebel![2]

## Setting Boundaries for Adult Children

When an adult child reacts in an immature way, parents tend to react as if he or she were still eight or twelve years old, worrying and trying to teach and control. This is part of a powerful pattern that developed at that age and is still activated.

Parents can break this cycle by changing how they view their adult child. When he or she reacts immaturely and wants the parent to rescue or give advice, the parent has other options.

Tamara was twenty-five and was still dependent on her parents for her life. She was rebellious and would act out by living with someone. But when things fell apart, she would come back to have her parents rescue her. The pattern started at age 14 when, against her parents' wishes, she had her first sexual relationship. Now, eleven years later, the same things were still happening.

Finally, the parents brought the situation into counseling. The father admitted that he had become very disgusted with his daughter. He was raised to work hard and could not understand his daughter's laziness and willingness to take handouts from others. The mother felt she had to protect her daughter and still saw her as a vulnerable little girl who could not handle things by herself.

The counselor focused on the father's disgust. "This is actually a good emotion, but misused. You are in a pattern of becoming disgusted and getting angry with your daughter. Then you feel guilty for pushing her away and getting your wife upset. Let's change the disgust into energy that will allow you to break away from being the provider for your daughter, but do it in love."

The father began to understand as he replied, "I have to let go of my expectations and start believing in my daughter. I will need Christ's help with this."

The counselor was not Christian, but he valued the father's faith. "Why don't you find several men at your church to be your spiritual mentors?" he suggested. "They can help you use your anger in a helpful way. Your daughter needs your blessing."

As he met with two of his friends from church, the father asked, "How can Christ help my disgust of my daughter? Our therapist said that it was good energy, but misused. I need to find out how to use my anger to help our daughter grow up."

One of the men said, "I actually struggled with our son. I had the same feeling when he started missing classes at the university."

As they talked and prayed, the father felt something different. "I know I love my daughter, and I can feel Christ taking my disgust and using it to break the bad pattern that we are in. The next time I think of my daughter, instead of being disgusted, I will put her in Christ's hands, confident that she will grow up."

The other man added, "Then the next time she has a crisis, you can look at her, smile, and say, 'You will find a way to handle this. I believe in you.'"

Adult children who are reacting in immature ways are usually "stuck" in this relationship with their parents, unable to grow up because of powerful forces that keep them either rebelling or searching for a blessing. With Christ's help, parents have the power to change their half of the relationship with such children. This can be a blessing to those struggling to grow up.

The spiritual practice of celebration is a wonderful way to give thanks to God when family boundaries are agreed on and maintained. God gives the gift of creativity and perseverance to parents and children as they ask for God's guidance in the determination of safe and reasonable boundaries for their family.

God's gift of agape is a source of celebration for families as well. Through being loved, parents are able to pass on spiritual maturity—a lifestyle of care and service to the next generations.

# Glossary

**Agape:** This is an expression of a love that does not exist in its natural form on earth, but is a function of the new self as Christ dwells within the believer's heart through faith. This love seeks nothing in return, but is completely selfless, its energy going outward in praise to God and service to one another. Such love is the basis for the fellowship within the Body of Christ and produces the unique healing possibilities of a faith community.

**Automated mood sequences:**
Like the automatic sequencing of physical DNA, damage to spiritual DNA causes automatic thinking, feeling, and behaving when situations similar to the original one occur. This automatic response defines a person's belief system about the situation, justifying the reaction to the situation.

**Becoming oinkey:**
When a person's mood shifts in a downward spiral in a relationship and is blaming the other, a good term to use is that the person has become oinkey. The person is now in a bad mood that is justified because of the perceived hurt or "not fair" feelings that are felt in the stomach area as sinking, angry and depressed energy.

**Blessing:** All children yearn for parental blessing. As children develop and form their own identity, parental interest and blessing are critical for the maturation process. Without parental blessing, the adolescent gets "stuck" trying to prove his or her worth, often in opposition to parental authority. An example of a blessing in the life of Jesus is recorded in Matthew 3:17: "A voice from heaven said, 'This is My beloved Son, with whom I am well pleased." A faith community can help with such a blessing from God in the re-parenting process.

**Body:** The body is the emotional force that searches for fulfillment of its energy. This force relentlessly pushes toward expression of its impulses (what it wants to do) and utilizes a "Who cares?" attitude as its rebellion over the controlling force of the mind. Impulses are sensed in the physical body, and fulfillment involves the physical body with its energy and actions.

**Constriction:** In a disordered body, soul, or relationship, the flow of blood, air, or energy is blocked and turned back into itself. Other terms for this constriction are "hardened arteries" or "a spiritually hardened heart." Constriction is just the opposite of neuroplasticity. See *Neuroplasticity*.

**Damage to spiritual DNA:**

Concrete, personal experiences that cause high anxiety or that give the child too much power (entitlement) cause dysfunctional strategies for later life. These are constrictive, self-protective strategies (a ME orientation) that turn energy inward. The natural self is on its own, without God's loving presence, and is forced to handle these situations privately. Such childhood strategies become the person's reality, forming personality traits that determine how situations are handled in the future.

**Defining moments:**

Concrete situations that remain vivid in a person's memory represent the moment when the child faced an emotionally important situation and had to develop a strategy to handle it. Sometimes, the child's only coping strategy is to disassociate or detach from the memory of the event. The child's coping strategy then becomes part of the spiritual DNA.

**Determinism:** A construct of scientific methodology, making it popular to relegate human behavior to genetic, environmental, or internal forces beyond a person's control. This tends to take away responsibility for a person's choices, making confession somewhat obsolete. The "God-breathed" nature of humans does give *free will*: the capacity to ponder reality and make choices. Without the revelation of God and the work of His Holy Spirit, however, a person cannot choose to believe in or love (agape) God and desire to follow His will. This is God's work of faith.

*DSM*-5: The diagnostic categories that are used by most health professionals are delineated in the *Diagnostic and Statistical Manual of Mental Disorders (DSM)*. This widely used classification is in its fifth revision and provides the most comprehensive description of the various mental and emotional disorders. These classifications are cited in this book.

**Faith as an added gift to healing:**

Psychology, through its empirical methodology and deep, intuitive insight, has given excellent understanding to the observable aspects of the human psyche. But all the research in the world can only give insight into a fallen world—a soul organized without the agape, a soul without its true guiding principle (*pneuma*). Faith that comes from the revealed Word of God through the Holy Spirit is the added gift for the healing of the soul. This blessing is conveyed through Word and Sacrament within a healthy faith community: the Body of Christ.

**Faith community:**

"For where two or three are gathered in my name, there am I among them" (Matthew 18:20). For most people, their primary faith community is a local congregation. This term is used in this sense, but is also used in a broader way to indicate the value of any gathering in Christ's name, sharing agape. Bible study groups, support groups, pastoral counselors, spiritual mentors, and deep conversations among Christian friends all qualify as elements of a person's faith community. Spiritual growth occurs within such faith communities that allow for intimate sharing and caring.

**Heart:** This is where direction in life is developed (Proverbs 16:9), where reality decisions are made. In this inmost chamber of the soul, the human spirit organizes reality and develops the person's attitudes and beliefs. This is the place of free will. What is pondered in the heart becomes what the person believes to be true.

**Human spirit:** The *spirit* is the unifying force of the psyche, providing a creative organizing principle for the direction and purpose of life. It is the timeless observer, the center of consciousness that forms the basic attitudes of the person toward life and toward others. The spirit organizes the person's reality—what the person deeply believes to be true.

**Incurvatus in se:**

This Latin term was first used by St. Augustine and then by Martin Luther to describe the effects of sin. The term means "curved into self" and is a graphic description of the flow of energy inward that takes away from the joy of loving God and serving others (energy flowing outward).

**Internal disorders:**

Faulty development of the personality can lead to internal struggles. St. Paul vividly describes his own internal disorder in Romans 7:21–23, identifying the natural war between the mind and the body. If the mind can take charge of the personality, the result is an overcontrol disorder. If the body can take over, the result is an impulse-control disorder. If the spirit does not form properly, the result is a reality disorder.

**Litany:**

A person's attitude becomes hardened toward another person, a situation, or to self when sufficient evidence is gathered to support a belief system. The key defining moment(s) for the development of such an attitude is (are) coupled with other observations that reflect this bias. Often hundreds of hours are spent in this process. Once the person's heart has hardened, this attitude is presented in the form of a *litany* that is endlessly repeated, trying to get others to go along with the belief system. It is as if all words are being sung to the same tune.

**Mind:**

The mind is the cognitive force within the psyche that knows what is right, operating out of the person's value system. This force relentlessly pushes toward what should be done and utilizes guilt in its effort to exert control over the impulses of the body.

**Motivation by joy:**

Christ modeled a caring ministry. His motivation was joy: "who for the joy that was set before him endured the cross" (Hebrews 12:2). He was always interested, stopping everything to connect with a person in the moment. For the Christian, a selfless (agape) act of caring produces deep joy as energy is going outward. Joy occurs in the act of caring: "But be doers of the word, and not hearers only" (James 1:22). Caregiving that is done out of guilt or obligation produces more and, ultimately, resentment.

**Natural self:**  See *Psychikos.*

**Neuroplasticity:**

A healthy body, a healthy soul, and healthy relationships are flexible with energy flowing freely outward. Neuroplasticity is a similar concept for a healthy brain that is creative and flexible when processing new information. The opposite of neuroplasticity is constriction. See *Constriction.*

**New self:**  See *Pneuma.*

**Painters and pointers:**

> This communication typology, developed by Dr. Ludwig, explores the difference in communication style that often leads to critical misunderstanding between two people. One "paints a picture" as he or she talks, and the other "sticks to the point." Pointers misunderstand by focusing on the first word of the painter as the point, missing the rest of the picture. Painters dismiss the summarizing first word of a pointer, not realizing that this word needs to be unpackaged to get to the detail.

*Pneuma* **(new self):**

> This Greek term describes the soul that has been reorganized by the Holy Spirit and is a new creation. The gift of Christ's presence within the heart of the believer through faith has the power to create a new reality. The new self is not the human spirit, but God's gift of love that can influence the person by renewing a right spirit within (Psalm 51:10). This is the basis of an extraordinary WE orientation to life and is the proper order for the soul.

*Psychikos* **(natural self):**

> This Greek term describes the development of a person's reality without the love of God and the direction of the Holy Spirit. This is a word picture that describes the struggle for meaning and fulfillment in life as the person is tossed about by cultural winds that blow promise for happiness. It describes one's sinful nature that is self-protective or curved back into self. This is the basis of a prevalent ME orientation to life and the dysfunctional order of the soul.

**Repairing spiritual DNA damage:**

> Physical DNA is constantly being damaged and needs to be repaired. Specialized proteins recognize the damage and repair the DNA, restoring its original code. By analogy, damaged spiritual DNA (ME-focused energy) needs to be recognized by comparing it with God's will (the function of the Law), leading to confession. The damage can be repaired as God's presence is received (God's selfless love as expressed in the Greek word *agape)*, restoring the original code (WE-focused energy).

**Soul:**

> This term (*psyche* in Greek) describes the inner world of a person, one's private thoughts and feelings that make up personal consciousness; one's "home" inside, where things of personal significance are stored. For purposes of this book, three forces within the psyche are addressed, utilizing St. Paul's terms in Romans 7–8: mind, body, and human spirit.

**Spiritual DNA:** The history of the formation of reality by the human spirit over the developmental stages in life is called a person's spiritual DNA. Like physical DNA, spiritual DNA is a way of passing on characteristics of the parental behavior, since the child's organization of reality begins within the context of the family unit. From early on, children form their own view of reality as they navigate through life experiences. This is the work of their creative spirit, which forms the automatic habits and personality characteristics based on what they believe to be true about life.

**Spiritual Growth and Formation:**

Spiritual growth is a gift of God that is passively received as the daily process of dying to sin and rising to a new life in Christ (Romans 6:4). This *renewal of a right spirit within* (Psalm 51:10) influences more of the thoughts, feelings, and behavior as the Christian grows in grace to be more Christlike. Spiritual formation is not a *doing* concept, but an outcome of *being* in God's Word: "Be still, and know that I am God" (Psalm 46:10). The "natural self" *(psychikos)* operates by the organizing principle that self must be protected (*incurvatus in se*). This "ME-oriented" stance toward life is a fatal flaw and cannot be corrected by trying to do better and live a life more pleasing to God. The "new self" (*pneumatikos)* is a perfect creation of God that sets a person free to consider the good of the whole (WE-orientation*).* See *Psychikos; Incurvatus in se; Pneuma.*

**Spiritual re-parenting:**

Belief that God is the Christian's new Father ("Abba! Father!" [Romans 8:15]) leads to a re-parenting process. Such belief can heal some of the dysfunction of the natural self. Repairing damage to one's spiritual DNA is accomplished by bringing concrete situations to the loving presence of Christ, thus reconstructing reality. Spiritual healing is enhanced in the context of a Christian community. Another term for this is "spiritual formation" or "reorganizing of the human spirit" by the witness of the Holy Spirit (Romans 8:16).

**Wellness Circle:**

This book utilizes a concept similar to the wellness wheel that the authors have worked with and used extensively in the many retreats for professional church workers and congregations organized by Grace Place Wellness Ministries. This chapter focuses on the areas of the wellness circle, giving specific suggestions as to how a faith community can organize its wellness emphasis.

# Suggestions for Further Reading

## CHAPTER 1

Kessler, R. C., W. T. Chiu, O. Demler, and E. E. Walters. "Prevalence, severity, and comorbidity of twelve-month DSM-IV disorders in the National Comorbidity Survey Replication (NCS-R)." *Archives of General Psychiatry* (2005 June): 62 (6), 617–27.
This article gives recent statistics of the prevalence of mental and emotional disorders in more detail than the NIMH website cited below.

Lenzenweger, M. F., M. C. Lane, A. W. Loranger, and R. C. Kessler. "DSM-IV personality disorders in the National Comorbidity Survey Replication." *Biological Psychiatry* (2007): 62(6), 553–64.
This article gives recent statistics of the prevalence of personality disorders in more detail than the NIMH website cited below.

Manji, H. K., et al. "Enhancing Neuronal Plasticity and Cellular Resilience to Develop Novel, Improved Therapeutics for Difficult-to-Treat Depression." *Biological Psychiatry* 53 (2003): 707–42.
This excellent technical article gives an engaging scientific analysis of the potential role that antidepressant medication may have in actually developing new neuronal circuits, thus enhancing neuronal plasticity.

www.nimh.nih.gov/health/publications/the-numbers-count-mental-disorders-in-america/index.shtml
The National Institute of Mental Health (NIMH) is a branch of the U.S. government that provides research and information on mental health issues. Its website gives current statistics and resource articles on various mental and emotional disorders. Most of the percentages of mental illnesses cited in this book are taken from the NIMH publications "The Numbers Count: Mental Disorders in America" and "Community Conversations about Mental Health"; see also store.samhsa.gov/shin/content//SMA13-4763/SMA13-4763.pdf.

www.thinkwenotme.com
This website was developed by Dr. David J. Ludwig, one of the authors, growing out of his position as director of the Center for the Study of Family and Community Relationships at Lenoir-Rhyne University, Hickory, North Carolina. It includes a discussion of the "painter/pointer" communication typology and materials for help both in the

marital relationship and in parenting.

## CHAPTER 2

Arbib, M., and M. Hesse. *The Construction of Reality*. Cambridge, U.K.: Cambridge University Press, 1986.
This book presents an integrated account of how humans "construct" reality through interaction with the social and physical world around them. It presents convincing detail of the individual's construction of reality as a network of schemas "in the head."

Beauregard, M., and D. O'Leary. *The Spiritual Brain—A Neuroscientist's Case for the Existence of the Soul*. New York: Harper, 2007.
This book raises the interesting question "Does religious experience come from God, or is it just the random firing of neurons in the brain?" Drawing on the brain research on Carmelite nuns that has attracted major media attention and provocative new research in near-death experiences, this book shows that genuine, life-changing spiritual events can be documented. The authors conclude that it is God who creates our spiritual experiences, not the brain.

Hay, D., and R. Nye. *The Spirit of the Child*. London: Jessica Kingsley Publishers, 2006.
This book argues for the inclusion of spiritual awareness as a cross-curricular element in the school syllabus to promote the development of morality and social cohesion. Children are, the authors maintain, capable of profound and meaningful beliefs from an early age. A three-year research study into young children's spirituality and its survival value informs Hay's view that education needs to adopt a theory of spirituality.

Twenge, J., and K. Campbell. *The Narcissism Epidemic: Living in the Age of Entitlement*. New York: Free Press, 2009. www.narcissismepidemic.com.
This book and webpage give convincing data reflecting the current ME-oriented society that is curved into itself.

## CHAPTER 3

Andreas, S. *Transforming Negative Self-Talk*. New York: Norton, 2012.
This is one of many books that show the connection between inner conflict and mental health disorders. The book shows how persistent inner negative chatter and rumination can lead to depression, anxiety,

phobias, and obsessive-compulsive thoughts.

www.iep.utm.edu/freud/
This is an easy-to-read summary of Sigmund Freud's groundbreaking theory of internal conflict between the *superego* and the *id*. In a limited way, these concepts have some similarity to St. Paul's use of the terms *mind* and *body*, to show the war going on inside.

## CHAPTER 4

Damasio, A. *Self Comes to Mind: Constructing the Conscious Brain*. New York: Vintage Books, 2012.
In this book, a neuroscientist seeks to explain how the primordial elements of the mind—all these body maps and recursive loops—get transformed into conscious experience, into that metaphysical figment we call the "self." These automated sequences define reality for the conscious mind.

Perry, B., and J. Marcellus. "The Impact of Abuse and Neglect on the Developing Brain." www.teacher.scholastic.com/professional/bruceperry/abuse_neglect.htm.
Bruce Perry and others have studied the effects of childhood trauma on the neuroplasticity of the brain, concluding that there are real effects that the child carries all through life that show up in thought patterns, emotional reactions, and behavioral habits. These findings are similar to the concepts of automated mood sequences that grow out of damaged spiritual DNA, which are presented in this book. See also the website of Child Abuse Academy, childtrauma.org.

## CHAPTER 5

Brettig, K., and M. Sims, editors. *Building Integrated Connections for Children, Their Families and Communities*. Newcastle, U.K.: Cambridge Scholars Publishing, 2011.
This groundbreaking work focuses on developing integrated child and family communities so that the powerful effects of childhood trauma can be mitigated by a supportive environment. This book shows the intricate connection between neuroscience, childhood experiences, and the benefit of a supportive family and community environment.

Kleinig, J. *Grace upon Grace*. St. Louis: Concordia Publishing House, 2008.
This powerful book shows how Christian spirituality is simply follow-

ing Jesus. Because God has joined us to Christ, He continually comes to give us life. See also Dr. Kleinig's website, www.johnkleinig.com.

Meaney, M. "Epigenetics and the Biological Definition of Gene x Environment Interactions." *Child Development* (2010a): 81(1), 41–79.
This article gives a good background for the understanding of "epigenetics" and the power of healthy parental signals over the perinatal period that can serve as a catalyst for remodeling.

Peterson, E. *Christ Plays in Ten Thousand Places: A Conversation in Spiritual Theology*. New York: Eerdmans, 2008.
This book shows how spirituality and theology have been estranged in modern times. It gives numerous examples of how healthy theology can shape spiritual lives.

## CHAPTER 6

Calhoun, A. *Spiritual Disciplines Handbook: Practices That Transform Us*. Downers Grove, IL: InterVarsity Press, 2005.
Foster, R. *Celebration of Discipline*. New York: Harper Collins, 1988.
These two books outline the various spiritual disciplines that have been practiced in the Christian tradition.

May, G. *Authentic Spiritual Experience*. Washington DC: Shalem Institute for Spiritual Formation, 2007.
This brochure explains the role of a spiritual director in the life of a Christian.

Tibbits, D. *Forgive to Live*. Nashville: Thomas Nelson, 2008.
This book explores forgiveness as a spiritual practice that affects emotional, physical, and spiritual well-being.

www.Oboedire.wordpress.com
A good website for attentive spiritual formation.

www.sdiworld.org
The website for Spiritual Directors International.

## CHAPTER 7

Anderson, R. *Creating a Healthier Church: Family Systems Theory, Leadership, and Congregational Life*. Minneapolis: Augsburg Fortress, 1996.

This book offers steps church leaders can take to become more positive forces for healing and cooperation.

Carr, N. *The Shallows: What the Internet Is Doing to Our Brains*. New York: Norton, 2010.
This book shows how current technology has taken the depth out of life, leading to shallow, momentary experiences.

Koch, R., and K. Haugk. *Speaking the Truth in Love: How to Be an Assertive Christian*. St. Louis: Stephen Ministries, 1992.
This classic book about assertiveness is written for Christians by Christians. There are eighteen topics on assertiveness for building healthy relationships in congregations.

Turkle, S. *Alone Together: Why We Expect More from Technology and Less from Each Other*. New York: Basic Books, 2011.
Based on interviews with hundreds of children and adults, this book describes new, unsettling relationships between friends, lovers, parents, and children, and new instabilities in how we understand privacy and community, intimacy and solitude. It is a story of emotional dislocation, of risks taken unknowingly. But it is also a story about returning to what is most sustaining about direct human connection.

www.drlarryrosen.com/2011/03/idisorder/
Dr. Rosen has coined the word *iDisorder* to show how the current technological culture takes the depth from life. In contrast to this, a healthy faith community can bring the needed depth back into people's lives by the deep, lasting relationships that are formed.

www.hisaor.org/
This website for the Ambassadors of Reconciliation presents teaching tools and practical intervention strategies for conflict within congregations, turning conflict into a means for growth.

www.ministrycare.net
This website utilizes a Wholeness Wheel to focus on resources for developing wellness ministries in all areas of life. The website is set up for professional church workers but also has implications for faith community wellness.

# CHAPTER 8

Clark, M., and J. Olson. *Nursing within a Faith Community: Promoting Health in Times of Transition.* New York: Sage Publications, 2000.
This book provides a unique outlook on the theoretical underpinnings for faith community nursing from perspectives of both theology and nursing.

Cummings, D. *Eight Secrets of a Healthy 100.* Maitland, FL: Florida Hospital Publishing, 2012.
This book delineates the principles of a healthy lifestyle as practiced by Adventist Christians based on a longitudinal, fifty-year study made possible by grants from National Institutes of Health and the Center for Aging. Information about this study is also available on the website www.healthy100.org.

*Faith Community Nursing: Scope and Standards of Practice.* American Nurses Association, 2005.
This manual describes the specialty practice of faith community nursing as an independent practice of nursing to promote health and healing in faith communities. It presents a scope of knowledge, standards of care, and professional performance based on ANA Standards of Clinical Practice for Nurses. *See also* www.nursingworld.org.

Kepple, A., and V. Madaan. "MEAN: How to manage a child who bullies." *Current Psychiatry* (April 2013): 04, 20–28. www.currentpsychiatry.com/index.php?id=22161&cHash=071010&tx_ttnews[tt_news]=177666)
This brief article explains childhood bullying behavior and strategies for managing behaviors.

Koenig, H., and G. Lewis. *The Healing Connection.* Nashville: Word Publishing, 2000.
Koenig, a physician and medical researcher, looks at questions of religion and healing.

Westberg, G. *The Parish Nurse.* Minneapolis: Augsburg Fortress, 1990.
The author describes a parish nursing program with nurses working in congregations as ministers of health.

www.Healthy100Churches.org.
This website describes faith community nursing and health ministry team building in the Adventist Health Care System, based in Central Florida.

www.parishnurses.org
In 2011, the International Parish Nurse Resource Center moved under
the umbrella of the Church Health Center in Memphis.

## CHAPTER 9

Acterberg, J., et al. *Rituals of Healing: Using Imagery for Health and Wellness.*
New York: Bantam Books, 1994.
This is the *"American Journal of Nursing* Book of the Year" award winner and is a practical guide to using the power of the mind and the
imagination to form rituals that can help the body restore and maintain health.

Cloud, H., and J. Townsend. *Boundaries: When to Say Yes, When to Say No.*
Grand Rapids: Zondervan, 1995.
This classic work provides biblically based answers to questions about
setting healthy boundaries. The accompanying workbook provides
practical exercises to help set healthy boundaries with parents, spouses, children, friends, co-workers, and self.

Droege, T. *The Healing Presence: Spiritual Exercises for Healing, Wellness, and
Recovery.* Minneapolis: Youth and Family Institute of Augsburg College, 1996.
This resource for guided imagery for healing is drawn from the stories,
parables, and metaphors of Scripture that are rich in powerful healing
images. It can be used on retreats, in workshops, and in healing worship services as well as individually for strengthening in body, mind,
and spirit.

Hartung, B. *Holding Up the Prophet's Hands.* St. Louis: Concordia Publishing
House, 2010.
This book is a good resource for caring and support for church work-
ers.

Oberdeck, J. *Eutychus Youth: Applied Theology for Youth Ministry in the 21st
Century.* St. Louis: Concordia Publishing House, 2010.
This penetrating book gives insight into developing healthy ministry
to the developing adolescent and the struggles faced during this critical period of life.

www.ACAPcommunity.com
This is an example of a community website that provides support for
those who are caregivers for aging parents.

## CHAPTER 10

Bruckner, G., et al. *Making Therapy Work: Your Guide to Choosing, Using, and Ending Therapy.* New York: Harper and Row, 1988.
This book provides practical suggestions by three professional therapists as to how to engage actively in therapy for a positive outcome. The topics include how to find a therapist, developing a working relationship with one's therapist, overcoming resistance, evaluating therapy, and knowing when to end therapy.

Haugk, K. *When and How to Use Mental Health Resources.* St. Louis: Stephen Ministries, 2000.
This book describes collegial relationships between Stephen Ministers, leaders, and mental health professionals and explains clear boundaries and the roles of each.

www.aacc.net
This is the website for the American Association of Christian Counselors, which has fifty thousand members and is a good referral source.

www.store.samhsa.gov/shin/content//SMA13-4763/SMA13-4763.pdf
A helpful list of government resources for mental health is found on page 19 of this website publication.

## INTERLUDE

www.nami.org/
This is a grassroots website for people with mental and emotional disorders, giving resources and providing interactive support.

Greene-McCreight, K. *Darkness Is My Only Companion: A Christian Response to Mental Illness.* Grand Rapids: Brazos Press, 2006.
This book is a first-person account of a Christian's journey through severe mental illness. Her insights are deep and well considered.

www.christchurchcharlotte.org/www/docs/351.2884 ("What Helped Me, Might Help You.")
"In two-minute videos, Christ Church parishioners share what enabled them to cope and sustain hope through some of life's hardest hurts." Issues discussed include alcohol addiction, depression/bipolar, eating disorders, suicide.

## CHAPTER 11

Collins, G. *Christian Counseling: A Comprehensive Guide.* New York: Nelson Reference and Electronic Publishing, 2007.
This guide in pastoral counseling for all types of disorders builds on biblical foundations and also current professional research and insight.

Walsh, W. *Nutrient Power: Heal Your Biochemistry and Heal Your Brain.* New York: Skyhorse Publishing, 2012.
Nutrient therapy is an emerging natural alternative that can complement drug therapy by either enabling medication to be reduced or substituting for it in cases of milder disorders. Because it makes use of naturally occurring substances such as vitamins, amino acids, and minerals, nutrient therapy exhibits very few of the side effects common to drug therapies.

## CHAPTER 12

Day, J. *Risking Connection in Faith Communities: A Training Curriculum for Faith Leaders Supporting Trauma Survivors.* Baltimore: Sidran Institute, 2006.
This training curriculum helps faith leaders use growth-promoting relationships to help those who have suffered psychological trauma, with special emphasis on the spiritual impact of trauma.

Martinson, J. *Clinical Depression—Recognition and Treatment within the Religious Community: A Manual for Clergy and Congregations.* Fairfax, VA: The American Association of Pastoral Counselors, 2003.
This resource is a manual for training faith communities in recognizing depression and understanding treatment approaches.

## CHAPTER 13

Chapman, G., and R. Campbell. *The Five Love Languages of Children.* Northfield, MN: Northfield Publishing, 2012.
This book provides parents with a guide for building a foundation of unconditional love for their children and for providing a blessing by understanding their children's love languages.

www.surgeongeneral.gov/library/reports/national-strategy-suicide-prevention/full_report-rev.pdf
This excellent website from the U.S. Department of Health and Human Services on suicide prevention gives the warning signs and specific steps to take when suicide is threatened. It includes "2012 National

Strategy for Suicide Prevention: Goals and Objectives for Action" issued by the Office of the Surgeon General and the National Action Alliance for Suicide Prevention.

## CHAPTER 14

Crits-Christoph, P., and I. Barber. "Psychosocial Treatments for Personality Disorders" in *A Guide to Treatments That Work*. Edited by P. Nathan and J. Gorman. New York: Oxford University Press, 2002.
This is a very good, comprehensive book for practical therapy techniques for all disorders. The article on personality disorders points to cognitive therapy approaches that have some positive effect for the borderline personality disorder.

## CHAPTER 15

Woodruff, R. *Spiritual Caregiving to Help Addicted Persons and Families: Pastoral Counselor's Curriculum for the Education of Faith Leaders*. Washington DC: National Association for Children of Alcoholics, 2006.
This is training material designed for clergy who wish to deepen their professional pastoral relationship with addicted persons and their families. See also www.nacoa.org.

gsa-alcohol.fmhi.usf.edu/Evidence-based%20Practices%20for%20Preventing%20Substance%20Abuse%20and%20Mental%20Health%20Problems%20 in%20Older%20Adults.pdf
This is a good resource for working with substance abuse problems of older adults.

## CHAPTER 16

Dawson, G., et al. "Randomized, controlled trial of an early intervention for toddlers with autism." *Pediatrics* (2010): 125, 17–23.
This excellent study shows that a combination of structured therapy and follow-through with precise instructions in naturalistic settings with family and community provides the most promising retraining for autistic tendencies when implemented at an early age.

Furman, L. "ADHD: Does New Research Support Old Concepts?" *Journal of Child Neurology* (2008): 23, 775–84.
This is a thorough review of the literature on ADHA, concluding that this disorder is not necessarily a neurological disorder requiring medi-

cation, but rather a constellation of symptoms that can be managed and helped by a variety of treatment strategies.

## CHAPTER 17

Meyer, R., and S. Deitsch. *The Clinicians Handbook: Integrated Diagnosis, Assessment, and Intervention in Adult and Adolescent Psychopathology.* Needham Heights, MD: Allyn and Bacon (4th edition), 1996.
This is a classic work in this difficult area of reality disorders, which are very difficult to treat since the person's belief system is at stake. The authors conclude that careful work at relationship building; collaboration with other professionals, family, and community members; and gradual challenging of beliefs offers the best hope of gradual improvement for such individuals.

## CHAPTER 18

Boss, P. *Ambiguous Loss: Learning to Live with Unresolved Grief.* Cambridge, MA: Harvard University Press, 1999.
Based on research and clinical experience, the author, a professor of Family Social Science, explores the emotions stirred up by losses such as chronic mental illness, addiction, or Alzheimer's disease. Strategies to cushion the pain and deal with such uncertain losses are shared.

Broyles, Frank. *Coach Broyles' Playbook for Alzheimer's Caregivers*, www.alzheimersplaybook.com, 2010.
This guide is designed like a coach's playbook and includes information and practical tips to help families meet the needs of their loved ones suffering from Alzheimer's disease. The book was inspired by personal experience of the author, who retired at the end of 2007 after more than fifty years as a head coach and athletic director, most recently at Arkansas. *See also* www.caregiversunited.com.

Gwyther, L. *You Are One of Us: Successful Clergy/Church Connections to Alzheimer's Families.* Durham, NC: Duke University Medical Center, 1995.
This booklet offers specific strategies to help families dealing with Alzheimer's disease and faith communities make valued connections.

Richards, M. "Elder Spirituality and Care for the Cognitively Impaired" in *Transformational Eldercare from the Inside Out: Strengths-Based Strategies for Caring* by J. Henry and L. Henry. American Nurses Association, 2007.
This interview-based chapter highlights the continued presence of

spiritual and emotional capacities in the older adult with physical and cognitive decline. Practical suggestions for spiritual-emotional care are offered. See also www.nursingworld.org.

*Steps to Understanding Challenging Behaviors: Responding to Persons with Alzheimer's Disease*. Alzheimer's Association, 2000.
www.alzheimersassociation.org
This is a guide to help understand the progression of Alzheimer's disease.

## CHAPTER 19

Ludwig, D. *Renewing the Family Spirit*. St. Louis: Concordia Publishing House, 1989.
David Ludwig offers a hopeful perspective on conflict and family relations, illustrating how different styles of communication between husband and wife, parent and child, affect the spirit of a family.

Ludwig, D. *The Power of WE*. St. Louis: Concordia Publishing House, 2009 (DVD-ROM).
This video-based course provides both the theoretical understanding of the WE and the practical, day-to-day wisdom that will help form a good marriage.

www.thinkwenotme.com
Dr. Ludwig's website includes materials for help both in the marital relationship and in parenting.

## CHAPTER 20

www.parentingfamilies.com
This website, developed by Lutheran Hour Ministries (LHM), gives help in Christian-based parenting to families. This site features a video series authored by Dr. Ludwig and developed by LHM.

www.thinkwenotme.com
Dr. Ludwig's website offers interactive dramas of parent/child situations at various ages. Parenting skills involving the use of the WE orientation are taught with cartoon characters.

# Endnotes

## CHAPTER 1

1. National Institute of Mental Health publications "The Numbers Count: Mental Disorders in America" (www.nimh.nih.gov/health/publications/the-numbers-count-mental-disorders-in-america/index.shtml) and "Community Conversations about Mental Health" (store.samhsa.gov/shin/content//SMA13-4763/SMA13-4763.pdf).

2. An excellent technical article on neuroplasticity and the potential for antidepressive medication to facilitate new neural connections is found in the *Journal of Biological Psychiatry*: H. K. Manji et al., "Enhancing Neuronal Plasticity and Cellular Resilience to Develop Novel, Improved Therapeutics for Difficult-to-Treat Depression," *Journal of Biological Psychiatry 53* (2003): 707.

3. This communication typology can be found on Dr. Ludwig's website, www.thinkwenotme.com. It is also available in two products authored by Dr. Ludwig and available from Concordia Publishing House: the book *Renewing the Family Spirit* (1989) and the DVD/CD-ROM *The Power of WE (2009).*

4. In a study of clinical psychologists, only 33 percent of the therapists listed their faith as a most important influence on their lives as compared to 72 percent of the general population. A. Bergin and J. Jenson, "Religiosity of Psychotherapists: A National Survey." *Psychotherapy: Theory, Research, Practice, Training 27*, no. 1 (1990): 3–7.

5. "Mental Health in the Community." *Communication Conversations about Mental Health: Information Brief.* store.samhsa.gov/shin/content//SMA13-4763/SMA13-4763.pdf.

## CHAPTER 4

1. For more information about the revised edition of *DSM*, go to the American Psychiatric Association webpage: www.dsm5.org.

## CHAPTER 5

1. In 2013, the U.S. Department of Health and Human Services: Substance Abuse and Mental Health Services Administration was charged to start a national conversation on mental health to reduce the shame and secrecy associated with mental illness. The first of these excellent community conversations can be found at store. samhsa.gov/shin/content//SMA13-4763/SMA13-4763.pdf.

## CHAPTER 6

1. This is a personal account of Dr. Jacob, one of the authors of this book.

## CHAPTER 7

1. This is a personal story from the life of one of the authors, Dr. Ludwig.

## CHAPTER 8

1. The International Parish Nurse Resource Center has extensive information on faith community nursing standards of practice, training, and health ministry resource: www.churchhealthcenter.org.

2. Resources for training wellness committees and health ministry leaders in congregations can be found in some hospital systems and community health organizations, as well as through private consultation (see the reading list).

3. This illustration is based on "The Ten Leading Causes of Death" in the Health Ministry Team Building Instruction Manual, © copyright 2007, Florida Hospital Center for Community Health Ministry, managed by Florida Hospital Healthy 100 Church Ministry. Used by permission. All rights reserved. Information pertaining to "Ten Leading Causes of Death" may be found in a PowerPoint lecture presentation, "Faith and Health Connections" by Candy Huber, FCN at http://www.wphf.org/wp-content/uploads/2010/10/Candy-Hubers-REVISED-presentation1.pdf.

4. Grace Place Lutheran Wellness Ministries (www.graceplacewellness.org) developed the wellness circle in connection with several other organizations, such as Concordia Plans (www.concordia-plans.org/DetailPage.aspx?ID=462) and Wheat Ridge Ministries

(www.wheatridge.org/wholenesswheel).

## CHAPTER 10

1. The website www.aapc.org provides a national directory of pastoral counselors and other information pertaining to pastoral counseling.

2. Friends and families of problem drinkers find strength and hope in support groups such as Al-Anon and Alateen. For information, see www.al-anon.alateen.org.

## CHAPTER 11

1. Most of the percentages of the various mental illnesses that are cited in this book come from the National Institute of Mental Health and their publication "The Numbers Count: Mental Disorders in America," available on the Web at www.nimh.nih.gov/health/publications/the-numbers-count-mental-disorders-in-america/ndex.shtml.

## CHAPTER 13

1. www.who.int/mediacentre/factsheets/fs369/en/.

2. Statistics for this chapter are taken from the National Institute for Mental Health website: www.nimh.nih.gov/statistics.

3. See www.gmhfonline.org, the website of the Geriatric Mental Health Foundation.

4. "2012 National Strategy for Suicide Prevention: Goals and Objectives for Action." Available at www.surgeongeneral.gov/library/reports/national-strategy-suicide-prevention/full_report-rev.pdf.

## CHAPTER 16

1. See the author's website, www.thinkwenotme.com, for further detail on this communication typology.

## CHAPTER 18

1. Alzheimer's Association 2013 Facts and Figures from website www.alz.org.

2. A listing of local chapters is available by calling the Alzheimer's Association at 1-800-272-3900 or by visiting the website: www.alz.org.

## Chapter 19

1. This communication typology was developed by one of the authors, Dr. Ludwig. More information can be accessed on his website: www.thinkwenotme.com. See also the discussion of painters and pointers on pages 248–52.

2. The concept of mood particles was developed by one of the authors, Dr. Ludwig, for the book and DVD produced by Concordia Publishing House, *Renewing the Family Spirit*. The DVD used a weatherman to show the predictable weather patterns that occur inside the home when mood particles accumulate.

## Chapter 20

1. For more practical advice on handling parenting situations with a We orientation, even as a single parent, go to the "Practice Your Parenting" section of the website www.thinkwenotme.com, which uses cartoon characters and an interactive process.

2. There is good modeling for the single parent to utilize the We orientation in relationship with the child in the video *Parenting Families: From Me to We* (www.parentingfamilies.com) and the book *Renewing the Family Spirit* from Concordia Publishing House, 1989; both by author David Ludwig. Also see "Practice Your Parenting" at www.thinkwenotme.com.

Dr. David J. Ludwig received his MDiv from Concordia Seminary, St. Louis in 1965 and a PhD from Washington University, St. Louis in 1966. His blending of theology and psychology has spanned over forty-five years as a university professor, licensed psychologist, and LCMS minister. Dr. Ludwig has written seven books and numerous articles. He helped develop the masters program in counseling, a certificate program in Christian counseling, and the Power of WE Center at Lenoir-Rhyne College, Hickory, North Carolina. He currently serves as a semi-retired professor of psychology at Lenoir-Rhyne and as assistant to the pastor at Christ Lutheran Church in Hickory. He maintains a private practice as a licensed therapist and continues to travel extensively with his wife, Kathy, giving presentations on family relationships with grants from Wheatridge, Thrivent, and various synodical organizations. The message of the healing power of WE has been shared with congregations and audiences in the United States, Canada, Brazil, Australia, New Zealand, Indonesia, Taiwan, Thailand, Korea, Kenya, and England.

Dr. Mary R. Jacob has served on the staff of Lutheran Counseling Services, Inc., in Winter Park, Florida, since 1999. She providing individual, marital, family, and group counseling as a Psychiatric Nurse Practitioner. She previously engaged in private practice and has taught psychiatric nursing at The Medical College of Georgia, University of South Carolina, and University of Central Florida. Dr. Jacob completed parish nurse preparation in 1999 (Marquette model) and has consulted with parish nurses on mental health issues throughout Central Florida. Since completing a three-year spiritual formation/spiritual direction training in 2007, she has provided spiritual direction to individuals. She consults with congregational health ministries throughout Florida and provides workshops and training on a variety of mental health topics. Dr. Jacob received the Excellence in Writing Award from the Florida Nurses Association.